THE RIGHT TO EMPLOYEE INVENTIONS IN PATENT LAW

Although employers are required to pay compensation for employee inventions under the laws in many countries, existing legal literature has never critically examined whether such compensation actually gives employee inventors an incentive to invent as the legislature intends.

This book addresses the issue through reference to recent, large-scale surveys on the motivation of employee inventors (in Europe, the United States and Japan) and studies in social psychology and econometrics, arguing that the compensation is unlikely to boost the motivation, productivity and creativity of employee inventors, and thereby encourage the creation of inventions. It also discusses the ownership of inventions made by university researchers, giving due consideration to the need to ensure open science and their academic freedom. Challenging popular assumptions, this book provides a solution to a critical issue by arguing that compensation for employee inventions should not be made mandatory regardless of jurisdiction because there is no legitimate reason to require employers to pay it. This means that patent law does not need to give employee inventors an 'incentive to invent' separately from the 'incentive to innovate' which is already given to employers.

The Right to Employee Inventions in Patent Law

Debunking the Myth of Incentive Theory

Kazuhide Odaki

·HART·

OXFORD · LONDON · NEW YORK · NEW DELHI · SYDNEY

HART PUBLISHING

Bloomsbury Publishing Plc

Kemp House, Chawley Park, Cumnor Hill, Oxford, OX2 9PH, UK

HART PUBLISHING, the Hart/Stag logo, BLOOMSBURY and the Diana logo are trademarks of Bloomsbury Publishing Plc

First published in Great Britain 2018

First published in hardback, 2018
Paperback edition, 2020

A catalogue record for this book is available from the British Library.

Library of Congress Cataloging-in-Publication Data

Names: Odaki, Kazuhide.

Title: The right to employee inventions in patent law / Kazuhide Odaki.

Description: Oxford, UK ; Portland, Oregon : Hart Publishing, 2018. | Includes bibliographical references.

Identifiers: LCCN 2018020968 (print) | LCCN 2018021740 (ebook) | ISBN 9781509920334 (Epub) | ISBN 9781509920310 (hardback : alk. paper)

Subjects: LCSH: Inventions, Employees'.

Classification: LCC K1521 (ebook) | LCC K1521 .O33 2018 (print) | DDC 346.04/86—dc23

LC record available at https://lccn.loc.gov/2018020968

ISBN: HB: 978-1-50992-031-0
PB: 978-1-50994-391-3
ePDF: 978-1-50992-032-7
ePub: 978-1-50992-033-4

Typeset by Compuscript Ltd, Shannon

To find out more about our authors and books visit www.hartpublishing.co.uk. Here you will find extracts, author information, details of forthcoming events and the option to sign up for our newsletters.

www.bloomsbury.com

ACKNOWLEDGEMENTS

This book was written based on my doctoral thesis submitted to The University of Manchester. I wish to thank David Booton, my doctoral supervisor, for his valuable comments on the draft and constant encouragement.

TABLE OF CONTENTS

PART II

OWNERSHIP OF EMPLOYEE INVENTIONS AND THE VALIDITY
OF THE INVENTOR PRINCIPLE

LIST OF FIGURES

TABLE OF CASES

Germany

Japan

New Zealand

The United States

TABLE OF LEGISLATION

China, including (draft) regulations

The Czech Republic

Denmark

Finland

France

Germany, including guidelines and an ordinance

Malaysia

Mexico

The Netherlands

Norway

Poland

Portugal

The Republic of Korea

Romania

Russia, including an order of the government

Singapore

Slovakia

Slovenia

Spain

Sweden, including a collective agreement

Switzerland

Taiwan

Turkey

The United Kingdom

The United States, including Bills and State Laws

1

Introduction

I. Background and Purpose of this Book

A. Compensation for Employee Inventions: Various Legal Schemes

Most inventions today originate from within organisations. Of the 210,454 patent applications which were made worldwide through the Patent Cooperation Treaty (PCT) route in 2016, 85.5 per cent were filed by businesses, 7.5 per cent by individuals, 5 per cent by universities, and 1.9 per cent by governments or research institutes.[1] Although individuals still accounted for a large share of PCT applications in many countries which do not belong to the high income group,[2] these data show that nowadays over 90 per cent of inventions patented in the whole world are created by employees working for companies, universities, governments and other organisations.

Employee inventors, who typically work in research and development (R&D) departments of companies, are often expected to contribute to the making of patentable inventions. According to the established principle in labour law that employers should enjoy the fruits of labour of their employees their employees' labour, there is no reason why employers have to offer compensation for inventions made in the course of employees' duties in addition to their salaries and benefits. However, patent laws or other related laws in some countries require employers to pay additional compensation for such inventions. For example, according to the German Act on Employees' Inventions,[3] employers based in Germany are required to pay employee inventors 'reasonable compensation' in principle if they claim patentable 'service inventions'.[4] Here, 'service inventions' refers to those made during the term of employment which either (i) resulted from an employee's tasks, or (ii) are essentially based upon experience or activities of the company.[5]

---

[1] WIPO, *Patent Cooperation Treaty Yearly Review 2017: The International Patent System* (WIPO 2017) 19, 28 Fig A11, www.wipo.int/edocs/pubdocs/en/wipo_pub_901_2017.pdf.

[2] ibid 29 Fig A12.

[3] Gesetz über Arbeitnehmererfindungen vom 25 Juli 1957 (BGBl I S 756).

[4] Act on Employees' Inventions, ss 2, 9(1). However, employers may conclude agreements which are less favourable to employees after service inventions have been reported to the employers: Act on Employees' Inventions, s 22.

[5] ibid, s 4(2).

The amount of 'reasonable compensation' shall be calculated by considering particularly the commercial applicability of the service invention, the duties and position of the employee in the company, and the company's contribution to the invention.[6] According to the Guidelines for the Remuneration of Employees' Inventions in Private Employment[7] which are issued by the Federal Minister of Labour,[8] its amount is 'value of invention' multiplied by 'share factor'.[9] According to the 'licence analogy', which is most frequently used in practice of the three calculation methods prescribed in the Guidelines,[10] the 'value of invention', or supposed licence fee, is calculated on the basis of total turnover and the usual royalty rate applied to each industrial sector.[11] 'Share factor' is a numerical value expressed in the form of percentage which represents the inventor's share in the supposed benefit from the invention, and is determined in consideration of the assignment and solution of the task and his position in the company.[12] Such an elaborate legal scheme for calculating additional compensation to employee inventors is unique to Germany.

Courts in other countries have awarded the additional compensation on a case-by-case basis pursuant to relevant statutory provisions. In Japan, a court decision in 2004 awarded ¥20 billion (then over £10.3 million) to an ex-employee of a company who had invented a blue Light-Emitting Diode during his tenure on the assumption that he had contributed to 50 per cent of company profits (the *Blue LED* case).[13] On appeal, however, both parties reached a court-mediated settlement, in which the company agreed to pay the ex-employee about ¥840 million (a little more than 4 per cent of the amount originally awarded to him).[14] In the United Kingdom (UK), the High Court of England and Wales in 2009 awarded £1.5 million to a pair of employee inventors who had synthesised a new compound during their tenure. The amount accounted for 3 per cent of the profits their employer had derived from a patented radioactive imaging agent which incorporated this compound (the *Kelly and Chiu* case).[15] Since 2000, French courts have been willing to award a substantial amount of 'additional remuneration' for 'inventions under mission', namely those made in the course of employees' duties.[16] Decisions which awarded between €10,000 and €100,000

---

[6] ibid, s 9(2).

[7] Richtlinien für die Vergütung von Arbeitnehmererfindungen im privaten Dienst vom 20 Juli 1959 (Beilage zum Bundesanzeiger Nr 156 vom 18 August 1959).

[8] Act on Employees' Inventions, s 11.

[9] Guidelines for the Remuneration of Employees' Inventions in Private Employment, no 39.

[10] ibid, no 3.

[11] ibid, nos 10, 11.

[12] ibid, nos 30–37.

[13] Tokyo District Court, judgment on 30 January 2004, 1852 *Hanrei jihō* 36. The employee inventor in this case was later jointly awarded the Nobel Prize in Physics in 2014 for the invention with a couple of Japanese academics.

[14] Tokyo High Court, settlement on 11 January 2005, 1879 *Hanrei jihō* 141.

[15] *Kelly and Chiu* v *GE Healthcare Ltd* [2009] EWHC 181 (Pat), [2009] RPC 12 [203].

[16] Intellectual Property Code, art L611-7(1).

to employee inventors are not rare, and a few courts have awarded €300,000 or more, with the maximum award being €600,000.[17]

By contrast, courts in the United States (US) generally allow employers to claim inventions made by employees without paying additional compensation, as long as both parties have made a proper contract in advance.[18] Nonetheless, employees of the Federal Government who have assigned the inventor's rights to the Government are entitled by special legislation to a fixed sum of $2,000 in the first year, and at least 15 per cent of licensing royalties after deducting patent costs thereafter.[19]

B. Rationale for Inventor Remuneration: The 'Incentive Theory'?

One question which arises is why statutory laws in many, if not all, countries make the payment of additional compensation to employee inventors mandatory under certain conditions. A simple view may be that these statutory laws are aimed at fair distribution of profits gained from an invention to its inventor(s). However, this view gives no theoretical explanation as to why only inventors should be given special treatment even though these profits would not have arisen without a contribution made by other employees such as those working in manufacturing and marketing departments.

Some may argue instead that such laws are social legislation intended to improve employee inventors' status as workers. This theory partly explains why the German Act on Employees' Inventions was introduced.[20] However, it does not apply to most countries where only a few employee inventors can receive the additional compensation. According to the Patents Act 1977 in the UK, for example, where 'having regard among other things to the size and nature of the employer's undertaking, the invention or the patent for it (or the combination of both) is *of outstanding benefit* to the employer, and' 'it is just that the employee should be awarded compensation', 'the court … *may* award him such compensation' 'as will secure for the employee a fair share … of the benefit which the employer has derived' from the invention or the patent.[21] It is hard to say that the Act has generally raised the social status of employee inventors in the UK since according to this provision the additional compensation shall be awarded only in exceptional circumstances at the court's discretion. Indeed, the *Kelly and Chiu* case has been the only example so far where the English court actually awarded

---

[17] Sanna Wolk, 'Remuneration of Employee Inventors – Is There a Common European Ground? A Comparison of National Laws on Compensation of Inventors in Germany, France, Spain, Sweden and the United Kingdom' (2011) 42 *International Review of Intellectual Property and Competition Law* 272, 284–85.

[18] See ch 6, s IV.

[19] Stevenson-Wydler Technology Innovation Act of 1980 (Public Law 96-480) § 14 (a)(1)(A)(i), as codified in 15 USC § 3710c (2012).

[20] See ch 9, s I.

[21] Patents Act 1977, ss 40(1), 41(1) (emphasis added).

compensation. Meanwhile, employee inventors may want to establish their right to additional compensation by collective agreements so that they can redress the social inequality between them and their employers. In Sweden, a collective agreement concluded in 2015 guarantees unionised employees a lump sum payment of either kr22,150 or kr44,300 (≒ €2,400 or €4,800, as of 2016) per invention claimed by their employers.[22] Yet in France, there are currently few enforceable collective agreements[23] despite a statutory provision that the conditions for the payment of the additional compensation shall be determined by collective agreements apart from company agreements and individual employment contracts.[24] In the US, employee inventors generally regard themselves as professional individualists, and as such are reluctant to unionise.[25] In most countries employee inventors have not sought the payment of the additional compensation by collective agreements which are aimed at improving employees' social status as a whole.

Traditional theories on the justification of the patent system may give a clue as to the rationale for the additional compensation employee inventors receive. However, the 'labour theory of property', which holds that an inventor has the natural property right in the fruits of his labour, is untenable on the grounds that the amount of monopoly profits gained by a patent depends on various social factors in the market, and that his idea itself is also fundamentally a social product based on the ideas of others ahead of him.[26] The 'reward theory', which holds that an inventor deserves reward for his labour rather than his natural talent or luck, has also attracted little support because a patent may bring him a considerable reward disproportionate to his effort.[27] Since the utilitarian argument that a patent offers the best incentive to invent gives a more acceptable explanation for the patent system,[28] the most plausible view may be that employee inventors receive additional compensation because this enhances or otherwise contributes to their overall motivation to invent. This 'incentive theory' claims that employee inventors need a special inducement to make inventions because, unlike independent inventors, they are on the regular payroll regardless of their job performance. This argument must be clearly distinguished from the 'reward theory' mentioned above, according to which the reward is given for inventors' effort rather than

---

[22] Agreement concerning the Rights to Employee Inventions between Swedish Enterprise and PTK, s 4(2).

[23] Thomas Bouvet, 'Employee-Inventor Rights in France' (Loyola Law School IP Special Focus Conference, Los Angeles, September 2006) 6-7, toscane2.veron.com/publications/Colloques/Employees_inventions.pdf.

[24] Intellectual Property Code, art L611-7(1).

[25] See ch 6, s IV.C.

[26] Edwin C Hettinger, 'Justifying Intellectual Property' (1989) 18 *Philosophy & Public Affairs* 31, 38–39. It should be noticed that the inventor is prevented from using his idea if someone else has obtained a patent on it before him: Fritz Machlup and Edith Penrose, 'The Patent Controversy in the Nineteenth Century' (1950) 10 *The Journal of Economic History* 1, 14.

[27] Machlup and Penrose (n 26) 20; Hettinger (n 26) 41–42. In addition, it does not explain why only the patentee deserves the reward, even though many useful inventions are usually created almost simultaneously by more than one inventor as the society evolves: Machlup and Penrose (n 26) 18.

[28] Machlup and Penrose (n 26) 21–22; Hettinger (n 26) 47.

their 'natural talent and luck' beyond their control.[29] The additional compensation may be justified as an incentive, but not as what is mentioned as 'reward' here because its amount is usually linked to the social value of the inventions rather than the inventors' effort.[30] Compensation offered to employee inventors is comparable to cash prizes historically offered to the general public by governments or other organisations to trigger important discoveries or inventions.[31] It may boost the creation of inventions by employees, even if only a few who have made fairly valuable inventions can receive it.

C. Does Inventor Remuneration Really Encourage Employees to Invent?

It has been taken for granted in the relevant literature of law and economics that money acts as an incentive for employee inventors to invent.[32] Policy makers in many countries may want to boost the creation of valuable inventions that are vital to the industrial development of the country by allowing employee inventors to receive more generous compensation for inventions made in the course of their duties. However, to date there has been no critical examination of whether invention compensation schemes can actually increase the number of inventions made by employees. First of all, employee inventors may not be generally enticed by money. For example, Thomas A Edison was quoted as saying as follows:

> One might think that the money value of an invention constitutes its reward to the man who loves his work. But, speaking for myself, I can honestly say this is not so. ... I continue to find my greatest pleasure, and so my reward, in the work that precedes what the world calls success.[33]

Employee inventors today may also be naturally motivated to invent by their passion for inventing itself rather than pecuniary rewards they may receive for the success of inventing. And yet they are different to heroic lone inventors like Edison in that they invent in teams in organisations. Today inventions are created in companies through the collaboration of scientists and engineers from various disciplines. However, not all of them are named as inventors according to the

---

[29] Hettinger (n 26) 42–43.

[30] ibid 42. The court in *Kelly and Chiu* held that '[t]he amount of compensation [awarded under the UK Patents Act] is to be determined ... so as to secure a just and fair *reward* to the employee': *Kelly and Chiu* (n 15) [59] (emphasis added). Yet the word 'reward' was not used in the sense that the inventor deserves reward for his labour, because the court assumed that the compensation is paid so as to reduce 'the disparity in benefit between employer and employee': ibid [52].

[31] Suzanne Scotchmer, *Innovation and Incentives* (Cambridge, Massachusetts, The MIT Press, 2004) 41–45.

[32] See, eg, Roland Kirstein and Birgit Will, 'Efficient Compensation for Employees' Inventions' (2006) 21 *European Journal of Law and Economics* 129, 135 fn 27.

[33] Orison Swett Marden, *How They Succeeded: Life Stories of Successful Men Told by Themselves* (Boston, Lothrop, 1901) 237 fn 1.

criteria of inventorship in patent law. Regarding pharmaceuticals, for example, scientists who do not work on drug synthesis are unlikely to be named as co-inventors of a successful drug even though they may play a key role in the whole drug discovery process.[34] It may adversely affect the morale and teamwork of employee inventors as a whole if they regard the award of the compensation to a few named inventors unfair. Relevant to this point are diverse societal norms on 'distributive justice', that is, whether people think named inventors should deserve more because they have made special contribution (eg, West Europe and North America) or that all the members of a project team should be given equal treatment regardless of their contribution so that group harmony will be maintained (eg, Confucian Asia).[35]

Meanwhile, it may be argued that the motivation of employee inventors is in fact not a crucial factor for the success of inventing. While incentives offered to unskilled workers may immediately improve the productivity of the work they do, such as assembling parts of an automobile, those offered to employee inventors may not, because, even if such incentives enhance their motivation, inventions cannot be made without creativity. Moreover, irrespective of their motivation, inventions may be created as a result of mere serendipity, or even failures, as is the case with Post-it® note adhesive to be mentioned later.[36] Needless to say, an incentive is worthless if it does not produce a good effect on the end result. Given the complex factors which determine the success of inventing, a reasonable doubt arises that invention compensation schemes cannot immediately boost the creation of useful inventions by employee inventors.

D. Problem of Harmonisation and the Purpose of this Book

Legal literature on employee inventions have tended to focus on the apparent differences of legal schemes for compensating employee inventors among jurisdictions and highlight the need for international harmonisation of these national laws in an era when many companies operate across borders and often cooperate with research partners overseas. The varied national laws cause not only legal uncertainty, which makes it difficult for multinational corporations to plan their business strategies, but also unequal treatment of employee inventors who engage in the same R&D project in subsidiary companies abroad or foreign companies they are posted to.[37] Harmonisation is a particularly critical issue for the European Union (EU) which is committed to strengthening the European single

---

[34] See ch 3, s II.
[35] See ch 3, s III.
[36] See ch 4, s V.
[37] Marie-Christine Janssens, 'EU Perspectives on Employees' Inventions' in Marilyn Pittard, Ann Louise Monotti and John Duns (eds), *Business Innovation and the Law: Perspectives from Intellectual Property, Labour, Competition and Corporate Law* (Cheltenham, Edward Elgar, 2013) 117–18.

market. In 1997, the European Commission suggested in its Green Paper that 'differences between national laws on employees' inventions are having an effect on the freedom to provide services in the single market and/or on the conditions of competition'.[38] Yet only two years later did the Commission declare that it '[did] not intend to take any legal initiative in this field' for the reason that 'the issue of employees' inventions is one which should be dealt with primarily at national level'.[39] Similarly, Article 60(1) of the European Patent Convention (EPC) only provides that 'the right to a European patent shall be determined in accordance with the law of the State' that either an employee or an employer is connected with.[40] As things stand, the relevant laws in European countries differ considerably.[41]

However, an obvious route to harmonisation, whether at the EU or the global level, is to abolish all the national laws which provide for compensation for invention made in the course of employees' duties. The ultimate purpose of this book is to push the case for the abolition of such compensation schemes that are purportedly aimed at giving employee inventors an incentive to invent. Through reference to the latest surveys on motivations of employee inventors in advanced countries and research findings in econometrics and social psychology I will challenge in this book the popular assumption that monetary rewards[42] can motivate employee inventors to create more invention, which most legal scholars have not even questioned. A further point to be made is that compensation for employee inventions is not justified as payment for the transfer of their ownership from employee inventors to employers since the rights in employee inventions should *ab initio* belong to employers in principle. This will reinforce my argument for repealing the diverse statutory laws which have lost their practicality and yet become an obstacle to cross-border operation of companies.

II. Scope and Contents of the Book

A. Employee Invention

This book deals with inventions made by employees in the course of their normal or specifically assigned duties during working hours using their employers' resources, which will be referred to as (i) 'employee inventions' in this book. Statutes

---

[38] Commission, 'Promoting Innovation through Patents: Green Paper on the Community Patent and the Patent System in Europe' COM (97) 314 final, 18.

[39] Commission, 'Promoting Innovation through Patents: The Follow-Up to the Green Paper on the Community Patent and the Patent System in Europe' COM (1999) 42 final, 14.

[40] Convention on the Grant of European Patents (European Patent Convention) of 5 October 1973, art 60(1).

[41] Wolk (n 17) 296; Janssens (n 37) 113.

[42] In the following text I will use the word 'reward' not to indicate 'reward theory' of the patent system mentioned earlier but in its ordinary sense.

in some jurisdictions state that employers may be required to pay compensation only when such inventions are either patentable or actually patented.[43] The terms 'invention' and 'patent' are interchangeable unless stated otherwise in this book.

Apart from 'employee inventions', (ii) employees may make inventions not in the course of their duties but during working hours or using their employers' resources. From the results of a survey conducted in six European countries, the US and Japan to be mentioned later, it is estimated that about 10 per cent of all the inventions made by employees are such 'incidental inventions'.[44] Employers are not naturally entitled to own or exploit them without special legislation or legal doctrines because employment contracts do not cover such inventions. In addition, (iii) employees may make inventions independently of their duties outside working hours without using their employers' resources. The ownership of such 'independent inventions' is naturally vested in the employees themselves regardless of jurisdiction since they are no different from those made by independent inventors. Those who want to acquire or exploit such inventions must enter into a contract with the inventors in accordance with the general principles of contract law. These (ii) incidental and (iii) independent inventions will be left out of consideration in principle although the treatment of incidental inventions will be briefly discussed in chapters five and six (the shop right rule in the US).

B. Employee Inventor

This book mainly covers inventions made by scientists and engineers working in companies. Whilst inventions made by government employees are treated in the same way as those made by company employees in Germany,[45] inventors working in the public sector receive a special bonus in the US[46] and France.[47] Such special bonus schemes for government employees will not be further investigated since they cover only a negligible number of inventions.[48] However, I will discuss inventions made by academics separate from those made by company employees in chapter eight since they may require special treatment because of the academic freedom university researchers enjoy.

C. Contents of the Book

This book is divided into two parts. Part I of this book will show through an interdisciplinary approach that compensation offered to employee inventors is in fact

---

[43] See, eg, Act on Employees' Inventions (Germany), s 2; Patents Act 1977 (UK), s 40(1)(a); Patent Act (Japan, as amended up to Act No 55 of 2015), art 35(4).
[44] See ch 3, fig 14.
[45] Act on Employees' Inventions, s 1.
[46] See text to n 19.
[47] Intellectual Property Code, arts L611-7(5), R611-14-1(II)(III).
[48] See text to n 1.

unlikely to have a positive effect on their motivation, productivity and creativity. The analysis will reveal that the legislature cannot expect to encourage the creation of valuable inventions by making compensation for some employee inventions mandatory.

Following this introductory chapter, chapter two will discuss the motivation and productivity of employee inventors and show that financial incentives are unlikely to encourage the vast majority of employee inventors to be more productive. The results of several empirical surveys that have examined job satisfaction and motivation of professional scientists and engineers are consistent with the theory about workers' motivation in psychology, which holds that values intrinsic in a job can motivate workers to higher levels of job performance whilst monetary rewards cannot. In addition, studies in econometrics have yet to confirm a causal relationship between financial incentives offered to employee inventors and their productivity measured by the number of inventions they make. These findings bring into question the effectiveness of the invention compensation schemes.

Chapter three will provide theoretical explanations as to why such schemes do not work in the context of inventive activities taking place in modern companies. In the contemporary commercial environment, inventions are usually created in organisations through the combined efforts of scientists and engineers from various disciplines. The incentives offered to a few who are named as inventors under patent law will influence the working relationships among all the employees who contribute to the creation of inventions in practice. Scholars in social psychology have noticed that there is a relationship between social norms and reward allocation rules generally adopted by organisations in each society. In the light of their theory, the invention compensation schemes clash with the social norm in 'collectivist societies' such as Confucian Asia where group harmony is a guiding principle of organisations in general, whilst the schemes are likely to promote egocentric behaviour of employee inventors especially in 'individualist societies' such as English-speaking countries where people tend to attach great importance to individual achievement. These observations will help to explain why the schemes are likely to fail in various societies. Furthermore, it will be shown that team-based incentives offered to employee inventors as a whole are also unlikely to work according to the theories in business management and social psychology.

Whilst the above discussions concern the influence of the invention compensation schemes on the quantity of inventions employee inventors make, chapter four will discuss their influence on the creativity of employee inventors, which determines the quality of employee inventions, so to speak. On the basis of contemporary research findings in psychology about the effect of financial rewards on creativity, it will be shown that the schemes are unlikely to encourage the creation of valuable inventions which embody highly creative ideas even if the amount of compensation paid to employee inventors is linked to the commercial value of the inventions. Furthermore, a specific case study of organisational practices to encourage workplace creativity in a multinational technology company will show that the schemes have little, if any, effect on the creativity of employee inventors because workplace creativity depends greatly on non-pecuniary factors such as the interpersonal relationships among colleagues and the vision of supervisors and top management.

Whilst it will be observed in Part I that compensation for employee inventions is unlikely to act as an effective incentive to invent, it may be argued that employers are still required to pay compensation for the transfer of employee inventions if their ownership is initially vested in employee inventors. Independently of the fundamental principle in labour law that employers naturally enjoy the fruits of labour expended by their employees, patent laws in some civil law countries have traditionally adopted the 'inventor principle', which holds that only natural persons capable of creative activities can become the initial owner of inventions made by them. In accordance with this principle, the German Patent Act,[49] for example, makes it clear that the right to a patent of an invention initially lies with its inventor(s).[50] The US Constitution also vests the ownership of inventions in their inventors on the assumption that it serves to promote the progress of science.[51]

Part II will show that compensation for employee inventions cannot be justified as payment for the transfer of their ownership in principle despite the 'inventor principle' or the US Constitution. Chapter five will provide the theoretical justification for this conclusion in terms of encouraging 'innovation' in society. The meaning of the term 'innovation' needs to be clarified here in connection with the aforementioned 'incentive theory' about the patent system. The theory suggests that incentives should be given to make inventions available to end users, not just to create inventions.[52] Current economic theory holds that patents generate an incentive to invent by enabling patentees to recoup the sunk costs of innovation.[53] 'Innovation', as the super-ordinate concept of 'invention', is composed of '(1) the generation of an idea or invention, and (2) the conversion of that invention into a business or other useful application'.[54] Recognising the risk of imitation by competitors, economic theory presumes that patents prevent rival firms from doing so for a limited time so that they can recoup the costs of innovation through monopoly pricing.[55] According to this theory, this prospect for monopoly profits generates an incentive to innovate[56] which conceptually includes that to invent.

---

[49] Patentgesetz vom 16 Dezember 1980 (BGBl 1981 I S 1).

[50] Patent Act, s 6 first sentence.

[51] US Constitution, art I, § 8, cl 8. This constitutional principle is utilitarian in nature and thus distinguished from the 'inventor principle', which merely focuses on the fact that only natural persons can make inventions.

[52] Hettinger (n 26) 48.

[53] Alexander Tabarrok, 'Patent Theory versus Patent Law' (2002) 1(1) *Contributions to Economic Analysis & Policy* 1, 1, mason.gmu.edu/~atabarro/PatentPublished.pdf.

[54] Edward B Roberts, 'What We've Learned: Managing Invention and Innovation' (1988) 31(1) *Research-Technology Management* 11, 12. As Roberts succinctly put it, 'Innovation = Invention + Exploitation': ibid 13.

[55] Tabarrok (n 53) 1.

[56] ibid.

It was assumed before the advent of corporate laboratories in the late nineteenth century in the US that inventors would become innovators who exploit their inventions themselves. However, this assumption is no longer sustainable today, when most employee inventors have neither the inclination nor the ability to do so. It will be proposed in this chapter that as between employers and employees employee inventions should belong to employers for the sake of innovation and that they should be allowed to exploit employee inventions without paying compensation in principle.

Next, it will be seen that employers are generally allowed to acquire employee inventions without paying compensation in the US (chapter six) and other common law jurisdictions such as England and Wales, Australia and Canada (chapter seven). The US Constitution, which was drafted in the late eighteenth century, vests the ownership of inventions in their inventors to make it clear that a patent is not such a monopolistic privilege as was arbitrarily granted by the English absolute monarchy. Nevertheless, employers in the US naturally acquire employee inventions even in the absence of explicit agreements to that effect where the inventors are 'hired to invent'. Otherwise employees become the owner of inventions they have made in principle although employers acquire a 'shop right', or the right to use the inventions without paying royalties, where the employees have made them during working hours or using employers' resources. Employers usually require prospective employees to sign pre-invention assignment agreements in order to eliminate the uncertainty about the rights in inventions made by employees, and such agreements have generally been held as enforceable even though the employees are usually not allowed to claim additional compensation for the inventions according to these agreements. It will be shown that US courts have virtually made the constitutional principle a dead letter so as to put priority on the need to encourage innovation in the society. Employers in other common law jurisdictions are generally not required to pay compensation for the transfer of employee inventions because they naturally become the initial owners of the inventions according to the employment contracts under which employee inventors owe a duty to invent.

However, inventions made by university researchers cannot be treated in the same way because they do not usually owe a duty to invent but only a duty to research under their employment contracts. Chapter eight will suggest an approach to the ownership of such inventions using recent decisions of the Australian courts as a basis for the discussion. There is a legitimate concern that if inventions made by academics should belong to universities, academics cannot publish their research results freely because they are required to protect the patentability of the inventions. Yet now most European countries have done away with the 'professors' privilege', which used to allow academics to retain their ownership, on the assumption that it created a barrier to innovation. Meanwhile, there is a strong argument that inventions made in academia should not be owned by someone in the first place because universities should essentially be the institution of 'open science' where it is expected that researchers disseminate their research results to the public freely to promote further scientific inquiry. Discussing the implications of this argument, the chapter will provide a theoretical analysis of the topic on the assumption that universities should be involved in patenting only on a limited basis.

In chapter nine the validity of the aforementioned 'inventor principle' adopted in some civil law countries will be questioned through analysis of the rationale for compensation to employee inventors under the German Act on Employees' Inventions and the latest amendment to the relevant provisions in the Japanese Patent Act in 2015. It will be shown that the 'inventor principle' has in fact been compromised to accommodate the need to promote innovation, which will shake the assumption that that principle still demands the payment of compensation for the transfer of employee inventions in theory.

Finally, chapter 10 will discuss the policy and theoretical implications of this study and conclude that compensation for employee inventions should not be made mandatory regardless of jurisdiction because there is no legitimate reason to require employers to pay it.

PART I

Financial Incentives
and the Motivation, Productivity
and Creativity of Employee Inventors

2

Motivation of Employee Inventors and the Effect of Incentives on their Productivity

I. Practice of Compensation to Employee Inventors

It may be taken for granted that financial incentives will always boost employees' motivation. As most workers will wish for wealth, it is reasonable to assume that they are likely to feel motivated if there is a good chance of gaining it. Wealth is often regarded as a symbol of social success, and as such it usually appeals to those with ambitions to succeed in a capitalist society. For example, in a passage which discusses the relationship between the capitalist order and the increase in the output of the system, the economist Joseph Schumpeter stated as follows:

> The promises of wealth ... are strong enough to attract the large majority of supernormal brains and to identify success with business success. ... Spectacular prizes much greater than would have been necessary to call forth the particular effort are thrown to a small minority of winners, thus propelling much more efficaciously than a more equal and more 'just' distribution would, the activity of that large majority of businessman who receive in return very modest compensation or nothing or less than nothing, and yet do their utmost because they have the big prizes before their eyes and overrate their chances of doing equally well.[1]

Those who argue for pro-employee legal rules tend to apply this 'commonsense', yet unproven, view to scientists and engineers who invent as employees in companies. Dratler argues that '[o]nly an extraordinary incentive, apart from the usual rewards of promotion and higher pay, could motivate people to incur ... risks [of being criticized in case of failures] and costs [of creating inventions] in the face of uncertain success'.[2] If this is true, the vast majority of companies should already have introduced generous financial incentive programmes to encourage employees to invent whether or not the payment of compensation for employee

---

[1] Joseph A Schumpeter, *Capitalism, Socialism and Democracy*, new edn (originally published 1943, London, Routledge, 1994) 73–74.

[2] Jay Dratler Jr, 'Incentive for People: The Forgotten Purpose of the Patent System' (1979) 16 *Harvard Journal on Legislation* 129, 181.

Figure 1 Description of Compensation Schemes in US Companies

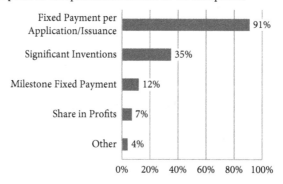

inventions is made mandatory according to the law of each country. However, employers in the US and Europe do not frequently offer a substantial amount of compensation for employee inventions.

Savitsky published the results of a survey of an 'employee invention compensation system' covering 118 'leading US companies' in 1991.[3] Only 50 per cent of these companies had 'a special monetary compensation system for employee inventions' separate from 'fixed salary'.[4] Figure 1 shows the description of the special compensation schemes.[5] Of the 50 per cent of the companies which had such schemes, 91 per cent offered compensation for 'fixed payment for every patent application filed and/or issued',[6] yet the sum was typically modest with most of them offering less than $1,000 per filing and/or issuance.[7] Only 12 per cent of the companies offered a bonus for certain 'milestones', such as '$1,000 for 10th application'.[8] Savitsky points out that these kinds of payments are 'related more to quantity than quality', and basically offered out of 'a management concern' to increase 'disclosure of inventions' and/or 'cooperation by the inventor in the patenting process'.[9]

Above and beyond these generally nominal awards, some companies adopt compensation schemes linked with the value of the invention, such as a bonus scheme for 'significant inventions' and a programme which allows employee inventors to 'share in profits or income derived from invention'.[10] Those schemes are 'related more to quality rather than quantity', and primarily expected to

---

[3] Thomas R Savitsky, 'Compensation for Employee Inventions' (1991) 73 *Journal of the Patent and Trademark Office Society* 645, 651.

[4] ibid 653.

[5] Adapted from Savitsky (n 3) 654 Fig 3.

[6] ibid 652, 654, 665.

[7] ibid 670–75.

[8] ibid 654, 673.

[9] ibid 659.

[10] ibid 665.

Figure 2 Rewards for Inventing in the US

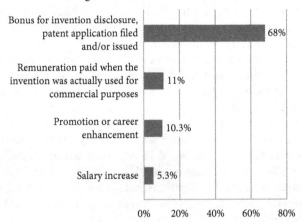

increase 'employee creativity or innovativeness'.[11] However, companies having such schemes were in the minority in Savitsky's survey. Only 35 per cent and 7 per cent of the companies having special payment schemes offered a bonus for 'significant inventions' and 'share in profits' respectively.[12] Thus, it would appear that US companies in his survey did not generally attach much importance to financial incentives for employee inventors.

A study conducted by the Intellectual Property Owners Association in the US in 2003, albeit less extensive, shows similar results to those of Savitsky's. Whilst 16 per cent, 61 per cent and 37 per cent of the 38 respondent companies paid their employees a nominal amount of money for invention disclosure, patent application and issuance respectively, only nine companies paid for a 'highly valuable' patent with its amount 'ranging from $300 to $37,500'.[13]

The results of the latest survey published in 2012 that are shown in Figure 2[14] also confirm the relatively rare occurrence of compensation linked to the economic value of employee inventions in the US. One question in this survey asked respondents about the rewards they had received from their employers as a result of making patented inventions.[15] Of the 1,923 US respondents who answered the question,

---

[11] ibid 659.
[12] ibid 654.
[13] Intellectual Property Owners Association, 'Employee Inventor Compensation Practices Survey: Report of the IPO Asian Practice Committee' (2004) 1–3.
[14] Adapted from Sadao Nagaoka and others, 'Innovation Process in Japan in the Early 2000s as Seen from Inventors: Agenda for Strengthening Innovative Capability' (in Japanese) (2012) *RIETI Discussion Paper Series 12-J-033*, 61 Table 3-4-2, www.rieti.go.jp/jp/publications/dp/12j033.pdf. Detailed account of this survey called 'PatVal EU-US/JP II' will be given in ch 3, s IV below.
[15] ibid.

68 per cent had received a generally nominal bonus for invention disclosure, patent application filed and/or issued, whilst only 11 per cent had received remuneration paid when the invention was actually used for commercial purposes.[16] However, there were 3,286 US respondents in this survey[17] and those who did not answer this question had presumably received no additional rewards for making inventions. It is said that the majority of US companies do not offer substantial inventor remuneration on the assumption that employees with ingenuity can naturally win promotion and salary increase which are thought to as sufficient incentives for them.[18] Nevertheless, these do not occur frequently according to this survey: only 10.3 per cent of the US respondents who answered that question had attained promotion/career enhancement, whilst 5.3 per cent had gained a salary increase.[19]

It is reasonable to say from the results of above recent surveys that the practice of compensation for employee inventions in US companies has changed little since Savitsky's survey. Meanwhile, in 2014 an international law firm carried out a survey on voluntary reward plans for employee inventors in 48 companies operating in Europe, of which 42 per cent had more than 10,000 employees.[20] It was found that 36 per cent, 92 per cent, and 68 per cent of respondent companies offered rewards upon the initial disclosure of the invention, filing of patent application and patent grant respectively, yet the amount was for the most part less than €1,000 per invention.[21] 44 per cent of them offered rewards upon the use of the invention by the company, and the amount was typically 0.5 to 1.5 per cent of the relevant turnover.[22] European companies, like their American counterparts, frequently offer a nominal amount of compensation for invention disclosure, patent application or grant, though most employee inventors are unlikely to receive substantial inventor remuneration whether in the US or Europe.

It may be argued that since it is hard to expect for employers to pay generous compensation for employee inventions on a voluntary basis, it is necessary to establish statutory compensation schemes which give employee inventors an adequate incentive to invent. However, one important question which arises is whether monetary rewards really motivate scientists and engineers who create inventions in companies. Here, in answer to this question, it is necessary to introduce the 'motivation-hygiene' theory in psychology presented by Herzberg. Although controversial, his theory on this topic is still influential among psychologists in this field.

---

[16] ibid 61 Table 3-4-2.

[17] See ch 2, s IV.

[18] Joseph Rossman, 'Rewards and Incentives to Employee-Inventors' (1963) 7 *The Patent, Trademark and Copyright Journal of Research and Education* 431, 447; Orin E Laney, 'Intellectual Property and the Employee Engineer' (IEEE-USA Professional Guideline Series, The Institute of Electrical and Electronics Engineers 2001) 15, www.ieeeusa.org/members/IPandtheengineer.pdf.

[19] Nagaoka and others (n 14) 61 Table 3-4-2.

[20] CMS Patents Team, 'Employee Inventor Rewards Survey' (CMS 2014) 3–5, downloadable from: cms.law/en/CHE/Publication/CMS-Employee-inventor-rewards-survey.

[21] ibid 8–10.

[22] ibid 11.

II. The Motivation-Hygiene Theory: Criticism and its Usefulness

Herzberg carried out his seminal empirical study on job motivation and first published his theory in 1959.[23] The basic assumption underlying his study was that what workers want from their jobs offers a clue for motivating workers.[24] He had learned from earlier literature on this topic that some factors would make a worker like his job whilst others not, and that these job attitudes might in turn have some effect on his output or productivity.[25] He tried to delineate this 'factors-attitudes-effects (F-A-E) complex'[26] by an empirical survey involving interviews with 203 accountants and engineers who worked for companies around Pittsburgh in the US.[27] The interviewees were asked to tell stories about times when they had felt exceptionally good or bad about their jobs.[28] Those stories were analysed afterwards by staff members of the survey so as to identify factors which had led to the interviewees' positive or negative attitudes toward their job and to assess their effects.[29]

In his study 'factors' meant 'concrete events or situations' 'antecedent to a person's attitude toward his job' 'reported by the respondent'.[30] It must be noted that 'factors' here are matters causing a certain job attitude of workers, whether positive or negative. For example, 'recognition' includes 'acts of criticism or blame', whilst 'achievement' includes 'its opposite, failure, and the absence of achievement'.[31] Similarly, 'salary' includes 'unfulfilled expectation of salary increases'.[32] Figure 3 below shows the frequency of each factor reported by respondents which resulted in their positive or negative job attitudes.[33]

These data suggest that five factors—achievement, recognition, work itself, responsibility and advancement—are more likely to increase job satisfaction because they appeared more in stories leading to positive job attitude than in those leading to negative job attitude.[34] Herzberg argued that these factors, which were related to tasks themselves or events accompanying successful performance of them, had led to positive job attitudes 'because they satisfy the individual's need

---

[23] Frederick Herzberg, Bernard Mausner and Barbara Bloch Snyderman, *The Motivation to Work*, 2nd edn (New York, John Wiley & Sons, 1967).

[24] ibid 6.

[25] ibid 7–8.

[26] ibid 11.

[27] ibid 30–32.

[28] ibid 35.

[29] ibid 39.

[30] ibid 27.

[31] ibid 45.

[32] ibid 46.

[33] Adapted from Herzberg, Mausner and Snyderman (n 23) 72 Table 6. Since more than one factor had been mentioned in any single sequence of events, the total percentage of all the factors which had appeared in the respondents' positive or negative job attitude exceeded 100 per cent: ibid 60.

[34] ibid 80.

Figure 3 Factors Appearing in Events that Led to Positive and Negative Job Attitudes

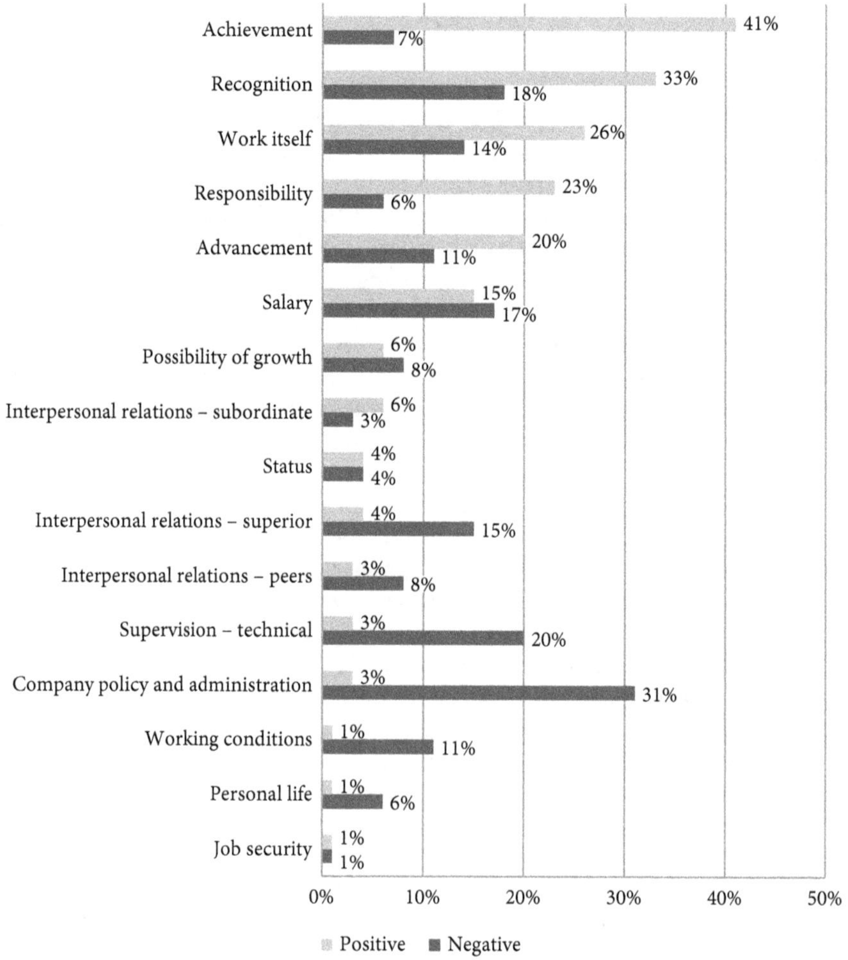

Achievement — 41% / 7%
Recognition — 33% / 18%
Work itself — 26% / 14%
Responsibility — 23% / 6%
Advancement — 20% / 11%
Salary — 15% / 17%
Possibility of growth — 6% / 8%
Interpersonal relations – subordinate — 6% / 3%
Status — 4% / 4%
Interpersonal relations – superior — 4% / 15%
Interpersonal relations – peers — 3% / 8%
Supervision – technical — 3% / 20%
Company policy and administration — 3% / 31%
Working conditions — 1% / 11%
Personal life — 1% / 6%
Job security — 1% / 1%

Positive ■ Negative

for self-actualization in his work'.[35] He argued that these factors, designated as *motivators* by him, 'serve to bring about the kind of job satisfaction and ... the kind of improvement in performance that industry is seeking from its work force'.[36]

On the other hand, the results suggest that 'company policy and administration, supervision (technical and human relations), and working conditions' are more likely to work as job dissatisfiers rather than satisfiers.[37] Herzberg designated

[35] ibid 113–14.
[36] ibid 114.
[37] ibid 82.

these factors, all associated 'with conditions that *surround* the doing of the job', as *hygiene* factors, on the assumption that 'they act in a manner analogous to the principles of medical hygiene'.[38] According to him, '[h]ygiene operates to remove health hazards from the environment of man' and thus '[i]t is not a curative; it is, rather, a preventive'.[39] Herzberg asserted by its analogy that improvement in hygiene factors, which form the basis for motivators to work, contributes to 'the prevention of dissatisfaction and poor job performance' by 'remov[ing] the impediments to positive job attitude', but 'does not motivate the individual to high levels of job satisfaction and … to extra performance on the job'.[40]

The question now arises as to whether monetary rewards are a motivator or a hygiene factor. Salary was mentioned with almost equal frequency in positive (15 per cent) and negative (17 per cent) job situations. Nevertheless, after some consideration Herzberg classified it as a hygiene factor.[41] He cited remarks of company managers that '[b]eyond enough for our real needs, money itself is valued less for what it will buy than as an evidence of successful skill in achievement'[42] and that '[e]arnings that are the reward for outstanding performance, progress, and responsibility are signs that he is a man among men'.[43] From these comments he claimed that what matters in monetary incentive schemes established in many companies was not money itself offered to employees, but 'achievement' and 'recognition' they experience.[44] According to him, where none of the motivators are present in a job, the correction of poor hygiene might lead to the elimination of 'voluntary restriction of output' commonly observed in industries.[45] Nevertheless, he stated that it was misleading to refer to it 'as a positive gain in performance' because '[t]he improvement produced under these circumstances is actually far less than one could obtain were motivators to be introduced'.[46]

Designating salary as a hygiene factor, Herzberg argued that money itself does not play a positive role in motivating employees or enhancing their productivity. Whether salary is a motivator or a hygiene factor, his study suggests that money itself is unlikely to give workers a high degree of job satisfaction as in that study salary was mentioned in only 15 per cent of events which had resulted in the respondents' positive job attitudes.[47]

Figure 4 shows the frequency of five motivators and salary (a hygiene factor) mentioned in the events which had led to the positive job attitudes of engineers and accountants surveyed in the study.[48] There were statistically significant

[38] ibid 113.
[39] ibid.
[40] ibid 113, 115.
[41] ibid 82–83.
[42] ibid 117.
[43] ibid 118.
[44] ibid 117.
[45] ibid 118.
[46] ibid.
[47] See Fig 3.
[48] Adapted from Herzberg, Mausner and Snyderman (n 23) 101 Table 16.

Figure 4 Frequency of *Motivators* and *Salary* Mentioned in the Positive Job Events of Engineers and Accountants

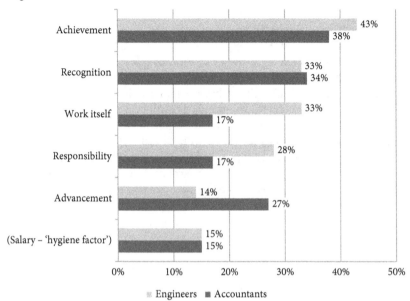

differences in the data for three factors, namely 'work itself', 'responsibility' and 'advancement'.[49] Engineers mentioned 'work itself' in positive job events nearly twice as frequently as accountants did. By contrast, the frequency of 'achievement', 'recognition' and 'salary' mentioned in positive job events differed little between these two groups of professionals.

On the basis of Herzberg's study, one may think that employers can motivate engineers by making their jobs more interesting because they are more likely to derive job satisfaction from 'work itself' as the above data suggest. However, Herzberg himself was sceptical about this idea. In his view, conscious effort to make jobs interesting does not necessarily bring the success in redesigning jobs because it is difficult to know what kind of job every employee finds interesting.[50] Meanwhile, he did not deny that economic incentives could still be 'applied to the hourly worker in a bonus or to the vice-president in an offer of a stock option'.[51] However, he assumed that there should be more effective ways of motivating workers because the nineteenth-century view of the economic man who 'sells his labor at the best price he can get for it' 'became untenable'.[52]

---

[49] ibid 101.
[50] ibid 134.
[51] ibid 126.
[52] ibid.

In sum, proposing the motivator-hygiene dichotomy, Herzberg argued that improving hygiene factors could prevent negative consequences caused by the low morale of workers.[53] However, while stating that '[h]ygiene is not enough', he did not present the precise way to strengthen motivators which should play a crucial role in boosting workers' motivation.[54]

Herzberg's motivation-hygiene, or dual-factor, theory has not won broad support from psychologists. It has been criticised on several grounds.[55] First, the results of the original survey by Herzberg and colleagues may have been biased by a possible tendency for respondents to attribute their job satisfaction to their personal achievement rather than factors surrounding the job and job dissatisfaction to their work environment rather than their own faults.[56] Moreover, their survey only covered 203 accountants and engineers, and thus it is not apparent whether their theory applied to workers in general. In less than a decade after the theory was first published in 1959, a number of psychologists conducted scores of surveys sampling workers from various occupations to test the general validity of the theory.[57] Whilst some of them claimed to replicate the original theory by Herzberg,[58] others showed that what he called motivators are no less related to job dissatisfaction than to job satisfaction, suggesting that motivators may not have unidirectional effects of increasing job satisfaction.[59]

The most fundamental criticism of the theory concerns its assumption that highly satisfied workers would have stronger motivation to work and thus achieve greater productivity.[60] It should be noticed that 'job satisfaction' is not necessarily a synonym of 'motivation'; the former meaning 'an emotional response accompanying thoughts or actions related to work', whilst the latter 'the process by which behaviour is activated'.[61] In theory, workers may be satisfied with their jobs without being motivated to work.[62] As Vroom commented, 'Herzberg loses sight of the distinction between recall of satisfying events and actual observation of motivated behavior'.[63]

---

[53] ibid 131.

[54] ibid 132.

[55] Robert J House and Lawrence A Wigdor, 'Herzberg's Dual-Factor Theory of Job Satisfaction and Motivation: A Review of the Evidence and a Criticism' (1967) 20 *Personnel Psychology* 369, 371.

[56] Victor H Vroom, *Work and Motivation* (originally published 1964, Malabar, Robert E Krieger, 1984) 129.

[57] House and Wigdor (n 55) 376–83.

[58] Frederick Herzberg, *Work and the Nature of Man* (originally published 1968, London, Staples Press, 1972) 128.

[59] Paul F Wernimont, 'Intrinsic and Extrinsic Factors in Job Satisfaction' (1966) 50 *Journal of Applied Psychology* 41, 44, 46; Robert B Ewen and others, 'An Empirical Test of the Herzberg Two-Factor Theory' (1966) 50 *Journal of Applied Psychology* 544, 548–49; Marvin D Dunnette, John P Campbell and Milton D Hakel, 'Factors Contributing to Job Satisfaction and Job Dissatisfaction in Six Occupational Groups' (1967) 2 *Organizational Behavior and Human Performance* 143, 169; House and Wigdor (n 55) 386–87.

[60] House and Wigdor (n 55) 373, 375, 384.

[61] David D Shipley and Julia A Kiely, 'Industrial Salesforce Motivation and Herzberg's Dual Factor Theory: A UK Perspective' (1986) 6(1) *The Journal of Personal Selling & Sales Management* 9, 9.

[62] ibid.

[63] Victor H Vroom, 'Some Observations Regarding Herzberg's Two-Factor Theory' (American Psychological Association Convention, New York, September 1966) 11.

Furthermore, it is open to question whether high job satisfaction and/or motivation of workers really result in high productivity. Although Herzberg and his colleagues claimed they observed 'an improvement in performance as a result of an improved attitude on the job'[64] based on the qualitative analysis of the respondents' reports about their job experiences, the researchers did 'no quantitative measure of changes in output'.[65] Even before the publication of Herzberg's theory, some psychologists had suggested by reviewing the previous empirical literature that there might be only a slight, if any, correlation between workers' satisfaction and performance.[66] Given that various factors, such as 'working conditions, the quality of leadership, the suitability of supplies and equipment, the efficiency of scheduling and coordinating procedures … [and] the abilities of the members of the work force', all involve productivity of workers, high satisfaction and/or motivation may have little causal relationship with total productivity.[67] Accordingly, 'the relation between [job satisfaction and productivity] is relatively complex' and thus 'one cannot conclude that a satisfied worker will necessarily be productive or that the conditions that promote satisfaction will necessarily promote productivity'.[68]

Herzberg's theory follows the need-satisfaction model of job attitudes, which 'has been the theoretical framework almost universally applied to understand job satisfaction and … motivation'.[69] The model posits that 'persons have basic, stable, relatively unchanging and identifiable attributes, including needs' and that 'jobs have a stable, identifiable set of characteristics that are relevant to those needs of individuals'.[70] However, some studies subsequent to Herzberg's have shown that there are individual differences in the way employees respond to various job aspects,[71] and psychologists since Herzberg have generally tried to formulate models of motivation in the workplace based on the assumption that 'different individuals have different need strength and … will respond differently to the same job characteristics'.[72] Herzberg's theory cannot avoid the criticism that it 'is an oversimplification of the relationships between motivation and satisfaction, and the sources of job satisfaction and dissatisfaction'.[73]

---

[64] Herzberg, Mausner and Snyderman (n 23) 86.

[65] ibid 85.

[66] Arthur H Brayfield and Walter H Crockett, 'Employee Attitudes and Employee Performance' (1955) 52 *Psychological Bulletin* 396, 420–21.

[67] House and Wigdor (n 55) 375, 384.

[68] Edward L Deci, 'Motivation Research in Industrial/Organizational Psychology' in Victor H Vroom and Edward L Deci (eds), *Management and Motivation: Selected Readings*, 2nd edn (Harmondsworth, Penguin, 1992) 169.

[69] Gerald R Salancik and Jeffrey Pfeffer, 'An Examination of Need-Satisfaction Models of Job Attitudes' (1977) 22 *Administrative Science Quarterly* 427, 427, 435–36.

[70] ibid 428.

[71] J Richard Hackman and Greg R Oldham, 'Motivation through the Design of Work: Test of a Theory' (1976) 16 *Organizational Behavior and Human Performance* 250, 251–52.

[72] Salancik and Pfeffer (n 69) 436.

[73] House and Wigdor (n 55) 387.

Nevertheless, as Vroom remarked, 'Herzberg and his associates deserve credit for directing attention toward the psychological effects of job content'.[74] His theory is still influential to this day across borders despite the above criticism. For example, in a recent study of employee suggestion schemes in 32 large organisations in the UK, factors corresponding to *achievement* and *work itself* in Herzberg's phraseology were far more frequently mentioned by employees as reasons for their having contributed ideas under the schemes than 'desire to win money or gifts'.[75]

This book discusses incentives for employee inventors rather than the general applicability of the motivation-hygiene theory or the relationship between job satisfaction, motivation and performance. Whether or not Herzberg's theory generally applies to all kinds of occupations, hereafter it will be examined in the light of his theory whether monetary rewards increase the job satisfaction, motivation and performance of scientists and engineers who create inventions in organisations. In the following analysis two points must be borne in mind. First, 'job satisfaction' is not equivalent to 'motivation'[76] or 'performance'. Although Herzberg's theory tends to focus on job satisfaction, the latter two demand adequate consideration to examine the effect of incentives for employee inventors comprehensively. Next, the range of this theory of US-origin may span across borders. If this theory applies to scientists and engineers outside the US, it will shake the assumption that monetary rewards can motivate employee inventors to create more inventions, not only in the US but also in other countries.

III. Job Satisfaction and Motivation of Scientists and Engineers

Herzberg's theory turns researchers' attention to job-intrinsic factors that may boost job satisfaction and motivation to work. In accordance with his theory scientists and engineers are more likely to derive job satisfaction and motivation from what Herzberg called *achievement* and *work itself* than from monetary rewards in general. For example, in a study published in 1931 which asked 710 US inventors about their motives for inventing, respondents who mentioned 'love of inventing' (193 inventors) or 'desire to improve' (189) outnumbered those who mentioned 'financial gain' (167).[77] In another empirical study published in 1967, sampled workers in six occupations in the US (engineers and scientists, machine equipment salesmen, secretaries, store managers, army reservists and night school

---

[74] Vroom (n 56) 129.

[75] Nigel Bassett-Jones and Geoffrey C Lloyd, 'Does Herzberg's Motivation Theory Have Staying Power?' (2005) 24 *Journal of Management Development* 929, 935–36.

[76] See text to n 61.

[77] Joseph Rossman, 'The Motives of Inventors' (1931) 45 *The Quarterly Journal of Economics* 522, 522–23 Table I.

Figure 5 Overall Means for *Achievement, Work Itself* and *Salary* in Six Occupational Groups

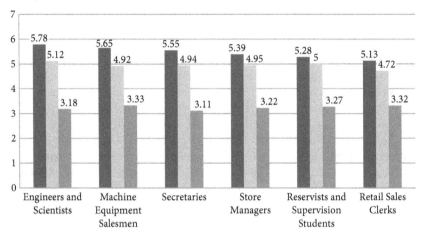

supervision students, and retail sales clerks) were asked to rate how likely they were to derive job satisfaction from some job factors mentioned in Herzberg's original study on a scale of '1' (the least likely) to '7' (the most likely).[78] Figure 5 below shows overall means of the ratings on three job factors, namely *achievement, work itself* and *salary*, which were calculated across the samples in six occupations.[79] It is noticeable that engineers and scientists rated *achievement* and *work itself* somewhat higher than any other occupational groups. Meanwhile, regardless of occupation, *salary* was rated lower than *achievement* or *work itself*. Care must be taken, however, in drawing a general conclusion from these data since the number of samples in this study was small.[80]

A far more extensive survey of 17,439 scientists and engineers working for the US Federal Government and 3,317 in industry, which was conducted between 1956 and 1957,[81] yielded similar results. Figure 6 below shows the percentages of those respondents who personally attached 'utmost importance' to 15 job elements 'in determining overall satisfaction with a research position'.[82] Respondents

[78] Dunnette, Campbell and Hakel (n 59) 149–50, 154–55.

[79] Compiled from Dunnette, Campbell and Hakel (n 59) 156–61 Table 4–9.

[80] The number of participants in each occupational group was 129, 49, 44, 133, 92 and 89 respectively: ibid 155.

[81] Committee on Engineers and Scientists for Federal Government Programs, 'Summary Report of Survey of Attitudes of Scientists and Engineers in Government and Industry' (Washington DC, United States Government Printing Office, 1957) 2–3.

[82] Compiled from Committee on Engineers and Scientists for Federal Government Programs (n 81) 72–74.

Figure 6 Job Elements to which Scientists and Engineers Attach Utmost Importance in Determining Overall Satisfaction with their Research Positions

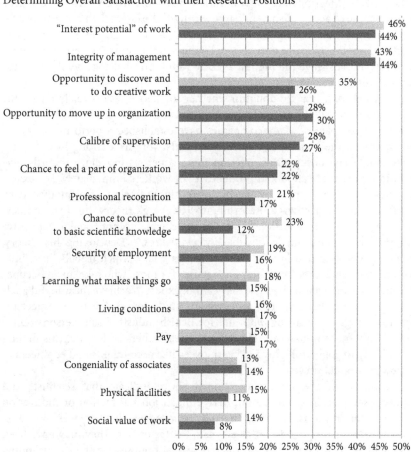

mentioned items that correspond to *work itself* in Herzberg's phraseology, such as "'[i]nterest potential" of work' (listed at the top) and '[o]pportunity to discover and to do creative work' (the third from the top), far more frequently than '[p]ay' (the fourth from the bottom).

Research personnel based in Europe are also likely to attach greater importance to *work itself* than to monetary rewards. As discussed in detail later in chapter three, Hofstede surveyed about 88,000 employees of the International Business Machines Corporation (IBM) across the world between 1967 and 1973.[83] In those

---

[83] Geert Hofstede, *Culture's Consequences: Comparing Values, Behaviors, Institutions, and Organizations across Nations*, 2nd edn (originally published 1980, Thousand Oaks, SAGE, 2001) 48.

surveys respondents were asked to rate the importance of various 'work goals' such as 'challenge' ('[h]av[ing] challenging work to do – work from which you can get a personal sense of accomplishment') and 'earnings' ('[h]av[ing] an opportunity for high earnings').[84] According to the data obtained from subsidiaries in 15 European countries,[85] of the 38 major occupational groups in the company 'research laboratory professionals' gave the highest average rating on 'challenge' whilst only the fourth lowest on 'earnings'.[86]

Nevertheless, it may be doubtful whether the above results really reflect the reality about the significance of monetary rewards for scientists and engineers working in companies. Many companies have established a performance-based pay system on the belief that monetary rewards work as a strong incentive for workers. In some occupations, offering more generous monetary rewards may result in higher motivation and productivity of workers immediately. For example, unskilled workers paid by the hour are highly likely to feel motivated by the rise in their hourly wage. According to Herzberg's theory, this can be interpreted merely as 'the correction of poor hygiene', which is not equal to 'a positive gain in performance' made possible by *motivators*.[87] Developing his theory, Myers hypothesised that *hygiene* factors such as salary, which usually 'have little motivational value', acquire greater importance for those who take up an occupation unattractive in nature because they cannot expect to achieve meaningful goals in their careers.[88] For example, an empirical study found that the prospect for higher earnings was a strong *motivator* for British industrial salespersons remunerated only by commission.[89] However, the researchers added that this finding was unlikely to apply to highly paid employees like accountants and engineers in Herzberg's original survey.[90]

The results of the surveys mentioned above indicate that scientists and engineers sampled in them did not derive much job satisfaction or motivation from monetary rewards. However, this may only suggest that they were not satisfied with the existing condition of pay as a matter of fact. They may have been better motivated if they had been offered special bonuses for their outstanding performance. Thus it is too early to conclude that potential inventors are generally indifferent to monetary rewards before discussing the results of more recent studies on incentives for them. For example, Staudt and colleagues published in 1990 the result of a survey of R&D personnel in Germany, which appears to highlight the importance of monetary incentives for employee inventors. In the survey, 522 employee inventors sampled from patent applications at the German

---

[84] ibid 256.
[85] ibid 257.
[86] ibid 488–89 Exhibit A3.4.
[87] See text to nn 45, 46.
[88] M Scott Myers, 'Who Are Your Motivated Workers?' (1964) 42(1) *Harvard Business Review* 73, 85.
[89] Shipley and Kiely (n 61) 12 Table 3.
[90] ibid 13.

Figure 7 Important Incentives for German Employee Inventors

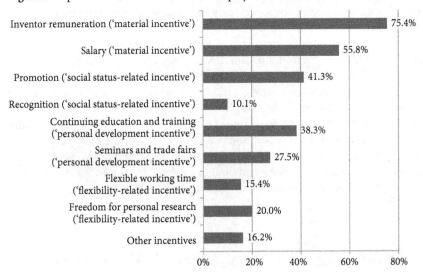

Patent Office were asked to name three most important incentives for their 'creative activity'.[91] As Figure 7 below shows,[92] nearly three out of four respondents mentioned 'inventor remuneration' as an important incentive and more than half of respondents 'salary'. These 'material incentives' were mentioned far more frequently than other incentives such as 'social status-related incentives' (eg, 'promotion' and 'recognition'), 'personal development incentives' (eg, 'continuing education and training' and 'seminar and trade fair attendance') and 'flexibility-related incentives' (eg, 'flexible working time' and 'freedom for personal research').[93]

Although the researchers concluded that those material incentives were particularly important for R&D personnel,[94] their findings must be interpreted cautiously for the following two reasons. First and foremost, no items which correspond to *achievement* and *work itself* in Herzberg's phraseology were included in the survey question. The survey only asked respondents' views on the importance of incentives listed in the Figure,[95] which were by no means exhaustive. Even though the majority of respondents in that survey regarded material incentives

---

[91] Erich Staudt and others, 'Anreizsysteme als Instrument des betrieblichen Innovationsmanagements – Ergebnisse einer empirischen Untersuchung im F+E-Bereich' [Incentive Systems as an Instrument of Corporate Innovation Management – Results of an Empirical Study in the R&D Sector] (1990) 60 *Zeitschrift für Betriebswirtschaft (ZfB)* 1183, 1185, 1194.

[92] Compiled from Staudt and others, (n 91) 1188 Abb 4, 1195 Abb 7.

[93] ibid.

[94] ibid 1197, 1198.

[95] ibid 1194.

as most important, the effect of such incentives may be negligible in fact because other factors not listed in the survey may have provided them with much greater motivation.

Next, although 60 per cent of respondents in the survey said they were not satisfied with the actual implementation of remuneration schemes in their companies,[96] their statements revealed that they complained mainly about 'justice' (the disparity between remuneration they received and their efforts in inventing or profits brought to their employers) and 'flexibility' or 'transparency' of criteria used in calculating remuneration rather than the sum itself.[97] To put it plainly, the main cause of their dissatisfaction was not 'the size of the received payment' but 'the "incomprehension" as to how the size of the payment came about'.[98] This suggests that just offering a larger amount of inventor remuneration is unlikely to make them feel more satisfied and motivated.

IV. Motivation to Invent:
Evidence from PatVal-I/II and RIETI Surveys

The data shown in Figure 7 do not tell the whole story about incentives for employee inventors according to the results of the recent three research projects conducted through the international cooperation of research institutes in Europe, the US and Japan. The PatVal-EU survey (hereinafter PatVal-I), the first instance of such research projects, was funded by the EU under its Fifth Framework Programme for Research and Technological Development (FP5),[99] which eventually developed into the PatVal EU-US/JP II survey to be discussed later. Although the primary goal of the programme 'was to gather information on the economic value of the European patents', it also provided information about the characteristics of the inventors in Europe which would bring about 'a better understanding of the relationship between the input and output variables of the innovation process'.[100]

The survey was conducted from 2003 to 2004 by sampling 27,531 patents granted by the European Patent Office (EPO) with a priority date between 1993

---

[96] ibid 1189.

[97] ibid 1189, 1192. These criteria are, for example, 'duration of the market success of the invention' and 'turnover achieved with the invention'.

[98] Peter Mühlemeyer, 'R&D – Personnel Management by Incentive Management: Results of an Empirical Survey in Research & Development' (1992) 21(4) *Personnel Review* 27, 33.

[99] Its official project name is '[t]he value of european patents: empirical models and policy implications based on a survey of european inventors'. See the Community Research and Development Information Service (CORDIS) website for the project information at: cordis.europa.eu/projects/rcn/60406_en.html.

[100] PatVal-EU, 'The Value of European Patents: Evidence from a Survey of European Inventors (Final Report of the PatVal EU Project)' (2005) 2–3, ec.europa.eu/invest-in-research/pdf/download_en/patval_mainreportandannexes.pdf.

and 1997, and the researchers received responses from 9,017 inventors in six EU countries, namely Germany, France, the UK, Italy, the Netherlands and Spain (hereinafter EU6).[101] Since 88.3 per cent of the respondents indicated that they had been employed in organisations at the time of the invention,[102] the results largely reflected the situation of employee inventors in EU6 countries.

Respondents were asked to rate the importance of six kinds of rewards for inventing, whether tangible or intangible, on a scale of '1' to '5', with '1' representing 'not important' and '5' 'very important'.[103] Figure 8 below shows the average ratings on these rewards among respondents in EU6 countries as well as those in Germany and the UK.[104] Some rewards correspond to 'material incentives' (eg, 'monetary rewards' and 'benefits in terms of working condition as a reward by the employer') and 'social status-related incentives' (eg, 'prestige/reputation' and 'career advances and opportunities or new/better jobs') in the classification adopted in Figure 7 above. In PatVal-I the rating on 'monetary rewards' was only the third lowest in EU6, or the second lowest in the UK, of the six items. It is interesting to note that in PatVal-I 'monetary rewards' was rated lower than 'prestige/reputation' by German respondents as opposed to the results shown in Figure 7. This weakens the conclusion drawn in that study that 'material incentives' bear higher importance for R&D personnel than any other incentive, including 'social status-related incentives'.[105] Factors that correspond to 'achievement' (eg, 'innovations increase the performance of the organization the inventor works for') and 'work itself' (eg, 'satisfaction to show that something is technically possible')[106] in Herzberg's phraseology were rated higher than 'material incentives' and 'social status-related incentives' listed in Figure 8. Overall, the results suggest that inventors in EU6 countries are more likely to feel motivated to invent by values which do not bring tangible gains to themselves directly.

A similar survey was conducted in the US and Japan in 2007 by the initiative of the Research Institute of Economy, Trade and Industry (RIETI), an incorporated administrative agency in Japan. It sampled 7,933 US inventors mentioned in patents with a priority date between 2000 and 2003, and 17,643 Japanese inventors mentioned in those between 1995 and 2001, from the Organisation for Economic Co-operation and Development (OECD)'s Triadic Patent Families database in 2006 which covers patents filed at both the EPO and the Japanese Patent Office (JPO) and granted by the US Patent and Trademark Office (USPTO).[107] The researchers

---

[101] ibid 3. The number of respondents was 3,346 (Germany), 1,486 (France), 1,542 (UK), 1,250 (Italy), 1,124 (Netherlands) and 269 (Spain), which reflected the relative size of each country's population.

[102] ibid Table C.1 in Annex II.

[103] ibid Question E.4 in Annex I.

[104] Adapted from PatVal-EU, 'The Value of European Patents' (n 100) 36 Table 5.1.

[105] See text to n 94.

[106] In the description of PatVal-II and RIETI survey to be discussed later, I similarly labelled the items of the same kind as 'work itself'. Yet, they may also be labelled as 'achievement' since inventors' satisfaction may result from the achievement of the task.

[107] John P Walsh and Sadao Nagaoka, 'Who Invents?: Evidence from the Japan-U.S. Inventor Survey' (2009) *RIETI Discussion Paper Series 09-E-034*, 30–32, www.rieti.go.jp/jp/publications/dp/09e034.pdf.

Figure 8 Average Level of the Importance of Rewards for Inventing in EU6 Countries (PatVal-I)

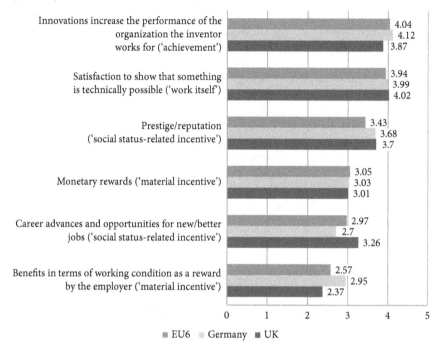

Innovations increase the performance of the organization the inventor works for ('achievement') — 4.04 / 4.12 / 3.87

Satisfaction to show that something is technically possible ('work itself') — 3.94 / 3.99 / 4.02

Prestige/reputation ('social status-related incentive') — 3.43 / 3.68 / 3.7

Monetary rewards ('material incentive') — 3.05 / 3.03 / 3.01

Career advances and opportunities for new/better jobs ('social status-related incentive') — 2.97 / 2.7 / 3.26

Benefits in terms of working condition as a reward by the employer ('material incentive') — 2.57 / 2.95 / 2.37

■ EU6   ▨ Germany   ■ UK

received responses from 1,919 US inventors and 3,658 Japanese inventors.[108] Since all but around 3 per cent of the respondents in both countries indicated that they had been employed by firms at the time of the invention,[109] the results largely reflected the situation of employee inventors in the US and Japan.

The researchers investigated inventors' motivation on the assumption that '[h]uman resources are increasingly seen as a key to innovation competitiveness'.[110] They asked respondents to rate the importance of various 'reasons to work on inventing' '[d]uring the research leading to the focal patent' on a scale of '1' to '5', with '1' representing 'not important' and '5' 'very important'.[111] Figure 9 below shows the total percentages of respondents who rated each reason as either '4' (important) or '5' (very important).[112] As in Figure 8 above, each reason is categorised into one of the following: 'achievement', 'work itself', 'material

---

[108] ibid 34 Table 1.
[109] ibid.
[110] ibid 1.
[111] Question C.5 in the questionnaire available at: www.prism.gatech.edu/~jwalsh6/inventors/InventorQuestionnaire.pdf.
[112] Adapted from Walsh and Nagaoka (n 107) 61 Figure 21.

Figure 9 Important Reasons for Inventing in the US and Japan (RIETI Survey)

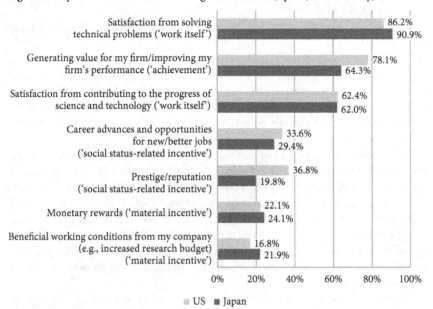

incentive' and 'social status-related incentive'. It is seen that factors that correspond to 'work itself' were important for most respondents in both countries. More than 60 per cent of them also mentioned the importance of contributing to the performance of the firm they worked for.[113] Meanwhile, only about 20 per cent of them indicated that 'monetary rewards' was important. More respondents in the US regarded 'social status-related incentives' as important than 'material incentives', though in Japan fewer respondents regarded 'prestige/reputation' as important than 'material incentives'.

The results of the latest PatVal EU-US/JP II survey which covered Europe, the US and Japan (hereinafter PatVal-II) also suggest that most inventors are not motivated by monetary rewards. This survey was conducted as part of the InnoS&T project funded by the EU under its Seventh Framework Programme for Research and Technological Development (FP7).[114] Developing the framework of PatVal-I, the project further explored 'key issues about invention process and

---

[113] The percentage of US respondents who mentioned this factor (78.1 per cent) was appreciably higher than that of their Japanese counterparts (64.3 per cent). Walsh and Nagaoka argued that the widespread use of stock options in the US might account for this: Walsh and Nagaoka (n 107) 24, 26. Yet their argument remains pure speculation since this factor was mentioned no less frequently by inventors outside the US than by US inventors in PatVal-II as shown in Fig 11 below.

[114] Its official project name is '[i]nnovative S&T indicators combining patent data and surveys: [e]mpirical models and policy analyses'. See CORDIS website for the project information at: cordis. europa.eu/project/rcn/89899_en.html.

the exploitation of patents' so that a direct comparison could be made between Europe, the US and Japan.[115]

The survey was conducted until July 2011 by sampling 124,134 patents granted by the EPO with a priority date between 2003 and 2005.[116] The researchers received responses from 13,451 inventors in 20 European countries including EU6 countries in PatVal-I and Israel, 3,286 in the US and 4,425 in Japan.[117] Since 84.1 per cent of the respondents in Europe, 90.5 per cent in the US and 95.5 per cent in Japan indicated that they had been employed at the time of the invention,[118] the results largely reflected the situation of employee inventors in the surveyed countries.

Respondents were asked to rate the importance of various motivations at the time when they had made the patented invention on a scale of '1' to '5', with '1' representing 'not important' and '5' 'very important'.[119] Figure 10 below shows the total percentages of European respondents who rated each factor as either '4' (important) or '5' (very important).[120] Around 70 per cent of them regarded as (very) important the three factors listed at the top of the Figure, which all correspond to 'work itself'. Meanwhile, 'monetary rewards' was (very) important for only about 15 per cent of them, which was the second lowest rate of the 12 factors listed in the Figure.

Figure 11 shows the international comparison of the average ratings on seven selected factors that correspond to 'work itself', 'achievement', 'material incentive' or 'social status-related incentive' between respondents in Europe (including Germany and the UK), Germany, the UK, the US and Japan.[121] As in Figures 9 and 10 factors that correspond to 'work itself' or 'achievement'

---

[115] InnoS&T, 'Final Report of the Inventor Survey in Europe, the US and Japan' (2012) 5, bcmmnty-qp.unibocconi.it/QuickPlace/innovativest/Main.nsf/$defaultview/6D9A810AEBB96DDFC125798900 2E1F30/$File/Final%20Report_inventors.pdf?OpenElement.

[116] InnoS&T, 'Final Report of PatVal-US/JP II: Survey Methods and Results US and JP' (2011) 2, 3, 9, bcmmnty-qp.unibocconi.it/QuickPlace/innovativest/Main.nsf/$defaultview/91E95FE59E5329CDC12 57911004A4EBC/$File/D3.4%20InnoS%26T.pdf?OpenElement.

[117] ibid 9, 10 Table 3.1. These 20 European countries are 'Germany, France, Great Britain, Italy, Netherlands, Switzerland, Sweden, Finland, Belgium, Austria, Denmark, Spain, Norway, Ireland, Greece, Slovenia, Hungary, Czech Republic, Poland, and Luxembourg': InnoS&T, 'Final Report of the Inventor Survey in Europe, the US and Japan' (n 115) 5. For reasons of expediency, Israel was included in European countries in this survey.

[118] InnoS&T, 'Final Report of PatVal-US/JP II' (n 116) 11 Table 3.3.

[119] ibid 16.

[120] Adapted from InnoS&T, 'Final Report of PatVal-EU II Survey: Methods and Results' (2010) 39 Table 4.11, bcmmnty-qp.unibocconi.it/QuickPlace/innovativest/Main.nsf/$defaultview/74EA6A339 19C1E4BC125775800683221/$File/D_2_5.pdf?OpenElement. Fig 10 shows the data obtained from responses received by June 2010.

[121] Compiled from InnoS&T, 'Final Report of PatVal-EU II Survey' (n 120) 40 Table 4.11a, 41 Table 4.11a; InnoS&T, 'Final Report of PatVal-US/JP II' (n 116) 16 Table 3.10. There were 5,277 responses from Germany and 820 from the UK by June 2010, whilst 13,451 from Europe (including Germany and the UK), 3,286 from the US and 4,425 from Japan by July 2011: InnoS&T, 'Final Report of PatVal-EU II Survey' (n 120) 17 Table 3.1; InnoS&T, 'Final Report of PatVal-US/JP II' (n 116) 10 Table 3.1. Fig 11 shows the data obtained from these responses.

Figure 10 Important Motivations for Inventing in Europe (PatVal-II)

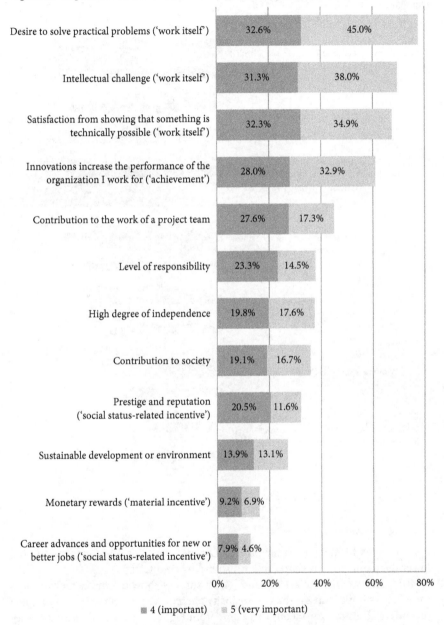

Desire to solve practical problems ('work itself') 32.6% 45.0%

Intellectual challenge ('work itself') 31.3% 38.0%

Satisfaction from showing that something is technically possible ('work itself') 32.3% 34.9%

Innovations increase the performance of the organization I work for ('achievement') 28.0% 32.9%

Contribution to the work of a project team 27.6% 17.3%

Level of responsibility 23.3% 14.5%

High degree of independence 19.8% 17.6%

Contribution to society 19.1% 16.7%

Prestige and reputation ('social status-related incentive') 20.5% 11.6%

Sustainable development or environment 13.9% 13.1%

Monetary rewards ('material incentive') 9.2% 6.9%

Career advances and opportunities for new or better jobs ('social status-related incentive') 7.9% 4.6%

0%   20%   40%   60%   80%

■ 4 (important)   ▩ 5 (very important)

were rated significantly higher than 'material incentives'. The average importance of 'monetary rewards' was lower than that of 'social status-related incentives' in general, though 'prestige and reputation' in Japan and 'career advances and

Figure 11 Average Level of Importance of Motivations for Inventing: International Comparison (PatVal-II)

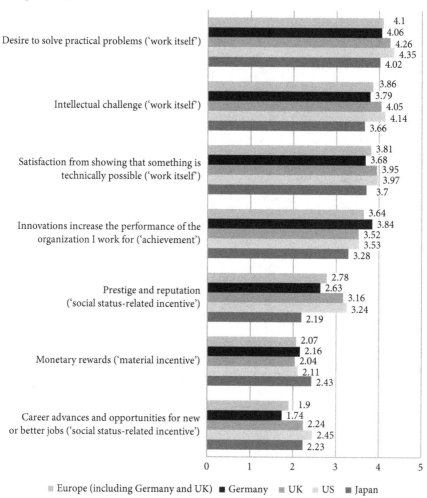

Europe (including Germany and UK) ■ Germany ■ UK ■ US ■ Japan

opportunities for new or better jobs' in Europe, Germany and Japan were rated lower than 'monetary rewards' in corresponding countries.

The results of the PatVal-I/II and RIETI surveys show that monetary rewards were far less important for the vast majority of employee inventors than intangible incentives. Thus it is erroneous to assume from Figure 7 shown earlier that monetary rewards will highly motivate employee inventors. It is unlikely that monetary rewards have been underestimated in these recent surveys because of possible biases. First, respondents may have been biased to choose socially desirable items such as 'challenging work' rather than 'monetary rewards' because they might have been influenced by 'social norms that view money as a less noble source of motivation'.[122] Yet the results shown in Figure 7 make it clear that respondents of surveys of this kind are not generally biased to choose socially desirable items. More respondents in that study indicated that 'inventor remuneration' and 'salary' were important for them than socially desirable items such as 'continuing education and training' and 'seminars and trade fairs'. Thus it can be safely said that respondents in these recent surveys show their honest views on important incentives for them independently of the influence of the social norms, if any, about the source of motivation.

Next, respondents in these surveys may have been preconditioned to underrate monetary rewards since most of them could not expect to receive considerable inventor remuneration as a matter of fact. According to PatVal-II, the median amount of remuneration paid for all the inventions made by respondents accounted for only 1 per cent (in Germany), 0.1 per cent (Europe, including Germany), zero per cent (the US) and 0.5 per cent (Japan) of their annual income.[123] However, even if there had been a greater possibility of inventor remuneration, it would have had little influence on the outcome of the surveys. This is evidenced by the fact that German respondents in PatVal-I/II did not highly rate monetary rewards any more than those in other countries even though the German Act on Employees' Inventions makes the payment of inventor remuneration mandatory in principle. In PatVal-I, the proportion of the respondents who had received inventor remuneration from their employers was substantially higher in Germany (61.3 per cent) than in the other EU6 countries such as the UK (28.2 per cent) and Italy (23.1 per cent).[124] Concerning PatVal-II, Figure 12 below shows rewards that respondents in Europe (including Germany), Germany, the US and Japan had received from their employers as a result of making patented inventions.[125] The proportion of those who had received remuneration paid when the inventions were actually used for commercial purposes was similarly higher in Germany (38 per cent) than in the US (11 per cent) and Japan (21 per cent). In contrast to generally nominal bonuses for invention disclosure, patent application filed and/or issued,[126] this kind of remuneration can be a substantial amount if it is linked to the revenue generated by the invention. Nevertheless, as shown in Figures 8 and 11 above, in both surveys the ratings on 'monetary rewards' in Germany were nearly as low as in other countries.

---

[122] Sara L Rynes, Barry Gerhart and Kathleen A Minette, 'The Importance of Pay in Employee Motivation: Discrepancies between What People Say and What They Do' (2004) 43 *Human Resource Management* 381, 382.

[123] Nagaoka and others (n 14) 62 Table 3-4-5.

[124] PatVal-EU, 'The Value of European Patents' (n 100) 37 Fig 5.1.

[125] Adapted from Nagaoka and others (n 14) 61 Table 3-4-2. The data on US respondents were already shown in Fig 2.

[126] See Fig 1 and accompanying text.

Figure 12 Rewards for Inventing: International Comparison (PatVal-II)

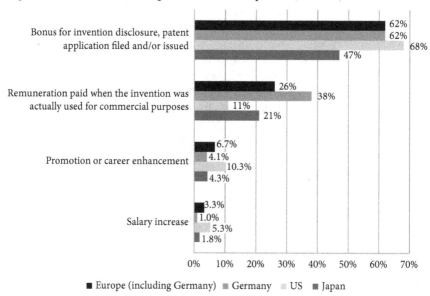

Europe (including Germany)   Germany   US   Japan

It can be presumed from the above analysis that respondents in the PatVal-I/II and RIETI surveys would have rated 'monetary rewards' low whether or not there was a greater possibility of earning substantial inventor remuneration. Therefore, independently of possible biases of respondents the results of these surveys show that what Herzberg called 'work itself' and 'achievement' are likely to generate powerful motivation in most employee inventors, whilst monetary rewards are not. To that extent his theory on workers' motivation applies to employee inventors today.

V. Financial Incentives and the Productivity of Employee Inventors

The results of the above comprehensive surveys of inventors in Europe, the US and Japan do not necessarily suggest that they are totally indifferent to monetary rewards. There is no doubt that monetary rewards are important to them at least as a *hygiene* factor in Herzberg's phraseology since they need to earn a livelihood in the same way as other kinds of workers do. Without sufficient earnings they cannot concentrate on inventing without being concerned about their economic lives. Csikszentmihalyi, a psychologist who has studied the lives of creative individuals, observed as follows:

> Probably very few creative persons are motivated by money. On the other hand, very few can be indifferent to it entirely. Money gives relief from worries, from drudgery, and

makes more time available for one's real work. It also enlarges the scope of opportunities: One can buy necessary materials, hire help if needed, and travel to meet people from whom one can learn.[127]

For minority inventors monetary rewards may be even a *motivator* which drives them to deliver above-standard job performance. Although German respondents in PatVal-I generally attached less importance to monetary rewards as shown in Figure 8 above, 59.5 per cent of them indicated that the German Act on Employees' Inventions still had some positive effect on their motivation,[128] and 57.2 per cent of those in favour of the legal scheme attributed the positive effect to 'financial incentives' among other things.[129] It must not be overlooked that in the RIETI survey and PatVal-II, 22.1 per cent of respondents in the US, 24.1 per cent in Japan, and 16.1 per cent in Europe regarded monetary rewards as important as shown in Figures 9 and 10 above. Since every worker has different needs, the offer of financial incentives may boost the performance or productivity of some employee inventors who are eager to earn as much money as possible even though such incentives do not generate great motivation in the majority of employee inventors.

It is hard to see whether the legal schemes that require employers to offer inventor remuneration improve the productivity of employee inventors in a country as a whole. Meanwhile, since the mid-2000s in particular, researchers in econometrics have attempted to show the correlation between financial incentive schemes implemented in companies or universities and the number of patent applications (grants) or technology licences by way of regression analysis.[130] If there is a positive correlation between them, it is reasonable to infer that the legal schemes similarly have some positive effect on the productivity of employee inventors at the country level. However, the following studies found no significant correlation at the company/university level:

(i)   An analysis of the data collected in 1993 on 352 'electrical engineers ... living within the Silicon Valley and Boston-Route 128 areas'[131] showed that there was a significant and positive correlation between 'the ratio of compensation from bonus or awards to compensation from salary' and both the amount of effort made by the

---

[127] Mihaly Csikszentmihalyi, *Creativity: Flow and the Psychology of Discovery and Invention* (New York, Harper Perennial, 1997) 334–35.

[128] Dietmar Harhoff and Karin Hoisl, 'Institutionalized Incentives for Ingenuity – Patent Value and the German Employees' Inventions Act' (2007) 36 *Research Policy* 1143, 1157 Fig 3.

[129] ibid Fig 4. Meanwhile, 18 per cent and 16.6 per cent of them attributed the effect to 'well-defined legal provisions' and 'acknowledgement of inventive performance' respectively.

[130] Regression analysis is a statistical method for assessing the quantitative effects one or more explanatory variables have on a dependent variable: Christine P Dancey and John Reidy, *Statistics without Maths for Psychology*, 5th edn (Harlow, Pearson Education, 2011) 384. In the studies mentioned in the text, for example, 'financial incentives offered to employee inventors' is an explanatory variable, whilst 'the number of inventions made by them' is a dependent variable.

[131] Todd R Zenger and Sergio G Lazzarini, 'Compensating for Innovation: Do Small Firms Offer High-powered Incentives That Lure Talent and Motivate Effort?' (2004) 25 *Managerial and Decision Economics* 329, 334.

engineers and their self-rated performance.[132] Nevertheless, it found no signifi-cant correlation between the ratio of bonus or awards to salary and the number of patents which the sampled engineers were credited with.[133]

(ii)   A survey conducted in 2003 of the directors of Technology Licensing Offices (TLOs) at 86 US and Canadian research universities found that performance-based pay schemes adopted in these universities had generally no significant correlation with the number of technology licences granted by them.[134]

(iii)   An analysis of the panel data on Japanese firms between 1990 and 2005 revealed that there was generally no significant correlation between the imple-mentation of invention compensation plans in the firms and the number of patent applications, whether the compensation was a fixed amount paid for patent application (registration) or a variable amount linked to sales, profits or licence royalties.[135]

On the other hand, the following studies generally found a positive correlation apart from study (vii) which showed mixed results:

(iv)   An analysis of the data on 57 high-technology firms in Connecticut between 1983 and 1988 found that more frequent award of variable bonuses for the issu-ance of patents was significantly associated with an increase in the number of patents granted to the firms.[136]

(v)   According to an analysis of the panel data on 102 research institutions in the US and Canada between 1991 and 1999, a 1 per cent increase in inventors' share of licence royalties significantly correlated with a 2.2 per cent increase in the number of licences granted by private universities.[137]

(vi)   Labour contracts of 160 researchers employed by three representative chemical and electrical engineering firms in Germany (Bayer, BASF and Siemens)

---

[132] ibid 335–36, 341 Table 5.

[133] ibid 341 Table 5.

[134] Sharon Belenzon and Mark Schankerman, 'University Knowledge Transfer: Private Ownership, Incentives, and Local Development Objectives' (2009) 52 *The Journal of Law and Economics* 111, 119–20, 133, 134 Table 6.

[135] Koichiro Onishi and Hideo Owan, 'Incentive Pay or Windfalls: Remuneration for Employee Inventions in Japan' (2010) *RIETI Discussion Paper Series 10-E-049*, 23, 38 Table 6, www.rieti.go.jp/jp/publications/dp/10e049.pdf; Koichiro Onishi, 'The Effects of Compensation Plans for Employee Inventions on R&D Productivity: New Evidence from Japanese Panel Data' (2013) 42 *Research Policy* 367, 368, 373, 374 Table 4.

[136] Sandra Honig-Haftel and Linda R Martin, 'The Effectiveness of Reward Systems on Innovative Output: An Empirical Analysis' (1993) 5 *Small Business Economics* 261, 262, 265 Table III, 266 Table IV.

[137] Saul Lach and Mark Schankerman, 'Incentives and Invention in Universities' (2008) 39 *The RAND Journal of Economics* 403, 426 Table 9, 429.

between 1877 and 1913 were collated with the number of patents granted to these firms between 1891 and 1913.[138] It was found that a 1 per cent increase in the proportion of bonus to the average amount of total compensation paid to the researchers significantly correlated with an approximately 0.1 per cent increase in the number of patents granted to the firms the following year.[139]

(vii)   In an analysis of the data collected in 2009 from 1,067 organisations in the Republic of Korea, it was seen that the implementation of invention compensation plans had a significant and positive correlation with the number of patent applications.[140] By contrast, the proportion of compensation for patents to the annual income of employee inventors had no significant correlation with the number of patent applications.[141] This suggests that increasing inventor remuneration is unlikely to boost the number of inventions made in organisations.

Whilst the above studies examined whether financial incentive schemes had a correlation with the number of patents or technology licences, some of these studies also confirmed a positive correlation between the schemes and the commercial value of inventions made by employee inventors. For example, study (v) showed that a 1 per cent increase in the inventors' royalty share significantly correlated with an approximately 4.3 to 5 per cent increase in the licensing revenues of private universities.[142] Study (vi) discovered a somewhat larger increase in the number of commercially valuable patents than in the total number of patents granted to the firms following a past increase in the proportion of bonus to total compensation paid to the employee inventors.[143] Interestingly, studies (ii) and (iii) also found that the implementation of invention compensation schemes had a significant and positive correlation with an increase in the licensing revenues and the number of commercially valuable patents respectively,[144] even though these studies showed no significant correlation between the schemes and the total number of technology licences or patent applications.[145] Similarly, study (vii) found that the proportion of compensation for patents to the annual income of employee inventors had a significant and positive correlation with the

---

[138] Carsten Burhop and Thorsten Lübbers, 'Incentives and Innovation? R&D Management in Germany's Chemical and Electrical Engineering Industries around 1900' (2010) 47 *Explorations in Economic History* 100, 104–08.

[139] ibid 109 Table 2, 110 Table 3.

[140] Yee Kyoung Kim, Tae-Kyu Ryu and Chan Sik Jung, 'Employees' Invention Compensation Plan as a Determinant of Patent Quality and Quantity: Findings of Inventor Survey in Korea' (2011) 6(1) *The Journal of Intellectual Property* 133, 141 Table 1, 155 Table 4.

[141] ibid 155–56 Table 4.

[142] Lach and Schankerman (n 137) 425–26 Table 9.

[143] Burhop and Lübbers (n 138) 109 Table 2, 110 Table 3.

[144] Belenzon and Schankerman (n 134) 129–31 Table 5; Onishi and Owan (n 135) 23, 38 Table 6.

[145] See text to nn 134, 135.

monetary value of patents indicated by respondents[146] in contrast to the number of patent applications.[147]

However, it is rash to conclude from the above findings that financial incentives have some positive effect on the productivity of employee inventors or the commercial value of inventions made by them. It must be noted here that 'correlation' is a distinct concept from 'causation' in statistics. Even though some studies indicated a positive correlation between them, it does not necessarily follow that financial incentives offered to employee inventors will boost their productivity or the commercial value of the inventions.[148] It is because the apparent positive correlation may be in fact attributed to 'reverse causation', where employee inventors made more (valuable) inventions, thereby bringing more profits to their employers, who in turn gave more generous inventor remuneration. For example, although study (iii) showed a significant and positive correlation between the implementation of revenue-based pay policies in firms and the number of commercially valuable patents, the researchers statistically confirmed that the former did not act as a cause of the latter.[149] They suggested instead the probability of reverse causation, where employee inventors may have recognised the remuneration policies only after patented technologies were commercialised.[150] Rather, given the mixed results in studies (i), (ii), (iii) and (vii), financial incentives may have no causal relationship with the productivity of employee inventors or the commercial value of inventions since they may actually be affected by other factors.

By way of contrast, another study of an autoglass company in the US empirically confirmed that a performance-based pay scheme improved the productivity of manual workers.[151] The study estimated that the company had achieved a 44 per cent gain in the productivity of autoglass instalments by switching hourly wages to a piece-rate system in which workers were paid according to the number of installed glass units (study (viii)).[152] It attributed the rise in the productivity not only to a 'pure incentive effect' which motivates average workers to produce more, but also to the recruitment of productive workers from outside of the company who wanted to earn more under the piece-rate system.[153] This finding is not necessarily inconsistent with Herzberg's theory, according to which monetary rewards should not motivate workers to a high level of productivity in general, because it acknowledges that monetary rewards may generate motivation to work in unskilled workers who do not find the work itself worthwhile.[154]

---

[146] Kim, Ryu and Jung (n 140) 153–54 Table 3.

[147] See text to n 140.

[148] See, eg, Lach and Schankerman (n 137) 428; Burhop and Lübbers (n 138) 110; Kim, Ryu and Jung (n 140) 156.

[149] Onishi and Owan (n 135) 25–26, 41 Table 9.

[150] ibid 26.

[151] Edward P Lazear, 'Performance Pay and Productivity' (2000) 90 *American Economic Review* 1346, 1346.

[152] ibid 1350, 1353 Table 3.

[153] ibid 1353 Table 3, 1354.

[154] See text to n 88.

The process of inventing in organisations today is generally characterised by what Cherensky called 'routinization of invention',[155] where professional engineers who have received technical education at universities engage in inventive activities collectively in industrial laboratories.[156] The following description of research laboratories that became prevalent among major industries in the US by the 1920s elaborates on this phenomenon:

> The giant firms which dominated the electrical and chemical industries pioneered in placing research work in industry on an organized basis. In doing so, they sought to institutionalize the foresight of those men who had laid the scientific foundations for the new industries, to transform what heretofore had been the result of random discovery and ingenious invention into the routine product of a carefully managed process. Systematic research, described by Frank Jewett as 'cooperative effort under control,' lessened their dependence upon the vagaries of genius; it made possible instead the creation of what GE's Phillip Alger called 'synthetic genii' – many specialists assembled as a team and 'held together by bonds of sympathy and understanding, as well as by the company management'.[157]

If inventions made in companies nowadays are 'the routine product of a carefully managed process' like autoglasses, financial incentives may stimulate the productivity of employee inventors as in the case of manual workers. Nevertheless, the inconsistent results in studies (i) to (vii) indicate the complexity of the relationship between financial incentives and inventors' productivity. In particular, study (i) deserves notice in that it did not confirm an increase in the number of patents despite the observed increase in the amount of the engineers' effort associated with bonus payment.[158] The result suggests that even if financial incentives have some positive effect on employees' motivation, it will not boost the creation of inventions immediately. Accordingly, inventing in companies is still qualitatively different from manual labour. The productivity of employee inventors is likely to depend greatly on other factors than financial incentives such as teamwork in inventing or their creativity as discussed in detail later in chapters three and four.

In sum, with all the results of the above econometrics studies, it remains unclear whether financial incentives can improve the productivity of employee inventors. In addition, two points need to be raised here to better understand the implications of the above studies.

---

[155] Steven Cherensky, 'A Penny for Their Thoughts: Employee-Inventors, Preinvention Assignment Agreements, Property, and Personhood' (1993) 81 *California Law Review* 595, 611.

[156] See ch 3, s II.

[157] David F Noble, *America by Design: Science, Technology, and the Rise of Corporate Capitalism* (Oxford, Oxford University Press, 1979) 118, citing George E Folk, *Patents and Industrial Progress: A Summary Analysis and Evaluation of the Record of Patents of the Temporary National Economic Committee* (New York, Harper & Brothers, 1942) 153; Philip L Alger, *The Human Side of Engineering: Tales of General Electric Engineering over 80 Years* (Schenectady, Mohawk Development Service, 1972) 7.

[158] See text to nn 132, 133.

A. Correlation between the Motives of Employee Inventors and their Productivity

Apart from its finding on the correlation between invention compensation plans in Korean organisations and the number of patent applications, study (vii) showed that there was a significant and positive correlation between the preference for monetary rewards indicated by employee inventors in private firms and the number of patent applications.[159] However, this finding has only a limited significance since other studies indicated that pecuniary motives of employee inventors had only a weaker correlation with their productivity than did their motivation provided by values intrinsic in inventing, such as intellectual challenge, or no significant correlation whatsoever. For example, according to an analysis of the data collected in 2001 and 2003 on 1,707 US employees with a PhD degree 'in a science, engineering, or health field',[160] their desire for intellectual challenge had a significant and more positive correlation with the number of patent applications and those resulting in licensing or commercialisation than did their desire for salary (study (ix)).[161] Meanwhile, an analysis of the data collected in 2007 on '5,091 Japanese inventors on 5,278 patents'[162] showed that their motivation provided by '[s]atisfaction from contributing to the progress of science and technology' and '[s]atisfaction from solving challenging technical problems' had a significant and positive correlation with both the number of patent applications and self-assessed economic value of the patents, whilst their desire for monetary rewards did not have a significant correlation (study (x)).[163]

Although it was stressed in the above study (ix) that pecuniary motives of employee inventors did have a weaker but positive correlation with their productivity,[164] it did not claim a causal relationship between inventors' motives and their productivity.[165] Accordingly, it is wrong to assume from that study that financial incentives offered to employee inventors are likely to improve their productivity by stimulating their desire for monetary rewards. On the contrary, short-sighted pursuit of monetary rewards by employee inventors may rather 'crowd out' their productivity in real terms. Study (iii) suggests that those inventors who work from pecuniary motives may learn to make trivial inventions that can be commercialised without difficulty.[166]

---

[159] Kim, Ryu and Jung (n 140) 156–58 Table 5. By contrast, inventors' preference for monetary rewards had no significant correlation with self-assessed value of patents.
[160] Henry Sauermann and Wesley M Cohen, 'What Makes Them Tick? Employee Motives and Firm Innovation' (2010) 56 *Management Science* 2134, 2137.
[161] ibid 2142, 2143 Table 4, 2147, 2148 Table 6.
[162] Hideo Owan and Sadao Nagaoka, 'Intrinsic and Extrinsic Motivations of Inventors' (2011) *RIETI Discussion Paper Series 11-E-022*, 7, www.rieti.go.jp/jp/publications/dp/11e022.pdf.
[163] ibid 9, 11, 41 Table 2, 42 Table 3.
[164] Sauermann and Cohen (n 160) 2150.
[165] ibid.
[166] Onishi and Owan (n 135) 26–27, 42 Table 10.

B. Inventor Remuneration Offered to Recruit Productive Inventors

As mentioned earlier, study (viii) concerning the piece-rate system introduced in an autoglass company suggests that the offer of financial incentives may not only improve the productivity of existing employees, but attract productive workers from outside the company.[167] Given that the best brains nowadays are willing to move across borders to find better employment opportunities, a question arises as to whether it is possible for a country to attract talented inventors from across the world if the national law provides that employee inventors working in the country will receive additional compensation when they make inventions.[168]

However, it is questionable whether employee inventors are lured by incentive schemes as in the case of unskilled workers working in an autoglass factory. Even companies cannot expect to attract productive inventors just because they have a policy to reward employee inventors. According to study (i), for example, the ratio of bonus to salary received by the engineers had no significant correlation with the number of patents[169] and their academic achievement such as possession of a Masters and/or a PhD degree, scores of the SAT (Scholastic Aptitude Test) used for the admission to US universities, and the rank of the engineer's graduate or under-graduate institution.[170] This can be interpreted in two ways: (a) a merit pay system did not attract graduates with good academic records; or (b) even if it attracted such graduates, their academic achievement was not related to their performance after they started working. In either case, it follows that the bonus system could not attract graduates who actually became prolific inventors after they joined the companies. Meanwhile, Figure 13 below shows the reasons for switching jobs mentioned by respondents in PatVal-II across Europe, the US and Japan who had changed their jobs during the past five years.[171] Whilst only about 20 per cent of them indicated that they had switched jobs because of 'higher salary', more than one third of them mentioned 'attractive research/inventive activities of the new employer', suggesting that more employee inventors attach importance to the contents of the work itself than to material incentives offered by new employers.

Whilst it has been seen that only a minority of employee inventors are attracted by a higher salary, even fewer will respond vigorously to the offer of variable inventor remuneration if employee inventors are generally risk-averse. The image of

---

[167] See text to n 152.

[168] This point was raised in the Japanese government's advisory panel which recently discussed the amendment to the Japanese patent law. See ch 9, s II.

[169] See text to n 133.

[170] Zenger and Lazzarini (n 131) 341 Table 5. Meanwhile, there was a weak but positive correlation between the engineers' share of their companies' equities and the number of patents, their possession of a PhD degree or SAT scores. Yet this book does not discuss employees' share option.

[171] Calculated according to the data available from Nagaoka and others (n 14) 22 Table 3-2-1.

Figure 13 Inventors' Reasons for Switching Jobs (PatVal-II)

inventors nowadays is generally not that of 'hero-inventors' until the late nineteenth century who took on financial risks by themselves to create brilliant inventions, but that of professionals working collectively in corporate laboratories as mentioned earlier.[172] Employee inventors may become risk-averse because of their financial investments in technical training at universities[173] or their general aspiration for higher managerial positions as illustrated by their reluctance to unionise to bargain with their employers.[174] Accordingly, they may avoid taking risks in inventing for fear that the failure will affect their prospects for promotion.[175]

Contrary to the above theory, however, PatVal-II found that nearly 75 per cent of respondents in the US, 60 per cent in Europe and 50 per cent in Japan regarded themselves as risk-loving rather than risk-averse[176] and that risk-lovers were more likely to produce valuable inventions.[177] In addition, it should be recalled here that according to Figure 7 above, more German inventors indicated that variable 'inventor remuneration' was important for them than 'salary'. Yet that study was not designed to discover the rank order of the respondents' preference for various incentives because it simply asked them to name three important incentives. In fact, in another experimental study specifically designed to measure the subjects' preference for five kinds of incentives based on their 'real-life decision-making processes',[178] it was found that German R&D personnel attached nearly twice as

[172] See text to nn 155-57 and ch 3, s II.
[173] Cherensky (n 155) 612.
[174] See ch 6, s IV.C.
[175] Dratler (n 2) 181, 183.
[176] Nagaoka and others (n 14) 19 Fig 3-1-10.
[177] ibid 18 Fig 3-1-9.
[178] Christopher Leptien, 'Incentives for Employed Inventors: An Empirical Analysis with Special Emphasis on the German Law for Employee's Inventions' (1995) 25 *R&D Management* 213, 217.

great importance to '[i]ncrease of fixed salary' as to 'variable bonus depending on the inventive performance'.[179] Even though many employee inventors see themselves as risk-loving today, offering variable inventor remuneration is unlikely to encourage them to take greater risks in inventing because they cannot know in advance how much profits will arise from inventions to be made and their share in the profits, which is usually determined normatively in consideration of the relative contribution of both employers and employees.[180]

Inventor remuneration to be paid according to statutory laws will be still less attractive for employee inventors if it is only a nominal amount or if there is a long time lag between the creation of the invention and the payment of the remuneration.[181] For example, the time lag can be several years under the German legal scheme since its amount is calculated only after the invention has been commercialised.[182] Inventors will need to wait even longer if they have to resort to litigation to receive the payment which often involves an intricate calculation based on various factors such as profits brought by the invention and the inventor's relative contribution.[183] According to PatVal-I, 'compensation too small', 'lack of transparency in calculation' and 'delays in the payment of compensation' were three major causes of disincentive mentioned by the German respondents who were sceptical about the motivational effect of the German Act on Employees' Inventions.[184] Thus it is naïve to think that each country can attract productive inventors in the world who contribute to the country's industrial development if it establishes an elaborate invention compensation scheme by a national law.

Several studies in econometrics mentioned in this section did not conclusively prove that financial incentives would improve the productivity of employee inventors. Rather, incentives offered to individual inventors are unlikely to affect their output directly because the actual inventive activities in organisations inevitably involve various factors beyond each inventor's effort and ability, such as serendipity, corporate hierarchy and teamwork. Since those who have played an important role in the teamwork do not always become inventors eligible for inventor remuneration, it is likely that the payment of the remuneration to a few eligible inventors will adversely affect communication among employee inventors as a whole, thereby hindering the creation of inventions in companies. These points will be discussed in detail in the next chapter.

---

[179] ibid 218 Table 1, 219–20 Table 3.

[180] Cherensky (n 155) 640.

[181] Klaus Brockhoff, 'Ist die kollektive Regelung einer Vergütung von Arbeitnehmererfindungen wirksam und nötig?' [Is the Collective Regulation of Remuneration for Employees' Inventions Effective and Necessary?] (1997) 67 *Zeitschrift für Betriebswirtschaft (ZfB)* 677, 683–84.

[182] Leptien, 'Incentives for Employed Inventors' (n 178) 223.

[183] In calculating the amount of compensation paid to employee inventors, the German Act on Employees' Inventions requires to consider the following factors in particular: (1) economic applicability of the invention, (2) duties and position of the employee in the company, and (3) proportion of the company's contribution to the invention: Act on Employees' Inventions, s 9(2).

[184] Harhoff and Hoisl (n 128) 1158 Fig 5.

3

Inventor Remuneration in the Organisational Context

I. Serendipity and Corporate Hierarchy

Many inventions are created simply as a result of serendipity. Thus compensation offered to employee inventors cannot have a direct influence on the creation of such inventions in theory. Figure 14 below shows the process of successful invention indicated by respondents in the PatVal-EU (PatVal-I) and Research Institute of Economy, Trade and Industry (RIETI) surveys.[1] Whilst nearly 50 per cent of inventions in EU6, 60 per cent in the US, and 70 per cent in Japan were either targeted achievements or expected by-products, serendipity may have played an important role in the other scenarios where inventions were created either unexpectedly or on the basis of ideas unrelated to inventive tasks. It would appear that an invention compensation scheme mainly intended to motivate R&D personnel could not have triggered inventions in the third and fifth scenarios shown in the Figure, where they expended no conscious effort to create these particular inventions. These accounted for about 25 per cent of inventions in EU6 and the US, and 15 per cent in Japan. Compensation paid for these inventions does not act as an incentive to invent but only means a congratulatory gift for good fortune.[2]

One may still argue that employee inventors will expend more effort in the hope of receiving additional compensation, which in turn will boost the likelihood of successful invention, whether it is made intentionally or coincidentally. However, their motivation alone will not produce inventions in companies because they must work under the supervision of the senior staff. Today middle-level managers and the supervisors of rank-and-file employee inventors, rather than employers, or top management and stakeholders who only frame fundamental company policies, usually play the role of investors in inventive activities by making day-to-day

---

[1] Compiled from PatVal-EU, 'The Value of European Patents: Evidence from a Survey of European Inventors (Final Report of the PatVal EU Project)' (2005) 32 Table 4.3, ec.europa.eu/invest-in-research/pdf/download_en/patval_mainreportandannexes.pdf; Sadao Nagaoka and John Walsh, 'The R&D Process in the US and Japan: Major Findings from the RIETI-Georgia Tech Inventor Survey' (2009) *RIETI Discussion Paper Series 09-E-010*, Figure 10, www.rieti.go.jp/jp/publications/dp/09e010.pdf. However, the comparison of the results between EU6 and US/Japan is invalid because each survey covered different range of patents.

[2] Note, however, that inventions in the fifth category do not usually fall within the scope of this book because they are not made in the course of employees' duties.

Figure 14 Scenarios of Creative Process Leading to Inventions (PatVal-I and RIETI Survey)

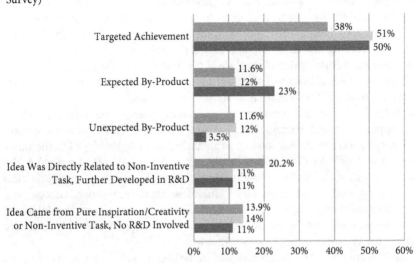

decisions on the allocation of economic resources to R&D activities.[3] It is no longer appropriate to presuppose investor-inventor dichotomy, or a strict separation between 'one with ideas and no money, and the other with money and no ideas',[4] which arguably reflects the image of inventors before the end of the Industrial Revolution who worked alone or in small businesses.[5] Accordingly, in discussing incentives which may boost the creation of inventions in companies it is necessary to focus not only on R&D personnel, who engage in inventing in a narrow sense, but also on their supervisors and middle-level managers.[6]

According to Dratler, the innovation process taking place in companies comprises several stages, beginning with 'the recognition of a need'.[7] Those who act as investors inside companies then collectively decide whether they will allocate resources to meet the need.[8] This stage is followed by decisions on the approach to the problem made by manager(s), inventor(s) or both, specifying the relevant technological field and assigning the work to individuals, groups and/or laboratories competent to tackle it.[9] Only after this stage does the most crucial stage of

---

[3] Jay Dratler Jr, 'Incentive for People: The Forgotten Purpose of the Patent System' (1979) 16 *Harvard Journal on Legislation* 129, 168, 178.

[4] ibid 168.

[5] ibid 166–67.

[6] ibid 178.

[7] ibid 168.

[8] ibid 169.

[9] ibid.

the innovation process occur, namely imaginative conception or 'flash of genius', which exclusively belongs to inventors.[10] Inventors then present the ideas to other participants in the process to urge them to decide whether they will further allocate resources to develop them into mass production and use.[11] Once the decision is made, a working model is built and refined thereafter for the purpose of exploitation and marketing, which takes place at the final stage of the process.[12]

Whilst individual inventors work out a solution to a technical problem, Dratler is correct in saying that 'conception alone is only a small part of the innovative process'.[13] In the actual innovation process taking place in modern companies, their supervisors and managers recognise a need and decide how to allocate resources between problem-solving, exploitation and marketing.[14] On the other hand, employee inventors normally play only a passive role throughout the process, devoting themselves to 'definition of the problem, conception, production of a working model, and refinement'.[15] Therefore, there is no way of encouraging the creation of inventions without incentivising their supervisors and middle-level managers who control the whole corporate innovation process even if employee inventors may be motivated in some other way.

Apart from several studies mentioned in the previous chapter which examined the correlation between financial incentives and the productivity of rank-and-file inventors, a recent econometrics study investigated the effect of incentives on managers responsible for corporate R&D. Collating the data on 'more than 300 publicly traded US firms' between 1988 and 1997 with those on patents granted to them two years later, the researchers identified the average time lag between patent filing and issuance.[16] By way of regression analysis, they found that long-term incentives (eg, share options) offered to corporate R&D heads significantly and positively correlated with patent citation, grants and originality, whilst short-term incentives (eg, bonuses linked to annual performance) did not.[17] According to them, 'equity-based incentives lead to better decisions [by R&D executives] about project selection at the corporate level',[18] which 'affect outcomes with a considerable [time] lag',[19] whilst short-term incentives may make them favour their 'private benefits at the expense of shareholders, such as funding "pet projects" or showing favoritism to select labs'.[20] Consistent with the aforementioned study

---

[10] ibid.

[11] ibid 170.

[12] ibid 170–71.

[13] ibid 179.

[14] ibid 191.

[15] ibid.

[16] Josh Lerner and Julie Wulf, 'Innovation and Incentives: Evidence from Corporate R&D' (2007) 89 *The Review of Economics and Statistics* 634, 635, 637, 638.

[17] ibid 638–41, Table 2 and 3. Study (i) mentioned in ch 2, s V showed the similar results: see ch 2, n 170.

[18] Lerner and Wulf (n 16) 642.

[19] ibid 634.

[20] ibid.

(iii) (outlined in chapter two) concerning rank-and-file R&D personnel in Japan,[21] this study indicates that the conventional form of compensation, namely cash awards, may cause myopic behaviour of potential recipients which can impair corporate innovation process on a long-term basis.

Since the creation of inventions by rank-and-file employees depends firstly on the project selection made by R&D managers, it is wrong to expect that the offer of additional compensation to employee inventors will have a direct effect on their output. The traditional investor-inventor dichotomy, which presumably causes a false impression to that effect, overlooks the fact that middle-level managers and the supervisors of R&D personnel usually lead inventive activities in companies. Without a perspective on corporate hierarchy, one will misjudge the effect of additional compensation offered to employee inventors.

II. Teamwork in Inventing

A. Social Change in the Process of Inventing: From Independent to Collective Project

Another fact that those who argue for invention compensation schemes tend to overlook is that today inventions are usually made through effective teamwork of scientists and engineers in organisations. Cherensky points out that the social change in the process of inventing in the nineteenth century generally replaced the image of 'hero-inventors' with that of 'team-as-hero'.[22] In the eighteenth and nineteenth centuries, it was generally thought that inventions were created by the courageous efforts of heroic inventors blessed with exceptional inventive faculties, such as Thomas Edison and Alexander Graham Bell, who formed the image of generalist 'hero-inventors' who did everything required for inventing by themselves.[23] However, in the late nineteenth century, corporations began to establish laboratories in which professional engineers who had completed technical education worked to create inventions.[24] Since then, inventions previously made by heroic independent inventors have been steadily replaced by routinised inventions made in industrial laboratories through the collaboration of professional engineers from various disciplines.[25] By the twentieth century it had become more appropriate to describe inventions as products which were for the most part created by 'team-as-hero' working in corporations.[26] Statistics on the issuance of

---

[21] See text to ch 2, n 166.

[22] Steven Cherensky, 'A Penny for Their Thoughts: Employee-Inventors, Preinvention Assignment Agreements, Property, and Personhood' (1993) 81 *California Law Review* 595, 605–16.

[23] ibid 606–07.

[24] ibid 608–10.

[25] ibid 610–11.

[26] ibid 605–06.

US patents support this observation with only 12 per cent of patents being issued to corporations in 1885 compared with 75 per cent in 1950.[27]

The importance of teamwork in inventing cannot be over-emphasised in the present context where growing technical complexity increasingly requires cross-functional and interdisciplinary knowledge.[28] It is especially true of the chemical industry due to highly complex steps in developing chemicals.[29] In practice, companies establish integrated development teams to cope with the technical complexity, apart from some small and medium-sized companies that lack sufficient resources.[30] According to the survey of German employee inventors referred to in Figure 7 (in chapter two), over 80 per cent of respondents worked regularly in teams and 74.7 per cent of those respondents who had filed more than 30 patents were inventors working in teams.[31] The latter data suggests that team inventors are likely to create more inventions in accordance with the theory that the performance of scientists positively correlates with the frequency of their contacts with specialist colleagues.[32]

The number of co-inventors involved in a single invention also reflects the importance of teamwork in inventing today. In PatVal-I, there was more than one inventor in 62.6 per cent of inventions in EU6,[33] whilst according to the RIETI survey there were on average 2.71 inventors per invention in the US, and 2.76 in Japan.[34] This is not to say that no inventions are created by sole inventors in companies. However, in the latest PatVal EU-US/JP II survey (PatVal-II) only 6.7 per cent of respondents in Europe, 4.6 per cent in the US and 11.4 per cent in Japan indicated that they had not used 'communication among colleagues' as a source of information during the process of inventing.[35] Even sole inventors often have subordinates or co-operators who are not named as inventors.[36] If they can make inventions without using human and material resources in companies, they should already become independent inventors. As long as they work in companies, other employees usually assist them in perfecting inventions. Thus it

---

[27] David F Noble, *America by Design: Science, Technology, and the Rise of Corporate Capitalism* (Oxford, Oxford University Press, 1979) 87 (citation omitted).

[28] Erich Staudt and others, 'Der Arbeitnehmererfinder im betrieblichen Innovationsprozeß – Ergebnisse einer empirischen Untersuchung' [The Employee Invention in Corporate Innovation Process – Results of an Empirical Study] (1992) 44 *Schmalenbachs Zeitschrift für betriebswirtschaftliche Forschung (zfbf)* 111, 127.

[29] ibid.

[30] ibid.

[31] ibid.

[32] ibid.

[33] PatVal-EU, 'The Value of European Patents' (n 1) 26 Fig 4.1.

[34] Nagaoka and Walsh (n 1) Fig 14.

[35] InnoS&T, 'Final Report of PatVal-US/JP II: Survey Methods and Results US and JP' (2011) 15 Table 3.9, bcmmnty-qp.unibocconi.it/QuickPlace/innovativest/Main.nsf/$defaultview/91E95FE59E53 29CDC1257911004A4EBC/$File/D3.4%20InnoS%26T.pdf?OpenElement.

[36] Sadao Nagaoka and others, 'Innovation Process in Japan in the Early 2000s as Seen from Inventors: Agenda for Strengthening Innovative Capability' (in Japanese) (2012) *RIETI Discussion Paper Series 12-J-033*, 26, 28, www.rieti.go.jp/jp/publications/dp/12j033.pdf.

is fair to assume that employee inventions are almost always created through the cooperation of employees.

B. Determination of Co-inventors

Nevertheless, according to the criteria of joint inventor or co-inventorship in each jurisdiction, not all the co-operators become co-inventors eligible for inventor remuneration even if they play an important role in inventing. Thus one may question whether invention compensation schemes are really serving their purpose to encourage the creation of inventions. For example, according to the US Court of Appeals for the Federal Circuit, 'to be a joint inventor, an individual must make a contribution to the conception of the claimed invention that is not insignificant in quality when that contribution is measured against the dimension of the full invention',[37] whilst 'a person will not be a co-inventor if he or she does no more than explain to the real inventors concepts that are well known and the current state of the art'.[38] A joint inventor must contribute to 'conception', or 'the formation in the mind of the inventor, of a definite and permanent idea of the complete and operative invention, as it is hereafter to be applied in practice'.[39] Thus 'one [person] of ordinary skill in the art who simply reduced the inventor's idea to practice is not necessarily a joint inventor'.[40] Despite the amendment to the Patent Code in 1984 that relaxed the requirements for joint inventorship,[41] joint inventors must contribute to at least one claim[42] and appreciate what has been invented through 'collaboration or concerted effort', or 'some open line of communication during or in temporal proximity to their inventive effort'.[43] Accordingly, US courts are unlikely to regard as joint inventors those who were not involved in a collaborative effort to form an inventive idea per se as expressed in claims.

Whilst US courts determine co-inventorship 'on a claim-by-claim basis' in accordance with infringement analysis,[44] English and Japanese courts consider further information relevant to the invention besides the claim. In order to

---

[37] *Fina Oil and Chemical Co v Ewen*, 123 F3d 1466, 1473 (Fed Cir 1997).

[38] ibid.

[39] *Hybritech, Inc v Monoclonal Antibodies, Inc*, 802 F2d 1367, 1376 (Fed Cir 1986).

[40] *Ethicon, Inc v US Surgical Corp*, 135 F3d 1456, 1460 (Fed Cir 1998).

[41] US patents could be unjustly invalidated before 1984 because it was not permitted to name 'as an inventor a person who did not share in the conception of the invention and who did not contribute to all of the claims of the patent': ibid 1469 (Newman, J, dissenting). In order to remove this pitfall, the Patent Code was amended in 1984 so that now '[i]nventors may apply for a patent jointly even though (1) they did not physically work together or at the same time, (2) each did not make the same type or amount of contribution, or (3) each did not make a contribution to the subject matter of every claim of the patent': 35 USC § 116(a) (2012).

[42] *Ethicon* (n 40) 1460.

[43] *Bard Peripheral Vascular, Inc v WL Gore & Associates, Inc*, 670 F3d 1171, 1179-80 (Fed Cir 2012) (citations omitted).

[44] Typically, US courts first interpret the claim to identify the subject matter encompassed therein, and then compare it with a purported joint inventor's contribution in order to determine whether or not the contributor is a joint inventor: *Trovan, Ltd v Sokymat SA, Irori*, 299 F3d 1292, 1302 (Fed Cir 2002).

determine a 'joint inventor', which means 'the actual deviser of the invention' under the Patents Act 1977,[45] English courts seek to establish '[w]ho was responsible for the inventive concept',[46] or '"the heart" of the invention',[47] which is identified by 'information in the specification rather than the form of the claims'.[48] Japanese courts regard as co-inventors those who contributed substantially to 'technical ideas' understood from claims, detailed explanation of the invention in the description, and the prior art.[49] However, neither English nor Japanese courts are likely to recognise as co-inventors those whose ideas are not at all embodied in the inventive concept itself.

In fact, the conception of many inventions may not have occurred without contributions of those who are not deemed as co-inventors. Regarding pharmaceuticals, for example, the pre-clinical stage of a drug discovery programme begins with (i) 'target identification' and (ii) 'target validation' where the relationship between biological entities, notably proteins, and the disease is elucidated and verified through the application of various experimental models.[50] After these phases, (iii) scientists screen compound libraries to identify molecules which act on the target proteins ('hit discovery').[51] Subsequently, (iv) they refine these hit molecules to produce more potent and selective compounds ('hit to lead'),[52] and (v) improve on their deficiencies while maintaining favourable traits to make them suitable for clinical trials ('lead optimisation').[53] The preclinical stage described here is followed by clinical development and the proper authorisation to sell a new drug.[54] In the whole process, which 'can take 12–15 years and cost in excess of $1 billion',[55] 'significant, intellectual input is required from scientists from a variety of disciplines and backgrounds'.[56]

Nevertheless, according to the general criteria of co-inventorship in the US, the UK (England and Wales) and Japan, epidemiologists, geneticists, pathologists and genome scientists who mainly work on (i) target identification and (ii) validation are unlikely to become the co-inventors of a successful drug since their activities are not intended to identify the structure of the drug to be developed. In addition, as the Intellectual Property High Court of Japan pointed out, biological scientists

---

[45] Patents Act 1977, s 7(3).

[46] *Henry Brothers (Magherafelt) Ltd v The Ministry of Defence and the Northern Ireland Office* [1997] RPC 693, 706.

[47] *Markem Corp v Zipher Ltd* [2005] EWCA Civ 267, [2005] RPC 31 [102].

[48] ibid [101].

[49] See, eg, Osaka District Court, judgment on 23 May 2002, 1825 *Hanrei jihō* 177; Tokyo District Court, judgment on 27 August 2002, 1810 *Hanrei jihō* 102.

[50] JP Hughes and others, 'Principles of Early Drug Discovery' (2011) 162 *British Journal of Pharmacology* 1239, 1239–42.

[51] ibid 1242.

[52] ibid 1246.

[53] ibid 1248.

[54] ibid 1240 Fig 1.

[55] ibid 1239.

[56] ibid 1248.

who (iii) screen candidate compounds are also unlikely to become the co-inventors unless they suggest to those who work on drug synthesis the structure of a new compound to be selected or a course of action to be taken thereafter.[57]

In the US it has been argued that those who reduce conception to practice may exceptionally become joint inventors of a chemical compound despite the principle to the contrary.[58] According to the Court of Appeals for the Federal Circuit, '[c]onception requires (1) the idea of the structure of the chemical compound, and (2) possession of an operative method of making it',[59] and 'conception of a chemical compound ... does not occur unless one has a mental picture of the structure of the chemical, or is able to define it by its method of preparation, its physical or chemical properties, or whatever characteristics sufficiently distinguish it'.[60] Where 'an inventor is unable to establish a conception until he has reduced the invention to practice through a successful experiment',[61] those who carried out that experiment may become joint inventors since 'the reduction to practice can be the most definitive corroboration of conception'.[62] This doctrine of 'simultaneous conception and reduction to practice'[63] may be invoked in the case of pharmaceuticals because of 'the unpredictability of the experimental sciences of chemistry and biology'.[64] However, it is erroneous to say that 'an inventor can never conceive an invention in an unpredictable or experimental field until reduction to practice' since '[i]t is this factual uncertainty [about the inventor's idea], not the general uncertainty surrounding experimental sciences, that bears on the problem of conception'.[65] Accordingly, the doctrine does not suggest that those who simply reduce conception to practice become the co-inventors of pharmaceuticals. In addition, given the 'claim-by-claim' approach to the determination of co-inventorship,[66] those who discover only the utility of a compound are unlikely to become joint inventors in the US because a patent on a pharmaceutical usually claims the compound per se whilst its utility is only disclosed in its description.[67]

---

[57] Intellectual Property High Court, judgment on 15 March 2007, www.courts.go.jp/app/files/hanrei_jp/337/034337_hanrei.pdf.

[58] See text to n 40.

[59] *Oka v Youssefyeh*, 849 F2d 581, 583 (Fed Cir 1988) (citations omitted).

[60] *Amgen, Inc v Chugai Pharmaceutical Co*, 927 F2d 1200, 1206 (Fed Cir 1991).

[61] ibid.

[62] *Burroughs Wellcome Co v Barr Labs, Inc*, 40 F3d 1223, 1229 (Fed Cir 1994).

[63] *Alpert v Slatin*, 305 F2d 891, 894 (CCPA 1962).

[64] *Burroughs Wellcome* (n 62) 1228.

[65] ibid 1229.

[66] See text to n 44.

[67] Aaron X Fellmeth, 'Conception and Misconception in Joint Inventorship' (2012) 2 *New York University Journal of Intellectual Property and Entertainment Law* 73, 132–33. However, the Court of Appeals for the Federal Circuit has recently relaxed the traditional 'claim-by-claim' approach in a case of a patented compound. It held that a scientist who had developed an original method for producing certain compounds, yet had not tried it himself, was a co-inventor of a compound which his supervisor had synthesised using his method. The Court reasoned that '[w]here the method requires more than the exercise of ordinary skill, ... the discovery of that method is as much a contribution to the compound as the discovery of the compound itself': *Falana v Kent State University*, 669 F3d 1349, 1358 (Fed Cir 2012).

In sum, regardless of jurisdiction, potential inventors of a drug are usually only a few scientists who identify one particular successful chemical compound out of 200,000 to over 1,000,000 candidates.[68] Other scientists are not eligible for inventor remuneration even though they all paved the way for the discovery of the drug. The example of pharmaceuticals discussed here shows that invention compensation schemes would not necessarily lead to the creation of inventions because those who made an important contribution to an invention may not become co-inventors eligible to receive inventor remuneration according to patent law. In particular, it tends to be overlooked that sometimes 'the most difficult and important part of the inventive process is understanding the problem to be solved',[69] yet those who merely identify that problem are left out of the consideration just because they do not solve it.

C. Practice of 'Co-inventorship of Superiors' in Germany

The determination of co-inventors in Germany will be given special consideration here to draw attention to the controversial practice of so-called 'co-inventorship of superiors', where those who are not named as inventors unlawfully claim inventor remuneration under the German Act on Employees' Inventions. According to the data on German inventors in PatVal-I, there were on average 2.5 inventors per invention and only 24 per cent of the inventions were made by sole inventors.[70] The German Patent Act remains silent on who can become a co-inventor despite its provision that the right to a patent jointly belongs to persons who made the invention together.[71] According to German precedents, a co-inventor of a patented invention is a person who made 'creative contribution' to the invention,[72] which is identified on the basis of not only claims but the entire invention and how it came about as disclosed in the patent application.[73] Although mere 'constructive assistance' in making the invention does not suffice, 'contribution' here does not need to meet all the requirements for the patentability of an invention when considered alone[74] since patentability is a separate issue from the question of who has a share in the granted patent.[75] A co-inventor does not need to make a contribution to 'the crux of the invention',[76] yet it cannot trigger co-inventorship if the contribution

---

[68] Hughes and others (n 50) 1248.

[69] Fellmeth (n 67) 108.

[70] Dietmar Harhoff and Karin Hoisl, 'Institutionalized Incentives for Ingenuity – Patent Value and the German Employees' Inventions Act' (2007) 36 *Research Policy* 1143, 1145.

[71] Patent Act, s 6 second sentence.

[72] *Bundesgerichtshof (BGH)* [Federal Court of Justice of Germany], judgment on 16 September 2003, X ZR 142/01, GRUR 2004, 50, 51 – *Verkranzungsverfahren* (citations omitted).

[73] *BGH*, judgment on 17 May 2011, X ZR 53/08, GRUR 2011, 903, *Rn* 16, 17 – *Atemgasdrucksteuerung* (citations omitted).

[74] *Verkranzungsverfahren* (n 72) 51.

[75] *Atemgasdrucksteuerung* (n 73) *Rn* 13.

[76] *BGH*, judgment on 17 October 2000, X ZR 223/98, GRUR 2001, 226, 227 – *Rollenantriebseinheit*.

has not affected the overall success of the invention, was insignificant for the solution, or was made according to the instructions given by the inventor(s) or a third party.[77]

On the face of it, the German approach to co-inventorship appears to be more flexible than that adopted in the US, the UK (England and Wales) or Japan not only because it considers the contribution made to the entire invention not limited to claims and the historical process of the creation, but also because it does not require that the contribution be made to 'the crux of the invention'. Accordingly, a contributor who offers only a partial solution to the technical problem becomes a co-inventor in Germany as long as the contribution is significant for the success of the invention.[78] However, in the case of pharmaceuticals, scientists who work on (i) target identification and (ii) validation are unlikely to become co-inventors of a drug as in other jurisdictions since their activities do not aim at discovering a solution, or a compound used for a drug. Those who conduct experiments to test the efficacy of candidate compounds are also unlikely to become co-inventors unless they devise the procedure for the experiments on their own initiative and find the properties of an active substance.[79]

The 'co-inventorship of superiors' refers to cases reported in Germany where inventors' superiors are added as co-inventors at their request, not because they actually contributed to the inventions, but because they simply occupy superior positions to the actual inventors within the companies.[80] In the survey of German inventors mentioned in Figure 7 (in chapter two), it was found that superiors were named as co-inventors in 27.9 per cent of the cases surveyed, of which 60 per cent were due to this controversial practice.[81] An article published in 1997 revealed that 'senior executives' of a large company in the German chemical industry had been named as co-inventors of nearly 45 per cent of all the inventions made in the company, earning them no less than 31 per cent of all the compensation paid by the company for inventions made by its employees during the preceding 18 years.[82] In the light of the criteria for deciding co-inventors in Germany, superiors do not normally become co-inventors if they merely suggest the aim of the invention without offering a solution to the technical problem.[83] Nevertheless, 'co-inventorship of superiors' can still happen because the German Patent Office

---

[77] *Verkranzungsverfahren* (n 72) 51 (citations omitted).

[78] BGH, Judgment on 18 June 2013, X ZR 103/11.

[79] Franz-Josef Zimmer and Svenja Sethmann, 'What Makes a Co-Worker a Co-Inventor?' (Grünecker 2005) 3, www.grunecker.de/files/inventor.pdf.

[80] Staudt and others (n 28) 124.

[81] ibid.

[82] Klaus Brockhoff, 'Ist die kollektive Regelung einer Vergütung von Arbeitnehmererfindungen wirksam und nötig?' [Is the Collective Regulation of Remuneration for Employees' Inventions Effective and Necessary?] (1997) 67 *Zeitschrift für Betriebswirtschaft (ZfB)* 677, 681.

[83] Michael Trimborn, *Employees' Inventions in Germany: A Handbook for International Businesses* (Alphen aan den Rijn, Kluwer Law International, 2009) para 65.

is not expected to verify the correctness of statements on inventorship made by applicants before granting patents under the German Patent Act.[84]

It is likely that nominal 'co-inventorship of superiors' will be nullified if the relevant parties bring the case ex post facto before the Board of Arbitration set up under the Act on Employees' Inventions.[85] However, it is said that '[h]istorically, fewer than 140 disputes each year are brought before the Arbitration Board out of the roughly 40,000 annual applications that are covered by the [Act]'.[86] Employees may become reluctant to refer to the arbitration because they are concerned that initiating legal disputes with their employers can jeopardise their career.[87] Some German companies have internal guidelines which allow the naming of superiors only if they substantially contributed to the creation of inventions in reality.[88] However, the law can similarly induce false assertions of inventorship even in other jurisdictions if it requires the payment of compensation to employee inventors extensively as in Germany.[89] The practice of 'co-inventorship of superiors' will thus widen the gap between the actual contributors to inventions and the recipients of additional compensation.

D. Inventors' Secrecy and the Adverse Effect on Communication among Employees

If there are many co-inventors, it will dilute each inventor's prestige and monetary rewards associated with the creation of the invention.[90] Thus inventors may want to maintain their inventive ideas in secrecy so that they can monopolise the rewards in case these ideas eventually develop into inventions. Their secrecy is likely to hold back the process of industrial research[91] because it will prevent communication among colleagues which should allow them to share experiences that are useful for the research.[92] The adverse effect on the communication may be also

---

[84] Patent Act, ss 7(1), 37(1) third sentence.

[85] The Board, which is set up within the German Patent Office, deals with all the disputes between employers and employees about the application of the Act: Act on Employees' Inventions, ss 28, 29(1). According to the Board, superiors do not become co-inventors where they just assigned a subordinate research work, conveyed information on previous development work to him, or where they provided those who performed final testing of an invention with a piece of advice which was considered as prior art: Trimborn (n 83) para 70.

[86] Jesse Giummo, 'German Employee Inventors' Compensation Records: A Window into the Returns to Patented Inventions' (2010) 39 *Research Policy* 969, 973. See also Harhoff and Hoisl (n 70) 1150 fn 17.

[87] Giummo (n 86) 973.

[88] Brockhoff (n 82) 681.

[89] Richard C Witte and Eric W Guttag, 'Employee Inventions' (1989) 71 *Journal of the Patent and Trademark Office Society* 467, 475.

[90] W Fritz Fasse, 'The Muddy Metaphysics of Joint Inventorship: Cleaning Up after the 1984 Amendments to 35 U.S.C. § 116' (1992) 5(2) *Harvard Journal of Law and Technology* 153, 157.

[91] Witte and Guttag (n 89) 474.

[92] Christopher Leptien, 'Incentives for Employed Inventors: An Empirical Analysis with Special Emphasis on the German Law for Employee's Inventions' (1995) 25 *R&D Management* 213, 224.

caused by the enviousness of employees who actually contributed to the creation of inventions, yet are not eligible for inventor remuneration.[93] Even after inventions are made the payment of inventor remuneration can block 'inter-functional communication flow' so as to disturb the process of innovation if employees in the production and marketing department are not rewarded for their work whilst only inventors can reap the benefits.[94]

Surveys also suggest that the German Act on Employees' Inventions is likely to stifle communication among employee inventors. In a survey published in 1996 of German researchers working in industry, 67 per cent of respondents indicated that the German legal scheme had a negative effect on communication among them whilst only 8.5 per cent had a favourable view on this point.[95] In PatVal-I, some German respondents reported that, albeit on rare occasions, some inventors had even hindered the creation of subsequent inventions for fear that these inventions would substitute earlier inventions they had made, thereby reducing the amount of compensation they would receive.[96]

Surprisingly, the adverse effect of the invention compensation scheme was already recognised at the early stages of industrial laboratories in the early twentieth century in the US. For example, Bell Laboratories, a research institute that originated from a joint research group set up within American Telephone & Telegraph Company (AT&T) in 1912 and was later incorporated under the current name in 1925,[97] introduced what is called 'the group method' to organise its laboratory departments and this 'eventually became the standard operating procedure of industrial research'.[98] EB Craft, the then Executive Vice-President of Bell Laboratories, described the characteristics of that method which made the institution into 'a military type of organization'[99] as follows:

> Perhaps the outstanding characteristic of this organization, the one that sets it apart a little from others, is its conduct of research and development by a group method of attack ... the result is the necessity of a high degree of specialization. So in all of these technical departments we have specialists, chemists, metallurgists, physicists, engineers, statisticians, mathematicians, men who are trained and skilled in their particular branches of science and engineering. Their activities are so coordinated by means of this organization, that their best brains can be brought to bear upon any specific problem. ... When a problem is put up to the Labs for solution, it is divided into its elements and each element is assigned to that group of specialists who know the most about that

---

[93] Harhoff and Hoisl (n 70) 1158.

[94] Leptien (n 92) 223.

[95] Christopher Leptien, *Anreizsysteme in Forschung und Entwicklung: unter besonderer Berücksichtigung des Arbeitnehmererfindergesetzes* [Incentive Systems in Research and Development: With Special Reference to the Employee Invention Law] (Wiesbaden, Deutscher Universitätsverlag, 1996) 168.

[96] Harhoff and Hoisl (n 70) 1158.

[97] Noble (n 27) 115–16.

[98] ibid 119.

[99] ibid 119, citing EB Craft, *Bell Educational Conference, 1925* (New York, Bell System, 1925) 25.

particular field but they all cooperate and make their contribution to the solution of the problem as a whole.[100]

The institution 'at first compensated employees for patents beyond their salaries', yet this became counterproductive to its operation because, according to Frank B Jewett, the first president of the institution, 'such incentive allowance encouraged the worker to work for himself rather than his employer, and in competition with his co-workers':[101]

> The incentive was to get as many patents that could pass the Patent Office as possible. An invention was made. It could be covered by one strong patent or it could be covered by a dozen minor patents. It was to the company's advantage to have one strong patent, but it was to the employee's advantage to have a dozen minor patents. ... It created a situation where men would not work with each other ... yet the problem which was before us was a problem which required team action; ... so some way had to be found to get over that.[102]

Eventually, '[t]he Bell System's solution was ... the elimination of patent reward for employees'.[103] The passage below also elaborates on an alternative method adopted by the institution which also addressed the issue of de facto contributors who were not fortunate enough to be named as co-inventors in law:

> Before [around 1912] Bell engineers were awarded $100 dollars for each new patent, a policy which Jewett perceived as counterproductive since it fostered individual rather than cooperative effort. Jewett eliminated such incentives altogether, labelling them anachronistic, vestiges of the fading 'era of the inventor'. In their place the laboratory adopted elaborate procedures for recognizing individual accomplishment in lieu of rewarding it. ... Craft explained, '... [we] assign to the individual the particular contribution that he has made. This is all very carefully recorded in our laboratory notebooks, a complete record of all the work that is done, and these are turned over to the patent organization and they determine who the inventors are.' Those research workers not fortunate enough to be recognized by patent lawyers as inventors were recognized in other ways, such as through the publication of their work in technical journals. In this regard the management encouraged joint authorship of articles by perhaps half a dozen workers, so as to allow as many as possible to 'share in the glory of the achievement.
>
> The managers of the large industrial research laboratories thus sought to resolve the needs of individual workers with the corporate imperatives of their 'military' operations. They offered incentives to boost the ego of the individual without cost to the company, and emphasized the spirit of loyalty and cooperation in order to elicit his best efforts.[104]

[100] Noble (n 27) 119, citing Craft (n 99) 43–44.
[101] Noble (n 27) 100–01.
[102] ibid 101, citing *Pooling of Patents: Appendix to Hearings before the House Committee on Patents on H.R. 4523, Part I, 74th Congress* (Washington DC, United States Government Printing Office 1935) 276.
[103] Noble (n 27) 101.
[104] ibid 119–20, citing W Rupert McLaurin, *Invention and Innovation in the Radio Industry* (New York, Macmillan, 1949) 156; Craft (n 99) 47.

Although it appears that the employee inventors in the episode of the Bell Laboratories responded to the inventor's bonus vigorously, it indicates that the bonus did not motivate them to a high level of job performance but only caused their egocentric behaviour, which was counterproductive to inventing in the research institution.[105] Meanwhile, if all the members of an inventive team receive monetary rewards whether or not they are named as inventors in law, the negative effect on communication among employee inventors may not occur. For example, internal guidelines in some German companies provide that de facto contributors to the creation of inventions be awarded complementary payments beyond the legal requirement.[106] A US federal law allows federal laboratories to 'provide appropriate incentives ... to laboratory employees who are not an inventor' of inventions made in the laboratories 'but who substantially increased the technical value of such inventions'.[107] However, it is another question whether such team-based incentives can really enhance the motivation of team members, thereby promoting the creation of inventions by them. This point will be discussed later.[108]

E. Employees' Sense of Unfairness and the Notion of Distributive Justice

Herzberg found that workers' 'feelings of unfairness' about 'salary' were closely associated with their job dissatisfaction and poor motivation to work.[109] Inventor remuneration can arouse a sense of unfairness in employees who do not receive it, which will lead to their poor motivation, stifle communication with potential inventors and eventually hinder the creation of inventions. Actual inventors may also feel a sense of unfairness if nominal contributors are added to inventors at their request as in the case of 'co-inventorship of superiors' in Germany.[110] However, as long as proper persons are named as inventors in law, offering inventor remuneration may be in fact fair to all the employees because inventors may have made a more important contribution to the invention than others. Judgement about the fairness of the remuneration depends on the concept of justice or, more specifically, 'distributive justice' accepted by employees. Deutsch, a social psychologist, identified at least 11 values such as 'needs', 'supply and demand of the market place' and 'the principle of reciprocity' according to which the fruits of group activities

---

[105] In other words, they were not truly motivated to invent but merely distracted from inventive activities that require effective teamwork. Thus the episode does not contradict Herzberg's theory of motivation.

[106] Brockhoff (n 82) 681.

[107] Stevenson-Wydler Technology Innovation Act of 1980 (Public Law 96-480) § 14 (a)(1)(A)(ii), as codified in 15 USC § 3710c (2012).

[108] See ch 3, s III.C below.

[109] Frederick Herzberg, Bernard Mausner and Barbara Bloch Snyderman, *The Motivation to Work*, 2nd edn (New York, John Wiley & Sons, 1967) 78 Table 9, 83.

[110] Brockhoff (n 82) 682.

are distributed among group members.[111] However, the discussion here will focus on a utilitarian standard of distributive justice which considers how the distributive norm within a group can facilitate the productivity of group activities which include inventing in organisations.

Adams argues that it discourages workers' effort or can even cause higher absenteeism/turnout among them to the detriment of their productivity if they perceive that their pay is disproportionate to their input.[112] Adams' formulation would lead to a principle of distributive justice whose emphasis is on 'proportionality between the individual's outcome of rewards ... and his inputs or contributions' (equity principle).[113] The equity principle may help the group to achieve 'economic productivity' since it assumes 'that people will be unwilling to make relatively high inputs unless they can look forward to relatively high individual outcomes'.[114] Inventor remuneration may accord with the equity principle in that inventors, who arguably have made higher inputs than others, receive more.

On the other hand, Deutsch argues that the equity principle is rather harmful to 'enjoyable social relations' between group members because it will cause 'conflict over the valuation' and/or 'envy, self-devaluation' of those who are not highly appreciated in the group.[115] He puts forward instead another principle of distributive justice which regards it as fair that members 'are all entitled to equal share' as long as they 'contribute as fully as they can' (equality principle).[116] According to the equality principle, offering inventor remuneration will cause the envy of those who do not receive it to the detriment of the productivity of employee inventors as a whole.

Social psychologists have since discussed which of the above principles of distributive justice can boost the productivity of group work in general. Although they share the view that unfair distribution of profits gained from a joint project among its participants will adversely affect their teamwork, people may have different views about what is unfair distribution. Scholars in cross-cultural psychology have noticed that cultural difference in 'individualism' or 'collectivism' among various societies may mediate the relationship between people's perception of distributive justice and group productivity. The next section will introduce their research findings and discuss the effect of invention compensation schemes in 'individualist' and 'collectivist' societies.

---

[111] Morton Deutsch, 'Equity, Equality, and Need: What Determines Which Value Will Be Used as the Basis of Distributive Justice' (1975) 31(3) *Journal of Social Issues* 137, 139.

[112] J Stacy Adams, 'Toward an Understanding of Inequity' (1963) 67 *Journal of Abnormal and Social Psychology* 422, 428, 431–32.

[113] Deutsch (n 111) 144.

[114] ibid 143–44.

[115] ibid 146.

[116] ibid 144, 146.

III. Individualism, Collectivism and the Effect of Inventor Remuneration

A. The Individualism–Collectivism Dichotomy

i. Hofstede's Survey and Reworked Theory by Triandis

According to the typology by Hofstede, individualism signifies 'a society in which the ties between individuals are loose' and '[e]veryone is expected to look after him/herself ... only', whilst collectivism is 'a society in which people ... are integrated into strong, cohesive in-groups, which ... protect them in exchange for unquestioning loyalty'.[117] He surveyed about 88,000 employees who worked in the subsidiaries of the International Business Machines Corporation (IBM) in 71 countries around the world between 1967 and 1973.[118] In the factor analysis[119] of respondents' answers to 14 questions about 'work goals', he extracted a latent factor which represented the degree of individualism or collectivism in each society[120] and computed each country's factor score.[121] He transformed the score into the country's Individualism Index, which ranges between 0 (denoting perfect collectivist society) and 100 (perfect individualist society) by a simple mathematical formula.[122]

According to Figure 15 below, which shows Individualism Indices of 55 countries or regions,[123] Western societies tend to be more individualistic than other societies. Hofstede argues that, in these individualist societies, an emphasis is generally put on individual achievements.[124] Hence, reward allocation within a group tends to follow the equity principle,[125] with those members who have made a greater contribution to the group having a larger share of rewards, whilst incentives are usually linked to the individuals' performance.[126] On the other hand, in

---

[117] Geert Hofstede, *Culture's Consequences: Comparing Values, Behaviors, Institutions, and Organizations across Nations*, 2nd edn (originally published 1980, Thousand Oaks, SAGE, 2001) 225.

[118] ibid 48. I mentioned this survey earlier: see ch 2, Fig 2 and accompanying text.

[119] Factor analysis is a statistical method to extract an underlying latent (hypothetical) factor which accounts for a high correlation observed between some variables: Christine P Dancey and John Reidy, *Statistics without Maths for Psychology*, 5th edn (Harlow, Pearson Education, 2011) 456.

[120] Hofstede (n 117) 214, 257. For example, IBM survey asked respondents how important it was for them to have a job which left them sufficient personal time or to have freedom in deciding their approach to the job. The answers to these questions suggest the relationship between individuals and the organisation they belonged to, which arguably manifests the degree of individualism in each society.

[121] Factor score is a 'composite score made up from the variables correlated with the factor': Dancey and Reidy (n 119) 482. The score denotes the degree of a sample's association with the factor.

[122] Hofstede (n 117) 214, 257.

[123] Compiled from Hofstede (n 117) 52, 215 Exhibit 5.1, 502 Exhibit A5.3.

[124] ibid 227 Exhibit 5.4.

[125] ibid 244 Fig 5.6.

[126] ibid 241, 245 Fig 5.6.

collectivist societies, which include most of Asian, African and Latin-American countries, an emphasis is generally put on being members of institutions or organisations.[127] Hence, reward allocation within a group tends to follow the equality principle,[128] with its members having equal share of rewards regardless of their contribution to the group, whilst incentives are usually given to the group as a whole, not to individual members.[129] Shortly after the publication of Hofstede's theory, several studies in social psychology verified Hofstede's observation that dominant societal norms generally determine the distributive norm within a group in each society. According to these studies, 'collectivistic' Chinese subjects showed a more egalitarian tendency in allocating rewards to in-group co-workers[130] than did 'individualistic' American subjects.[131] Researchers statistically confirmed that the egalitarian tendency demonstrated by the Chinese subjects was rooted in their collectivistic orientation,[132] arguing that the cultural collectivism functions 'to avoid conflict and embarrassment and to promote group harmony and solidarity over time.'[133] These studies suggest that people in different societies are likely to regard different principles of allocation as fair.

Nevertheless, Hofstede's theory has received substantial criticism from his fellow social psychologists. Some doubt if the factor Hofstede extracted in his factor analysis actually indicates each society's degree of individualism or collectivism in his phraseology.[134] It is also questionable whether employees of a multinational corporation really represent each society.[135] For example, considering the impression dominant in the West that 'Japan is made up of a uniform race of pliant, obedient robots, meekly conforming to rigid social rules and endlessly repeating the established patterns of their society',[136] Japan's Individualism Index ('46')

[127] ibid 227 Exhibit 5.4.
[128] ibid 244 Fig 5.6.
[129] ibid 241, 245 Fig 5.6.
[130] Kwok Leung and Michael H Bond, 'The Impact of Cultural Collectivism on Reward Allocation' (1984) 47 *Journal of Personality and Social Psychology* 793, 802. Meanwhile, this study found that both Chinese and American subjects were more likely to endorse equitable allocation of rewards to out-group members.
[131] Michael H Bond, Kwok Leung and Kwok Choi Wan, 'How Does Cultural Collectivism Operate? The Impact of Task and Maintenance Contributions on Reward Distribution' (1982) 13 *Journal of Cross-Cultural Psychology* 186, 194; C Harry Hui, Harry C Triandis and Candice Yee, 'Cultural Differences in Reward Allocation: Is Collectivism the Explanation?' (1991) 30 *British Journal of Social Psychology* 145, 151.
[132] Kwok Leung and Saburo Iwawaki, 'Cultural Collectivism and Distributive Behavior' (1988) 19 *Journal of Cross-Cultural Psychology* 35, 43; Hui, Triandis and Yee (n 131) 154.
[133] Bond, Leung and Wan (n 131) 196.
[134] Youtaro Takano and Eiko Osaka, 'An Unsupported Common View: Comparing Japan and the U.S. on Individualism/Collectivism' (1999) 2 *Asian Journal of Social Psychology* 311, 319; Maxim Voronov and Jefferson A Singer, 'The Myth of Individualism-Collectivism: A Critical Review' (2002) 142 *The Journal of Social Psychology* 461, 467. For example, a question in Hofstede's survey about the importance of having 'good physical working conditions', which arguably assessed workplace satisfaction, as opposed to personal satisfaction, may have little to do with collectivism.
[135] Voronov and Singer (n 134) 466.
[136] Edwin O Reischauer and Marius B Jansen, *The Japanese Today: Change and Continuity* (Cambridge, Massachusetts, Harvard University Press, 1977) 159.

Figure 15 Hofstede's Individualism Indices in 55 Countries or Regions

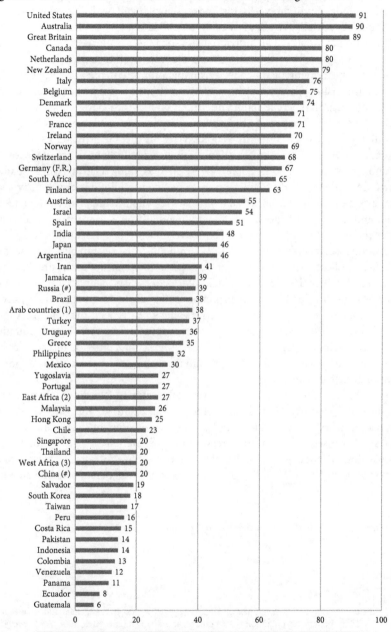

Notes: (1) Egypt, Iraq, Kuwait, Lebanon, Libya, Saudi Arabia and United Arab Republic;
(2) Ethiopia, Kenya, Tanzania and Zambia;
(3) Ghana, Nigeria and Sierra Leone;
(#) estimated values for countries not included in the original analysis by Hofstede.

appears to be higher than might be expected. Since Hofstede's survey researchers have done more studies to verify his findings, which will be discussed later.

Above all, social psychologists came to notice that people in some countries which Hofstede identified as individualistic societies are more likely to prefer the *equality* principle of distribution in fact. Triandis tried to explain this point by combining the individualism–collectivism dichotomy with the horizontal–vertical cultural dimension advanced by himself. According to him, 'the horizontal dimension emphasizes that people should be similar on most attributes, especially status', whilst 'the vertical dimension accepts inequality [where] rank has its privileges'.[137] This dichotomy which concerns people's view on their relative status ('same or different') is theoretically independent of Hofstede's individualism–collectivism dichotomy which concerns people's views on self–other relations ('independent or interdependent').[138] By combining these two cultural dimensions, four types of culture pattern can be identified, namely 'horizontal individualism (independent/ same) and horizontal collectivism (interdependent/same), vertical individualism (independent/different) and vertical collectivism (interdependent/different)'.[139]

Triandis' perspective is useful for explaining the relationship between the individualism–collectivism dimension and people's preference for a certain allocation principle. Whether they are individualists or collectivists, people living in vertical societies tend to value the equity principle which allows for people's difference in status, whilst those in horizontal societies value equality with the belief that there should be little difference in status among people. Unlike *vertical* individualists, who pursue achievement in their social life,[140] *horizontal* individualists are 'not … enthusiastic about differential compensation', despite their respect for autonomy in their relationship with others.[141]

Horizontal-individualist societies typically refer to Nordic countries, such as Norway,[142] Sweden[143] and Denmark.[144] For example, the Swedes 'do not like people who … stick out',[145] and tend to be envious of personal success of others[146] because of their 'group pressure towards sameness'.[147] The Danes, who share a similar language and culture, also tend to have distaste for 'conspicuous success and braggarts',[148] and thus put little emphasis on personal achievement as

---

[137] Harry C Triandis, *Individualism and Collectivism* (Boulder, Westview Press, 1995) 44.
[138] ibid (citation omitted).
[139] ibid.
[140] ibid 47.
[141] ibid 45.
[142] ibid 99.
[143] ibid 45.
[144] Michelle R Nelson and Sharon Shavitt, 'Horizontal and Vertical Individualism and Achievement Values: A Multimethod Examination of Denmark and the United States' (2002) 33 *Journal of Cross-Cultural Psychology* 439, 440.
[145] Triandis (n 137) 45.
[146] Åke Daun, 'Individualism and Collectivity among Swedes' (1991) 56 *Ethnos* 165, 169.
[147] ibid 170.
[148] Nelson and Shavitt (n 144) 440 (citations omitted).

a guiding principle in their lives as was demonstrated in a laboratory study that compared Danish samples with their US counterparts.[149] Often included among horizontal-individualists are the Australians,[150] who tend to want 'to cut down "tall poppies" (or those who have been conspicuously successful)' in the belief that 'success should not lead to inequalities and differences in status'.[151] These horizontal-individualists are likely to prefer the *equality* principle of distribution despite their high degree of individualism identified in Hofstede's survey.[152]

ii. Results of Subsequent Studies

There are a couple of studies which clearly illustrate the regional variations in the degree of individualism or collectivism in the world. First, Oyserman and colleagues conducted a meta-analysis[153] of 50 relevant studies published between 1980 and 2000.[154] They compared the level of 'individualism' or 'collectivism' observed among Americans (including Canadians) with that among people from eight other regions by calculating effect sizes,[155] which indicate the extent to which Americans are more individualistic (or less collectivistic) than people from other regions. The data are shown in Figure 16 below.[156] Their analysis confirmed that America is more individualistic (or less collectivistic) than any other region in the world. The difference in the degree of individualism or collectivism was generally small between America and English-speaking countries, Central Europe, or Western Europe, whilst large between America and Middle East or Africa. These results largely replicated the results of Hofstede's study. There was a moderate difference between America and Asian regions or Latin/South America in general, though some particular countries showed a large difference.[157] With respect to

---

[149] ibid 452 Table 5.

[150] Triandis (n 137) 46.

[151] Norman T Feather, 'Values and Cultures' in Walter J Lonner and Roy S Malpass (eds), *Psychology and Culture* (Boston, Allyn & Bacon, 1994) 183.

[152] However, studies mentioned in Figs 16 and 17 below did not provide clear evidence that the Australians prefer egalitarian principle of distribution.

[153] Meta-analysis is '[a] research technique which involves comparing the outcomes of a number of different studies in the same area, and examining the general themes or trends which can be identified as a result': Nicky Hayes and Peter Stratton, *A Student's Dictionary of Psychology*, 4th edn (London, Arnold, 2003) 169.

[154] Daphna Oyserman, Heather M Coon and Markus Kemmelmeier, 'Rethinking Individualism and Collectivism: Evaluation of Theoretical Assumptions and Meta-Analyses' (2002) 128 *Psychological Bulletin* 3, 10.

[155] ibid 10. The 'effect size' calculated in this meta-analysis was 'the mean difference' in scores on measures of individualism or collectivism 'between an American sample and a sample from another country' 'divided by the pooled standard deviation': ibid 11.

[156] Compiled from Oyserman, Coon and Kemmelmeier (n 154) 13 Fig 1, 18 Fig 3. These eight regions are as follows: English-speaking countries (South Africa, New Zealand, Australia), Western Europe (Spain, Italy, France), Central Europe (Poland, Greece, Bulgaria), East Asia (Vietnam, PR China, Japan), Other Asia (Pakistan, Nepal, India), Africa (Zimbabwe, Nigeria), Middle East (Turkey, Egypt), and Latin/South America (Puerto Rico, Mexico, Brazil).

[157] ibid 14 Fig 2, 19 Fig 4, 28.

Figure 16 Degree of Individualism/Collectivism: Comparison between America and Eight Regions

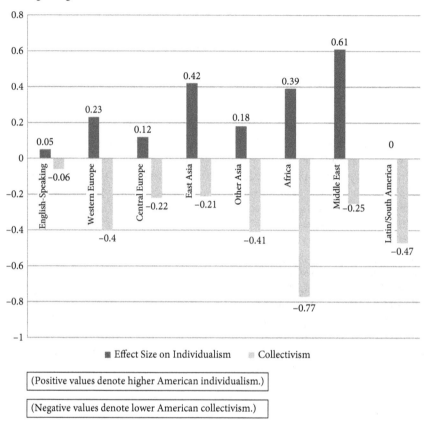

■ Effect Size on Individualism   ▨ Collectivism

(Positive values denote higher American individualism.)

(Negative values denote lower American collectivism.)

East Asia, the difference was large between America and China, Hong Kong, or Taiwan, whilst relatively small between America and Japan or South Korea.[158] This suggests that East Asians of Chinese origin are truly collectivistic, whilst the Japanese and the Koreans are not necessarily. However, it needs to be taken into account that most of the studies examined in the analysis sampled undergraduates as research participants.[159] Concerning Japanese undergraduates, their later socialisation, or the inculcation of collective values into their minds in companies they have joined may account for the Westerners' impression of Japan's rigid social norm mentioned earlier[160] or the image of collectivistic 'Japanese management'

[158] ibid 28.
[159] ibid 6.
[160] Takano and Osaka (n 134) 326.

acclaimed in the 1980s.[161] Conversely, it may be argued that the Japanese are in fact getting more individualistic (or less collectivistic) as a whole through the dispositional change found in younger generations[162] or the situational change after Japan achieved high economic growth.[163]

Another study published in 2004 was carried out by the Global Leadership and Organizational Behavior Effectiveness Research Program (hereinafter GLOBE). This has been the most extensive research programme ever published since Hofstede's. 170 'social scientists and management scholars from 62 cultures' participated in this 10-year research programme 'to increase available knowledge that is relevant to cross-cultural interactions'.[164] The researchers developed 735 questionnaire items to explore the differences among these societies in nine cultural dimensions and received responses from 'about 17,000 managers from 951 organizations functioning in 62 societies throughout the world' in three industries, namely financial services, food processing and telecommunications.[165] Relevant to this book are the findings on 'institutional collectivism', one of the nine cultural dimensions examined in this study, which means 'the degree to which organizational and societal institutional practices encourage and reward collective distribution of resources and collective action'.[166] Respondents were asked to indicate their views on statements about 'societal-level institutional practices' on a 7-point scale, with '1' representing 'low collectivism' and '7' 'high collectivism'.[167] These statements include, for example, '[i]n this society, leaders encourage group loyalty even if individual goals suffer', and '[t]he economic system in this society is designed to maximize [individual or collective interests]'.[168] Figure 17 below shows the mean scores on societal-level institutional collectivism practices calculated across all these statements in 10 cultural clusters in the world.[169] Consistent

---

[161] The Japanese management style has been characterised by its 'strong orientation to collective values' reflected in such aspects as lifetime employment, collective decision making and responsibility: William G Ouchi, *Theory Z: How American Business Can Meet the Japanese Challenge* (Reading, Massachusetts, Addison-Wesley, 1981) 47, 58.

[162] Takano and Osaka (n 134) 326.

[163] ibid 329.

[164] Robert J House, 'Illustrative Examples of GLOBE Findings' in Robert J House and others (eds), *Culture, Leadership, and Organizations: The GLOBE Study of 62 Societies* (Thousand Oaks, SAGE, 2004) 10–11.

[165] ibid.

[166] ibid 12.

[167] Michele J Gelfand and others, 'Individualism and Collectivism' in House and others (n 164) 463.

[168] ibid 464 Table 16.4a.

[169] Adapted from Gelfand and others (n 167) 477–78 Table 16.10a. These 10 cultural clusters are as follows: Nordic Europe (Finland, Sweden, Denmark), Confucian Asia (Taiwan, Singapore, Hong Kong, South Korea, China, Japan), Anglo (England, Ireland, Australia, South Africa (white sample), Canada, New Zealand, the US), Southern Asia (India, Indonesia, Philippines, Malaysia, Thailand, Iran), Middle East (Qatar, Morocco, Turkey, Egypt, Kuwait), Sub-Saharan Africa (Namibia, Zambia, Zimbabwe, South Africa (black sample), Nigeria), Eastern Europe (Hungary, Russia, Kazakhstan, Albania, Poland, Greece, Slovenia, Georgia), Germanic Europe (Austria, Switzerland, Netherlands, Germany (former East and West)), Latin Europe (Israel, Italy, Portugal, Spain, France, Switzerland (French-speaking)), and Latin America (Argentina, Bolivia, Brazil, Colombia, Costa Rica, Ecuador, El Salvador, Guatemala, Mexico, Venezuela).

with Hofstede's survey and Triandis' theory, Nordic Europe and Confucian Asia show higher scores on institutional collectivism practices than other clusters. Whilst Nordic countries are categorised as horizontal-individualist societies, Confucian societies in East Asia are generally collectivistic because of their emphasis on principles such as diligence and self-sacrifice[170] and their structural 'reliance upon "networks" which are co-ordinated through the mechanism of trust'.[171] Organisations in these cultural clusters are likely to adopt the equality principle of distribution in general.

In contradiction to the results of Hofstede's survey shown in Figure 15 above, Latin America shows the lowest score on institutional collectivism practices. However, this does not necessarily suggest that Latin America has totally become an individualistic society, for the GLOBE study also showed that regardless of the actual institutional practices respondent managers in this cultural cluster were more likely to agree that the social system *should* be designed to foster collectivistic values than those in any other cluster.[172] Meanwhile, according to the data on individual countries, Iran's score on institutional collectivism practices is among the lowest, reflecting people's distrust of collectivistic systems at the societal level caused by its long history of oppressive regimes and highly competitive education system.[173] Although Iran is generally regarded as a collectivistic society because of the people's strong 'loyalty and cohesiveness toward small groups such as family and close friends',[174] the country's score on institutional collectivism practices suggests that organisations there are less likely to adopt the equality principle of distribution than those in other collectivistic societies in Middle East or Southern Asia.

Continental (Eastern, Germanic and Latin) Europe generally shows a lower degree of institutional collectivism. Although some countries in 'Anglo', such as New Zealand, Ireland and South Africa (white sample), show a relatively high degree of institutional collectivism,[175] people in this cultural cluster generally devalue institutional collectivism 'because of the historical distrust of collective structures and goals imposed through colonization'.[176]

Although organisational cultures, as opposed to societal cultures, appear to determine the distribution principle in organisations,[177] the researchers in the

---

[170] Vipin Gupta and Paul J Hanges, 'Regional and Climate Clustering of Societal Cultures' in House and others (n 164) 189.

[171] Sid Lowe, 'Culture and Network Institutions in Hong Kong: A Hierarchy of Perspectives. A Response to Wilkinson: 'Culture, Institutions and Business in East Asia" (1998) 19 *Organization Studies* 321, 328.

[172] Gelfand and others (n 167) 477–78 Table 16.10a.

[173] Mansour Javidan and Ali Dastmalchian, 'Culture and Leadership in Iran: The Land of Individual Achievers, Strong Family Ties, and Powerful Elite' (2003) 17(4) *The Academy of Management Executive* 127, 131–32.

[174] ibid 130.

[175] Gelfand and others (n 167) 468 Table 16.7a.

[176] ibid 476.

[177] Hofstede (n 117) 213; Elizabeth A Mannix, Margaret A Neale and Gregory B Northcraft, 'Equity, Equality, or Need? The Effects of Organizational Culture on the Allocation of Benefits and Burdens' (1995) 63 *Organizational Behavior and Human Decision Processes* 276, 283.

Figure 17 Mean Scores on Societal-Level Institutional Collectivism Practices in 10 Cultural Clusters

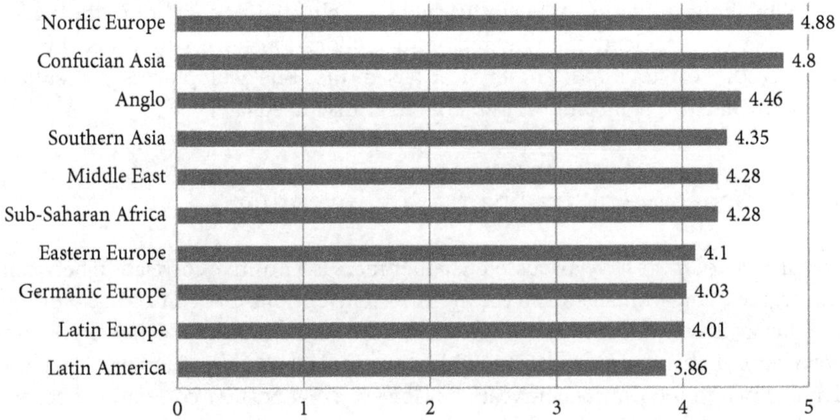

GLOBE study found that 'practices for societal Institutional Collectivism have a significant and strong positive relationship with organizational Institutional Collectivism practices', suggesting that 'societal cultural values and practices affect organizational cultural values and practices'.[178] Accordingly, 'organizations in societies with high scores on institutional collectivist values tend to emphasize collective rewards over individual rewards'.[179] This is consistent with the view generally accepted by '[t]extbooks in human resource management and organizational behavior' that 'organizations must "localize" their practices to fit the national culture of the country where operations are located'.[180]

So far it has been seen that Hofstede's individualism–collectivism dichotomy still provides a useful framework for analysing societal cultures. However, there are a couple of points to note regarding his theory. First, as in the case of the authoritarian Nazi regime and post-war East Germany, governments may sometimes impose collectivism on societies which are otherwise individualistic by nature.[181] Since historical factors may influence societal cultures, the results of Hofstede's survey are not necessarily static.[182] Second, Hofstede's aim was not to predict the behaviour of individuals but to analyse cultures at the societal level.[183] One cannot assume from Hofstede's indices that individuals within particular societies are always individualistic or collectivistic because every person's behaviour may be

---

[178] Gelfand and others (n 167) 491.

[179] ibid.

[180] Barry Gerhart and Meiyu Fang, 'Pay for (Individual) Performance: Issues, Claims, Evidence and the Role of Sorting Effects' (2014) 24 *Human Resource Management Review* 41, 49.

[181] Triandis (n 137) 88, 95.

[182] Hofstede (n 117) 253–54.

[183] ibid 216.

situation-specific: one may become individualistic at work whilst collectivistic in other social situations.[184]

With all the limitation of the individualism–collectivism dichotomy, the correlation between societal cultures and reward allocation norms indicated by the above studies carries important implications for the issue of employees' perception about the fairness of inventor remuneration as discussed later.

B. Influence of Cultural Norms on Inventing

Social psychologists have discussed whether there is a positive correlation between the degree of individualism and the number of inventions made in a society or the number of creative ideas generated in a group. Shane reported a strong positive correlation between Hofstede's Individualism Indices and the number of patents granted in a country in specific years.[185] However, that positive correlation became weaker, or even disappeared, when controlling for the wealth level of the country and other 'economic variables such as research and development expenditure, technical infrastructure, and [the] number of technical employees'.[186]

Recent laboratory studies on the relationship between individualism and the number of creative ideas generated by participants, which can be seen as substitutes for inventions in the real world, have shown seemingly inconsistent results. Goncalo and Staw found that groups made up of individualistic participants who had been manipulated to 'stand out' from others generated more creative ideas in a brainstorming task, in terms of both quantity and quality, than collectivistic groups who had been manipulated to 'blend in' with others.[187] In contrast, Bechtoldt and colleagues found that groups with collectivistic value orientation, whose members focused on group gains, produced more creative ideas than those with individualistic value orientation whose members focused on individual gains.[188] Whilst the former study only manipulated the participants' self-construal concerning how they saw themselves compared to others, the latter study further manipulated the participants' value orientation concerning what motivated them.[189] Amalgamating these conflicting findings, the researchers in the latter study argue that 'creativity in groups seems to flourish when collectivistic values combine with people's individualistic self-construal'.[190]

---

[184] Triandis (n 137) 27.

[185] Scott A Shane, 'Why Do Some Societies Invent More Than Others?' (1992) 7 *Journal of Business Venturing* 29, 38 Table 3.

[186] ibid 38–39 Table 4.

[187] Jack A Goncalo and Barry M Staw, 'Individualism-Collectivism and Group Creativity' (2006) 100 *Organizational Behavior and Human Decision Processes* 96, 100–02, 103 Fig 1, 104 Fig 2.

[188] Myriam N Bechtoldt, Hoon-Seok Choi and Bernard A Nijstad, 'Individualism in Mind, Mates by Heart: Individualistic Self-Construal and Collective Value Orientation as Predictors of Group Creativity' (2012) 48 *Journal of Experimental Social Psychology* 838, 841, 842 Table 1.

[189] ibid 840.

[190] ibid 843.

Many scholars in this field believe for the present that conformity found in a collectivistic culture is detrimental to inventing because they believe it will supress the free expression of unique ideas.[191] Yet they have not drawn a firm conclusion on whether individualism or collectivism affects the number of inventions created in a certain society or organisation. A recent laboratory study has partly proven the theory that cohesion which characterises a collectivistic culture can boost the creation of inventions if the norm requires members to adhere to divergent thinking, which is an attribute of individualism.[192] As inventions are usually made through teamwork in organisations, it is arguable that collectivism may foster the creation of inventions by employee inventors. A notable example is once successful Japanese corporations, where interpersonal communication promotes sharing of information and coordination between different organisational units.[193] Although their collectivistic practices encouraged teamwork so as to produce numerous inventions, this may not be the case with a company which has a highly individualistic culture where workers may tend to favour their own ideas and be reluctant to endorse the superior ideas of others.[194] However, some companies in the 'individualistic' US society have tried to introduce 'collectivistic' Asian business practices,[195] which suggests that collectivism, which is likely to create cooperative working environment, may remedy the disadvantage of individualism.

Nevertheless, it must be noticed that all the studies mentioned above discuss the influence of cultural norms on inventing, and thus do not specifically examine whether the equity principle or the equality principle of reward allocation will facilitate the creation of inventions by employee inventors. In explaining why individualism is more suitable for making inventions than collectivism, Shane mentions 'the importance to people of being compensated for doing more than others',[196] suggesting that the equity principle associated with individualism might encourage people to generate more inventive ideas than the equality principle associated with collectivism. However, his theory has not been sufficiently endorsed by subsequent experimental studies. A recent laboratory study by Goncalo and Kim found that groups endorsing the equity principle in the distribution of rewards generated significantly more ideas in a brainstorming task than those endorsing

---

[191] Francis J Flynn and Jennifer A Chatman, 'Strong Cultures and Innovation: Oxymoron or Opportunity?' in Cary L Cooper, Sue Cartwright and P Christopher Earley (eds), *The International Handbook of Organizational Culture and Climate* (Chichester, John Wiley & Sons, 2001) 266–67; Goncalo and Staw (n 187) 98.

[192] Flynn and Chatman (n 191) 273; Jack A Goncalo and Michelle M Duguid, 'Follow the Crowd in a New Direction: When Conformity Pressure Facilitates Group Creativity (and When It Does Not)' (2012) 118 *Organizational Behavior and Human Decision Processes* 14, 18–20.

[193] Miriam Erez, 'Interpersonal Communication Systems in Organizations, and Their Relationships to Cultural Values, Productivity and Innovation: The Case of Japanese Corporations' (1992) 41 *Applied Psychology* 43, 59.

[194] Flynn and Chatman (n 191) 277.

[195] Goncalo and Staw (n 187) 96.

[196] Shane (n 185) 34.

the equality principle when both kinds of groups were all made up of people with 'independent' (or more competitive) orientation.[197] Yet the study did not yield similar results when all the groups were made up of people with 'interdependent' (or less competitive) orientation.[198] Although all the participants in this study were from the 'individualistic' US society,[199] it suggests that the equity principle may not always encourage teams to produce more inventive ideas even in individualistic societies, depending on the competitiveness of the team members. Overall, social psychologists since Hofstede have not clarified the relationship between distributive norms and the performance of employee inventors.[200]

C. Effect of Inventor Remuneration

i. Adverse Effect of 'Unfair' Inventor Remuneration on the Performance of Employee Inventors

Whether the equity principle is more likely to encourage the creation of inventions than the equality principle or vice versa, invention compensation schemes are likely to backfire if employees regard the inventor remuneration as unfair. According to meta-analyses of organisational justice studies in social psychology, people's perceived justice positively correlates with their job satisfaction and productivity in general, whilst it negatively correlates with counterproductive work behaviour such as high absenteeism and turnover.[201] In sum, when workers feel reward allocation is unfair, they are likely to experience lower job satisfaction, which will eventually cause their counterproductive work behaviour and lower productivity. Similarly, a recent laboratory study shows that the perception of distributive injustice has a negative effect on creative performance of those who possess creative potential.[202]

As long as employee inventors do not change their jobs they continue to make more inventions in the same companies even after inventor remuneration is given

---

[197] Jack A Goncalo and Sharon H Kim, 'Distributive Justice Beliefs and Group Idea Generation: Does a Belief in Equity Facilitate Productivity?' (2010) 46 *Journal of Experimental Social Psychology* 836, 838–39, Fig 1.

[198] ibid.

[199] ibid 837.

[200] Flynn and Chatman (n 191) 281.

[201] Yochi Cohen-Charash and Paul E Spector, 'The Role of Justice in Organizations: A Meta-Analysis' (2001) 86 *Organizational Behavior and Human Decision Processes* 278, 296 Table 4, 298 Table 6, 299–300 Table 7, 304–07; Jason A Colquitt and others, 'Justice at the Millennium: A Meta-Analytic Review of 25 Years of Organizational Justice Research' (2001) 86 *Journal of Applied Psychology* 425, 434, 436 Table 5; Jason A Colquitt and others, 'Justice at the Millennium, a Decade Later: A Meta-Analytic Test of Social Exchange and Affect-Based Perspectives' (2013) 98 *Journal of Applied Psychology* 199, 208 Table 3, 209 Table 4.

[202] Aneika L Simmons, 'The Influence of Openness to Experience and Organizational Justice on Creativity' (2011) 23 *Creativity Research Journal* 9, 18 Table 2 Fig 1, 19–20.

for a single invention. According to PatVal-II, the median number of inventions respondents had made was 10.0 in Europe, 20.0 in the US and 30.0 in Japan.[203] However, it follows from the findings in organisational justice studies mentioned above that inventor remuneration is likely to cause negative reactions of employees who regard it as unfair. This will adversely affect the teamwork in inventing in the future and thus eventually impede the creation of subsequent inventions.

This is not to say that employees all around the world would regard inventor remuneration as unfair. People in different societies are likely to have different views on distributive justice. Those in individualistic societies may regard it as fair on the assumption that those who have made a significant contribution should naturally deserve rewards. However, those in collectivistic societies may regard it as unfair on the assumption that all the employees should be treated equally regardless of the significance of their contribution. Alternatively, they may favour evaluation based on loyalty or seniority.[204]

According to the meta-analysis by Taras and colleagues, more than half of earlier studies on individuals' preference for reward allocation rules examined by them showed a significant and positive correlation between individualism and the equity principle, whilst a significant and negative correlation between individualism and equality or seniority principle.[205] However, about 25 per cent of the studies showed the opposite correlation and thus the predictive power of the individualism–collectivism dichotomy on reward allocation rules is comparatively weak.[206] Some social psychologists suggest that Triandis' horizontal–vertical cultural dimension may better explain reward allocation behaviour.[207] Therefore, it is reasonable to assume for the present that the reward allocation rule usually follows the equity principle in vertical-individualist societies, and the equality or seniority principle in collectivist and horizontal-individualist societies. The influence of inventor remuneration on the teamwork of employee inventors in various societies will be discussed below according to this distinction.

ii. Inventor Remuneration in Vertical-individualist Societies

Vertical-individualist societies typically refer to English-speaking and European countries apart from horizontal-individualist societies such as Australia and

---

[203] Nagaoka and others (n 36) 12 Table 3-1-10.

[204] Triandis (n 137) 79.

[205] Vas Taras, Bradley L Kirkman and Piers Steel, 'Examining the Impact of *Culture's Consequences*: A Three-Decade, Multilevel, Meta-Analytic Review of Hofstede's Cultural Value Dimensions' (2010) 95 *Journal of Applied Psychology* 405, 418 Table 2. 15 out of 26 studies on the relationship between individualism and equity principle showed a positive correlation, whilst nine out of 16 studies on the relationship between individualism and equality or seniority principle showed a negative correlation.

[206] ibid 418 Table 2, 432. See also Ronald Fischer and Peter B Smith, 'Reward Allocation and Culture: A Meta-Analysis' (2003) 34 *Journal of Cross-Cultural Psychology* 251, 258.

[207] Fischer and Smith (n 206) 259-60.

Nordic countries and collectivist societies in Southern and Southeast Europe,[208] notably southern Italy and rural Greece.[209] It appears that inventor remuneration is consistent with the equity principle of reward allocation generally accepted in vertical-individualist societies. As long as proper persons are named as inventors, people in these societies are likely to see inventor remuneration as fair on the assumption that named inventors have made a special contribution to the invention. Yet the degree of individualism varies from region to region.[210] There is also a gender difference in this respect. Several studies consistently show that women in the US society are more likely to stress the collectivistic value of 'relatedness to others' than men, who generally stress 'independence from others'.[211] People's opinions about the equity principle and inventor remuneration may differ according to their attributes.[212]

However, empirical studies in both laboratory and organisational settings have already confirmed that setting individual goals which will result in pay dispersion among workers is counterproductive in interdependent tasks.[213] This is because establishing an individual goal in an interdependent task makes workers focus on their own outcomes, and thus causes more competition and less cooperation among them to the detriment of interdependence, resulting in their lower performance as a team.[214] This theory applies to inventing in organisations, which essentially requires teamwork among scientists and engineers from various disciplines. Consistent with this theory patent reward gave rise to the secrecy of inventors, who wanted to monopolise the reward, in the episode of Bell Laboratories mentioned earlier.[215] Inventors' secrecy is likely to occur especially in

---

[208] However, collectivism in Southern and Southeast Europe manifests itself more clearly in family or group cohesiveness than in institutional practices such as reward allocation: Jorge Correia Jesuino, 'Latin Europe Cluster: From South to North' (2002) 37 *Journal of World Business* 81, 85; Gyula Bakacsi and others, 'Eastern European Cluster: Tradition and Transition' (2002) 37 *Journal of World Business* 69, 75.

[209] Harry C Triandis, 'Collectivism and Individualism as Cultural Syndromes' (1993) 27 *Cross-Cultural Research* 155, 160.

[210] Triandis (n 137) 168–69.

[211] Susan E Cross and Laura Madson, 'Models of the Self: Self-Construals and Gender' (1997) 122 *Psychological Bulletin* 5, 9.

[212] For example, a field study found that German organisations were less likely to adopt the equity principle of distribution than their US and UK counterparts: Ronald Fischer and others, 'How Do Organizations Allocate Rewards? The Predictive Validity of National Values, Economic and Organizational Factors Across Six Nations' (2007) 38 *Journal of Cross-Cultural Psychology* 3, 11 Table 1. Female subjects in a laboratory study showed less preference for the equity principle than their male counterparts: David G Wagner, 'Gender Differences in Reward Preference: A Status-Based Account' (1995) 26 *Small Group Research* 353, 365 Table 2.

[213] Terence R Mitchell and William S Silver, 'Individual and Group Goals When Workers Are Independent: Effects on Task Strategies and Performance' (1990) 75 *Journal of Applied Psychology* 185, 190 Table 2; Jason D Shaw, Nina Gupta and John E Delery, 'Pay Dispersion and Workforce Performance: Moderating Effects of Incentives and Interdependence' (2002) 23 *Strategic Management Journal* 491, 504, 507 Fig 4. However, the latter study suggests that the negative effect of pay dispersion is somewhat attenuated if individual incentive is offered as a legitimate rationale for the dispersion: ibid 504, 508.

[214] Mitchell and Silver (n 213) 190 Table 3, 191 Table 4; Shaw, Gupta and Delery (n 213) 508.

[215] See text to nn 102, 104.

vertical-individualist societies, where people tend to demand rewards for individual achievements. If inventors receive inventor remuneration thanks to the secrecy maintained by them, other employees would no longer regard it as fair. Inventors' secrecy caused by the offer of inventor remuneration thus adversely affects the teamwork of employee inventors.

Although the teamwork in inventing will not be affected if inventor remuneration is not offered, it is another question whether it will undermine the morale of those who are properly named as inventors. They may expect that their status as a named inventor should naturally accompany monetary rewards. However, most named inventors, even those in vertical-individualist societies who generally support the equity principle of reward allocation, are unlikely to lose the motivation to invent if they receive no monetary rewards for the successful inventions since their motivation comes from values intrinsic in inventing rather than material incentives as demonstrated in recent surveys mentioned earlier.[216]

It needs to be added here that inventorship does not legally entitle inventors to some economic benefits. Inventors have the moral right to be named as such in patents regardless of jurisdiction.[217] In the US, whether under its 'first-to-invent' system since the inception of its patent law, or the 'first-inventor-to-file' system effective from 16 March 2013 under the Leahy-Smith America Invents Act (AIA),[218] false inventor(s) mentioned in patent applications can lead to the cancellation of claims pursuant to either 'interferences' (pre-AIA) or 'derivation proceedings'(post-AIA).[219] Apart from these points, the status of a named inventor essentially carries no legal significance. Although it is assumed in the US or under the 'inventor principle' in some civil law countries that named inventors initially retain the ownership of inventions they have made in theory, as discussed later in Part II of this book, most of them are not entitled to additional compensation when they assign the inventions to their employers except in Germany, where the Act of Employees' Inventions makes inventor remuneration mandatory in principle.

Fundamentally, it is open to question whether people in vertical-individualist societies really believe that named inventors naturally deserve monetary rewards. If inventors' 'flash of genius' is still regarded as invaluable as that of historical 'hero-inventors' such as Edison and Bell, the equity principle should require that

---

[216] See ch 2, s IV.

[217] Paris Convention for the Protection of Intellectual Property of 20 March 1883 (as amended on 28 September 1979), art 4*ter*.

[218] The Leahy-Smith America Invents Act replaced the traditional 'first-to-invent' system, where a patent had been granted to the first inventor, with the 'first-inventor-to-file' system, where a patent is granted to the inventor who is the first to file the application: Public Law 112-29 § 3(b)(n); 35 USC § 102(a) (2012).

[219] 35 USC § 135 (pre-AIA, post-AIA). Derivation proceedings apply to patent applications on and after 16 March 2013. False inventorship can still invalidate claims under the AIA despite the repeal of 35 USC § 102(f), since the US Constitution and 35 USC § 101 still require that patentees should be true inventors: Joe Matal, 'A Guide to the Legislative History of the America Invents Act: Part I of II' (2012) 21 *Federal Circuit Bar Journal* 435, 451.

named inventors be given monetary rewards today. However, this anachronistic view of heroic lone inventors until the late nineteenth century no longer applies to the present situations, where inventions are created in organisations through the teamwork of staff from a variety of backgrounds. It should be recalled that employers in the US seldom award generous rewards to employee inventors[220] even though it is said that more than 90 per cent of US companies offer some kind of financial incentives to workers in general.[221] This suggests that even Americans who generally endorse the equity principle may not agree that named inventors should always receive inventor remuneration. Rather, offering inventor remuneration in vertical-individualist societies is likely to promote the secrecy of employee inventors to the detriment of their teamwork and productivity. Manly pointed out as early as 40 years ago that since the German Act on Employees' Inventions had come into force in 1957, the number of patents issued to the citizens of West Germany at the time had declined steadily until the late 1970s.[222] He already foresaw that the Act, which 'singles out one cog in the innovative wheel—the inventor', would not serve its intended purpose when Congressperson Moss in the US proposed a Bill similar to the German Act in the 1970s.[223]

iii. Inventor Remuneration in Collectivist and Horizontal-individualist Societies

Although pay differentials occur even in collectivistic and horizontal-individualist societies due to the hierarchy of staff in organisations as a matter of course, the question here is how to distribute profits gained from inventive projects among the participants from various departments, regardless of their positions in organisations. In these societies, people are likely to regard it as fair to distribute profits equally among participants in the projects regardless of the significance of their contribution. In view of the results of various studies in cross-cultural psychology mentioned earlier, it can be said that the following regions are typically collectivist societies: Confucian Asia, Middle East, Russia, Southern Asia, Sub-Saharan Africa and Latin America.[224] Yet there are some anomalies such as Iran, whose culture is individualistic at the organisation level.[225] In general employees other than named inventors are likely to see inventor remuneration as unfair in these societies, so that it can provoke negative reactions from such employees to the detriment of teamwork in inventing and eventually hinder the creation of subsequent inventions. Meanwhile, some employee inventors in these societies may

---

[220] See ch 2, Figs 1, 2 and accompanying text.

[221] Shaw, Gupta and Delery (n 213) 492.

[222] Donald G Manly, 'Inventors, Innovators, Compensation and the Law' (1978) 21(2) *Research Management* 29, 30, 32 Fig 1.

[223] ibid 30. For the outline of Moss Bill, see ch 6, s IV.C.

[224] Southern and Southeast Europe are also included in collectivist societies: see text to n 208.

[225] See text to n 173.

want to monopolise inventor remuneration, but their secrecy is less likely to occur than in vertical-individualist societies because their social norm generally gives group interest priority over private interest.

In horizontal-individualist societies, notably Nordic countries, people generally endorse equal distribution of rewards. The collective agreement in Sweden mentioned earlier, according to which all the unionised inventors shall receive either kr22,150 or kr44,300 no matter how commercially valuable their inventions are,[226] may partially reflect the Scandinavian values that everyone should enjoy an equal social status in principle.[227] However, the agreement can still adversely affect the teamwork of employee inventors because it treats named inventors differently from other employees who also contribute to the creation of inventions.

People in collectivist societies might become vertical-individualists in the future, influenced by affluence and mass media which foster individualistic values.[228] For example, a field study found that some Chinese, who tended to show strong collectivistic orientation under traditional 'Confucian values of cohesion'[229] and post-1949 communist ideology, had been increasingly prepared to accommodate themselves to differential reward allocation rules since the Chinese government initiated economic reform a few decades ago.[230] However, unless individualism becomes predominant over collectivism, most Chinese employees who do not receive inventor remuneration are likely to take a negative attitude because group harmony generally takes precedence over individual achievements in their society.

It may still be argued that offering inventor remuneration in a collectivistic culture is still useful for creating an individualistic climate that may facilitate employees' free expression of inventive ideas. Whilst those in individualist societies generally focus on successes in their social life, those in collectivist societies tend to focus on failures and fear deviating from their societal norms.[231] Thus the offer of inventor remuneration may serve as a kind of a seal of approval which allows workers in collectivist societies to break through their psychological barrier to exhibiting their unique ideas. However, an individual goal established in an interdependent task generally has an adverse effect on teamwork as mentioned earlier.[232] It should be recalled here that in the study by Bechtoldt and colleagues groups whose members focused on individual gains generated less creative ideas

---

[226] See text to ch 1, n 22.

[227] See text to nn 142–49.

[228] Triandis (n 137) 82–83.

[229] ibid 45.

[230] Chao C Chen, James R Meindl and Raymond G Hunt, 'Testing the Effects of Vertical and Horizontal Collectivism: A Study of Reward Allocation Preferences in China' (1997) 28 *Journal of Cross-Cultural Psychology* 44, 50–51, 62, 63 Table 5. Japan may also be shifting toward an individualistic society: see text to nn 162, 163.

[231] Chen, Meindl and Hunt (n 230) 70–71.

[232] See text to nn 213, 214.

than those on group gains.[233] This suggests that even if individualistic personality is advantageous for inventing in general,[234] financial incentives offered to individuals will not enhance group creativity.

According to the analysis so far, the offer of inventor remuneration will promote the secrecy of employee inventors especially in vertical-individualist societies where people tend to demand rewards for individual achievements, whilst the remuneration will cause negative reactions of employees who do not receive it in collectivist and horizontal-individualist societies where group harmony is a guiding principle of organisations in general. Inventor remuneration will thus adversely affect the teamwork of employee inventors in both kinds of societies in different ways: the adverse effect is mainly triggered by the attitude of employees who try to monopolise inventor remuneration in vertical-individualist societies or those who do not receive it in collectivist and horizontal-individualist societies. Accordingly, invention compensation schemes are likely to fail whether in individualist or collectivist societies.

iv. Effectiveness of Team-based Incentives

Then in view of the reality that inventions are created through teamwork in organisations, what if the law were to require employers to offer team-based incentives to employee inventors? With this imaginative law, all the contributors to an invention, whether or not they are legally named as inventors, would receive some amount of compensation from profits that employers would gain by exploiting the invention. Can this kind of law induce employee inventors to create more inventions?

In business administration, an incentive plan in which the reward is tied up with organisational profits is called 'profit-sharing'.[235] The team-based incentives discussed here also qualify as profit-sharing as team members who create an invention through their joint effort will share a certain percentage of the profits it eventually brings to their company. However, an invention itself does not generate company profits unless it is exploited through an innovation process,[236] which necessarily entails not only knowledge procurement but successful manufacturing, marketing and financing.[237] In theory, employee inventors cannot control

---

[233] See text to n 188.

[234] See text to n 191.

[235] Jody R Hoffman and Steven G Rogelberg, 'A Guide to Team Incentive Systems' (1998) 4 *Team Performance Management* 22, 22.

[236] Ralf Kesten, 'Innovationen durch eigene Mitarbeiter: Betriebswirtschaftliche Aspekte zur monetären Beurteilung von Diensterfindungen nach dem Gesetz über Arbeitnehmererfindungen' [Innovations by Individual Employees: Economic Aspects of Monetary Evaluation of Employee Inventions under the Law on Employee Inventions] (1996) 66 *Zeitschrift für Betriebswirtschaft* (*ZfB*) 651, 653.

[237] ibid 653, 654 Abb 1.

the financial outcomes of the company directly.[238] This can diminish the effectiveness of the incentive plan because employee inventors are unlikely to work hard to improve their productivity when the goal is out of their immediate control (so-called 'line-of-sight' problem).[239] This is especially true of composite products such as automobiles which are made of numerous patented technologies because the connection between one component invention and the company profits derived from the sales of the product becomes even more obscure.[240]

The above problem may be resolved if the incentive plan sets outcomes that can be achieved by the team of workers independently.[241] However, team-based incentive schemes generally entail the problem of 'social loafing'. This refers to 'the reduction in motivation and effort when individuals work collectively compared with when they work individually',[242] and it has actually been observed in a number of studies in social psychology.[243] Some researchers explain that workers engaged in collective tasks tend to be demotivated because 'factors other than the individual's effort frequently determine performance, [whilst] valued outcomes are often divided among all of the group members'.[244]

Laboratory studies have revealed that collectivists are less likely to exhibit social loafing than individualists, especially when group members share a common goal which requires a high level of cooperation,[245] they are from homogeneous backgrounds,[246] or when they show a strong preference for group work.[247] According to Earley, this is because collectivists share a social motive of pursuing group goals, and thus tend to derive their satisfaction from successful group outcomes, whilst individualists, who generally have a self-interest motive of maximising their personal gains, have little incentive to contribute to group outcomes unless their individual contribution is recognised and rewarded.[248] Even in the case of individualists, social loafing can be reduced by enhancing the

---

[238] Hoffman and Rogelberg (n 235) 23.

[239] ibid (citations omitted).

[240] Brockhoff (n 82) 680.

[241] Hoffman and Rogelberg (n 235) 25.

[242] Steven J Karau and Kipling D Williams, 'Social Loafing: A Meta-Analytic Review and Theoretical Integration' (1993) 65 *Journal of Personality and Social Psychology* 681, 681.

[243] ibid 689–93 Table 1.

[244] ibid 684. There are several other theories which attempt to explain the cause of social loafing: ibid 682–84.

[245] P Christopher Earley, 'Social Loafing and Collectivism: A Comparison of the United States and the People's Republic of China' (1989) 34 *Administrative Science Quarterly* 565, 572–73, 576 Fig 1.

[246] P Christopher Earley, 'East Meets West Meets Mideast: Further Explorations of Collectivistic and Individualistic Work Groups' (1993) 36 *Academy of Management Journal* 319, 331–32, 336 Fig 2, 341.

[247] Eric M Stark, Jason D Shaw and Michelle K Duffy, 'Preference for Group Work, Winning Orientation, and Social Loafing Behavior in Groups' (2007) 32 *Group & Organization Management* 699, 710, 711 Table 2, 715. Consistent with these studies, the result of a meta-analysis shows that people from Eastern cultures (mostly collectivists) are less likely to social loaf than those from Western cultures (mostly individualists): Karau and Williams (n 242) 697, 698 Table 4.

[248] Earley (n 245) 577.

identifiability of each member's performance.[249] However, this is not to say that offering financial reward for individual performance at the same time can settle the problem without harming team performance. Researchers in this field generally observe that mixing team-based and individual-based incentives often only ends up creating 'a social dilemma', in which each member of the team is inclined to pursue their personal interests to the detriment of cooperation with other members.[250] Reducing group size can also be a solution to the problem of social loafing[251] because it makes 'the line of sight between pay and performance' visible to the members, and thus improves their motivation to work.[252]

Although some studies show that rewards contingent on group performance have no independent effects on the level of cooperation among workers,[253] some researchers in social psychology have argued that the offer of team-based incentives may still enhance group performance because it may diminish intra-group competition, thereby creating an enjoyable working environment.[254] Despite the problem of social loafing, studies have generally confirmed that team-based incentives are no less effective in boosting the productivity of general workers than individual incentives when the group size is small.[255] For example, a recent field study has found that a factory in the US which 'assembles a large assortment of security metal locks' achieved 'a 31% rise in productivity and a 95% drop in product defects' after it switched from a piece-rate system to an incentive plan which linked the rewards with performance at both the team and plant level.[256]

---

[249] ibid 573, 576 Fig 1; John A Wagner III , 'Studies of Individualism-Collectivism: Effects on Cooperation in Groups' (1995) 38 *The Academy of Management Journal* 152, 165 Table 3, 166 Fig 2; Robert C Liden and others, 'Social Loafing: A Field Investigation' (2004) 30 *Journal of Management* 285, 297 Table 3.

[250] Christopher M Barnes and others, 'Mixing Individual Incentives and Group Incentives: Best of Both or Social Dilemma?' (2011) 37 *Journal of Management* 1611, 1612, 1623–26 Table 3-7, 1631.

[251] Wagner (n 249) 165 Table 3, 166 Fig 2; Liden and others (n 249) 298 Table 4.

[252] Jacquelyn S DeMatteo, Lillian T Eby and Eric Sundstrom, 'Team-Based Rewards: Current Empirical Evidence and Directions for Future Research' in Barry M Staw and LL Cummings (eds), *Research in Organizational behavior*, vol 20 (Greenwich, Connecticut, JAI Press, 1998) 161–62 (citation omitted).

[253] Ruth Wageman, 'Interdependence and Group Effectiveness' (1995) 40 *Administrative Science Quarterly* 145, 169, 170 Table 4, 173; Ruth Wageman and George Baker, 'Incentives and Cooperation: The Joint Effects of Task and Reward Interdependence on Group Performance' (1997) 18 *Journal of Organizational Behavior* 139, 153 Table 3, 154, 155, 156 Table 5.

[254] Wageman and Baker (n 253) 151 Table 1, 156; Jason D Shaw, Michelle K Duffy and Eric M Stark, 'Interdependence and Preference for Group Work: Main and Congruence Effects on the Satisfaction and Performance of Group Members' (2000) 26 *Journal of Management* 259, 268–69, 271 Table 2, 272, 273 Table 3, 274–75.

[255] Judith A Honeywell-Johnson and Alyce M Dickinson, 'Small Group Incentives: A Review of the Literature' (1999) 19 *Journal of Organizational Behavior Management* 89, 102–05; Yvonne Garbers and Udo Konradt, 'The Effect of Financial Incentives on Performance: A Quantitative Review of Individual and Team-Based Financial Incentives' (2014) 87 *Journal of Occupational and Organizational Psychology* 102, 116, 117 Table 4.

[256] Francisco J Román, 'An Analysis of Changes to a Team-Based Incentive Plan and its Effect on Productivity, Product Quality, and Absenteeism' (2009) 34 *Accounting, Organizations and Society* 589, 590–91, 602–05 Table 3, 609 Fig 2.

Nevertheless, it is questionable whether team-based incentives can boost the creation of inventions in companies, for the success of inventing does not depend on the sum of individual worker's effort alone as the assembly of security metal locks does. What needs to be considered is the task structure unique to inventing in organisations in which a team of employee inventors try to find a solution to a technical problem. In Steiner's typology of group tasks, it qualifies as a 'disjunctive task', in which 'groups are required to select one of two or more discretely different options as the group product'.[257] Unlike assembling security locks, its aim lies not in maximising outputs but in optimising intellectual resources to produce 'the best' outcome.[258] For the success of disjunctive tasks the group must have at least one competent member who can arrive at the correct solution, and follow a feedback process whereby '[a]ny individual with the necessary resource should proceed to solve the problem and announce his solution to other members of the group', whilst '[t]he latter should, in turn, renounce incorrect solutions in favor of the correct one'.[259] It has been pointed out that this kind of task is highly susceptible to social loafing because individual contributions of group members, especially those who take part in the correction of solutions alone, cannot be identified from the single solution per se submitted by the group, and thus it can 'invite undetectable free riding on other's contributions'.[260]

Moreover, evidence has shown that a group is likely to fail to reach an optimal solution

> when (a) a majority of the group members initially favor an outcome other than that generated by the most competent person; (b) the most competent person has low status in the group; (c) the most competent person is not very confident of his own ability to perform the task; or (d) the most competent person does not present his contribution very aggressively and does not evoke supportive reactions from others.[261]

Because the group process involved in disjunctive tasks is thus subject to complex interpersonal factors, team-based incentives are unlikely to boost the creation of inventions in companies immediately as in the case of the lock assembly plant. Although many studies in social psychology have quantitatively confirmed that team-based incentives have more or less positive effects on the productivity of tasks which maximise outputs, it remains unclear whether they have similarly positive effects on disjunctive tasks which optimise intellectual resources to find a solution to a particular problem.[262]

---

[257] Ivan D Steiner, *Group Process and Productivity* (New York, Academic Press, 1972) 17. He sorted group tasks into four categories ('disjunctive', 'conjunctive', 'additive' and 'discretionary' task) according to 'ways they permit members to combine their individual products' and discussed the productivity of each kind of task: ibid 4, 16–18.

[258] ibid 16–17.

[259] ibid 21.

[260] Harold H Kelley and others, *An Atlas of Interpersonal Situations* (Cambridge, Cambridge University Press, 2003) 243–44.

[261] Steiner (n 257) 28.

[262] Little is known as to how group incentives affect the performance of disjunctive tasks: Honeywell-Johnson and Dickinson (n 255) 111–14.

Irrespective of whether team-based incentive plans have positive effects on workers' productivity in general, it must be critically examined whether it is really feasible to adopt such plans for employee inventors. The most problematic is how to set goals to be achieved by them. As the aforementioned 'line-of sight' problem suggests, the goals, or the criteria for measuring team performance, must be what employee inventors can influence; otherwise they would not know what they should devote their energies to.[263] Since employee inventors cannot control the profits to be brought to their companies in theory,[264] possible goals include the objective value of the invention measured without reference to the resultant company profits. However, setting aside the problem of establishing realistic criteria for measuring the value of an invention, this goal is still out of the immediate control of rank-and-file employees because its value depends on the technical problem to be solved which is usually set by their supervisors or middle-level managers.[265] In addition, inventions are not suited to a numerical target defined in terms of the number of created inventions since they are not mass-produced goods like security locks. Furthermore, even if practical goals for employee inventors can be defined under the team-base incentive plans, their effect is questionable because the reward size for each member will be substantially reduced when the team size is large.[266]

It is worth mentioning that the description of the 'line-of-sight' problem and the 'disjunctive task' discussed here essentially holds true for incentives offered to individual inventors, not teams of employees. Viewed in this light, financial compensation linked to the creation of inventions is not a suitable measure for boosting the creation of inventions in companies, whether it is offered to individual inventors or to teams of inventors. Of course, some inventors who have made a more significant contribution to the creation of an invention than others may still feel unhappy about not getting a special reward for their contribution. Yet it appears reasonable to leave its recognition to the normal personnel evaluation in their companies which may eventually lead to their promotion and let those contributors expect that 'such inequities … [will] balance out in the long run'.[267] Meanwhile, earlier discussion suggests that salient rewards for a significant contribution should be avoided because it will either promote the secrecy of employee inventors or arouse a sense of unfairness in those who do not receive it, so that it will adversely affect the teamwork in inventing.

In summary, I pointed out in this chapter that invention compensation schemes are unlikely to encourage the creation of inventions immediately in actual industrial settings in view of serendipity, corporate hierarchy and teamwork in

---

[263] DeMatteo, Eby and Sundstrom (n 252) 164.
[264] See text to nn 236–40.
[265] See text to n 3.
[266] DeMatteo, Eby and Sundstrom (n 252) 155.
[267] Kelley and others (n 260) 245.

inventing. Following that, I argued through reference to the notion of distributive justice and Hofstede's individualism–collectivism dichotomy that such schemes are likely to fail in any society. All the theories mentioned in this chapter apply to workers in general. No further discussion is necessary to confirm this conclusion if employee inventors do similar works to those done by other kinds of workers.

Nevertheless, inventing is qualitatively different to other kinds of work in that it requires 'creativity'. As will be seen later, psychologists argue that monetary rewards can either undermine people's creativity or help people bring out their creativity. Although the discussions so far deal with the influence of financial incentives on the quantity of inventions made by employees, they reveal nothing about their effect on the creativity of employee inventors which determines the quality of the inventions, so to speak. In the next chapter it will be examined whether monetary rewards for employee inventors can enhance the value of inventions they make. Furthermore, it will be shown that invention compensation schemes have little, if any, effect on the creativity of employee inventors because factors other than monetary rewards actually play an important role in harnessing workplace creativity.

4

Monetary Rewards and the Creativity
of Employee Inventors

I. Controversy over the Effect of Monetary Rewards

A. Deci's Theory on Intrinsic Motivation and Amabile's Theory on Creativity

There are various definitions of 'creativity' resulting from the diverse theories on this topic put forward by psychologists.[1] According to Amabile's phraseology, creativity is composed of three elements, namely 'creative-thinking skills', 'motivation' and 'expertise'.[2] Although some people tend to focus on the first element alone, which 'determine[s] how flexibly and imaginatively people approach problems',[3] many researchers in this field agree that an outburst of creativity inevitably necessitates the other two factors, namely 'an intense enthusiasm and involvement' in creative activity,[4] and 'technical, intellectual and procedural knowledge in a specific area [which] helps in the identification and solution of problems of real importance in the area'.[5]

The question to be examined here is whether financial rewards can induce people to exhibit their creativity often necessary for making inventions. It must be noticed that the current question is different to that of inventors' motivation which was examined in chapter two since motivation is just one component of creativity according to Amabile's phraseology. The current question may seem to stray from the scope of this book which discusses incentives for employee inventors since 'incentive' is usually understood as a word concerning solely people's motivation. However, one cannot make inventions without creativity. The legal compensation schemes will be irrational if they adversely affect inventors' creativity and thereby hinder the creation of inventions. Therefore, their effect on creativity needs to be discussed here as a topic closely related to the subject matter of this book.

---

[1] Eunice ML Soriano de Alencar, 'Creativity in Organizations: Facilitators and Inhibitors' in Michael D Mumford (ed), *Handbook of Organizational Creativity* (Amsterdam, Academic Press, 2011) 88–90.

[2] Teresa M Amabile, 'How to Kill Creativity' (1998) 76(5) *Harvard Business Review* 77, 78.

[3] ibid.

[4] Alencar (n 1) 93.

[5] ibid 94.

Amabile's theory on creativity is based on Deci's seminal laboratory study which examined the effect of financial rewards on people's behaviour. In the study Deci used what is called a 'Soma puzzle', a cube which 'is made up of seven pieces of plastic' each comprising three or four one-inch cubes, and asked two groups of subjects to reproduce various configurations designated in advance during three sessions.[6] The experimental group received $1 for each configuration completed during the second session but no financial reward for the task during the first and third sessions.[7] The control group received no financial reward during all these sessions.[8] Each group was allowed to decide freely whether they would work on the puzzle or get some diversion for eight minutes in the middle of each session, and Deci measured the amount of time each spent on the task during this period of time, which was thought to represent spontaneous display of motivation of the subjects in each group for the creative activity.[9] The result showed that the experimental group spent considerably less time working on the puzzle in the third period than in the first period.[10] Since the control group spent more time in the third period than in the first, it could be assumed that the decrease of time spent by the experimental group was not due to boredom or an increased familiarity with the task.[11]

Deci replicated the study with similar results in the subsequent studies.[12] These studies suggest that people are likely to lose their motivation to perform tasks that are inherently interesting after monetary rewards are offered for it. Deci explained the reason as follows:

> When [a person] is intrinsically motivated, the perceived locus of causality ... of that behavior is within himself. He is doing it because it provides him with some sort of internal satisfaction. However, when he performs the activity for external reinforcements such as money, he comes to perceive that he is doing it for the money. The perceived locus of causality changes from within himself to the environment; that is, he cognitively re-evaluates the activity as one which he does because it provides him with external rewards.[13]

Developing Deci's theory that financial rewards have a negative effect on people's 'intrinsic motivation', Amabile argues that 'intrinsic motivation is conductive to creativity whereas extrinsic motivation is detrimental'.[14] Here, 'intrinsic motivation' is what 'arises from the individual's positive reaction to qualities of the task

---

[6] Edward L Deci, 'Effects of Externally Mediated Rewards on Intrinsic Motivation' (1971) 18 *Journal of Personality and Social Psychology* 105, 108.

[7] ibid 108–09.

[8] ibid.

[9] ibid 109.

[10] ibid 109 Table 1, 110.

[11] ibid.

[12] ibid 110–12; Edward L Deci, 'Intrinsic Motivation, Extrinsic Reinforcement, and Inequity' (1972) 22 *Journal of Personality and Social Psychology* 113, 115–18.

[13] Edward L Deci, 'The Effects of Contingent and Noncontingent Rewards and Controls on Intrinsic Motivation' (1972) 8 *Organizational Behavior and Human Performance* 217, 223 (citation omitted).

[14] Teresa M Amabile, *Creativity in Context* (Boulder, Westview Press, 1996) 91.

itself' whilst 'extrinsic motivation' is what 'arises from sources outside of the task itself'.[15] She argues that financial rewards adversely affect people's performance in tasks which require creativity, citing several studies such as Glucksberg's.[16] Using what is called Duncker's candle problem,[17] the researcher in that study instructed the subjects to 'mount a candle on the wall' using a 'cardboard match and thumb-tack boxes, matches, and thumbtacks' as quickly as possible.[18] Under conditions in which the boxes were filled with the tacks and matches, some of the subjects were offered monetary reward for solving the problem whilst the others were not.[19] Glucksberg found that the latter could find the solution, namely 'tacking an emptied box to the wall and placing the candle in or on it',[20] significantly faster than the former.[21] The result suggests that monetary rewards may adversely affect the performance of those who work on a problem requiring creative-thinking skills to solve.

According to Amabile's theoretical explanation, financial rewards undermine people's creativity because they would impose 'social constraints'[22] on their mental attitude which can drive them into 'exploration, set-breaking, and risk-taking' often necessary for creative thinking.[23] She elaborates on this point as follows:

> Extrinsically motivated behaviour is narrowly directed toward achieving the extrinsic goal that has been imposed, whether that goal be attaining a reward, meeting a dead-line, achieving the approval of an observer, or obtaining a positive evaluation from an expert. In order for a creative response to be produced, however, it is often necessary to temporarily "step away" from the perceived goal ... to direct attention toward seem-ingly incidental aspects of the task and the environment. The more single-mindedly a goal is pursued, the less likely it may be that alternative solution paths will be explored.[24]

Based on the theory above, she argues that 'people will be most creative when they feel motivated primarily by the interest, satisfaction, and challenge of the work itself—and not by external pressures',[25] whilst monetary reward cannot enhance their creativity 'especially when it leads [them] to feel that they are being bribed or controlled'.[26] According to her theory, the key to creativity lies in what Deci and Ryan call 'self-determination', or people's psychological propensity to act 'out of

---

[15] ibid 115.

[16] ibid 155–58.

[17] For an interesting account of Duncker's candle problem and the concept of 'intrinsic motiva-tion', see TED, 'The Puzzle of Motivation | Dan Pink' (*YouTube*, 25 August 2009), www.youtube.com/watch?v=rrkrvAUbU9Y.

[18] Sam Glucksberg, 'The Influence of Strength of Drive on Functional Fixedness and Perceptual Recognition' (1962) 63 *Journal of Experimental Psychology* 36, 36–37.

[19] ibid 37. The conditions made the problem more difficult to solve than when the boxes were presented empty.

[20] ibid.

[21] ibid 37 Table 1.

[22] Amabile (n 14) 107.

[23] ibid 111.

[24] ibid 110 (citation omitted).

[25] Amabile (n 2) 79.

[26] ibid.

choice rather than obligation,[27] which even defies control by the lure of monetary rewards.

Sometimes workers may feel that they are 'being bribed or controlled' depending on the way rewards are offered. For example, based on his general observation that 'working-people ... are born lazy or inefficient,[28] the management guru Frederick Taylor proposed a 'differential rate system of piece-work' at the turn of the twentieth century.[29] Under the system, a worker would be paid at a higher rate if he got his job done flawlessly in the shortest time imaginable,[30] whilst at a lower rate if his performance fell below that standard in terms of quantity or quality.[31] According to Taylor, this reward system promotes efficiency in that it forces inherently 'lazy' workers to do their best with the lure of 'unusually high wages', and it drives out those who end up earning 'below even the ordinary' as punishment for poor performance.[32] He stressed the need for 'vigorous and rapid inspection' of workers' performance that enables day-to-day 'stimulus to maximum exertion', on the assumption that few of them would be motivated effectively by large rewards after 'a comparatively short period of time'.[33] This authoritarian incentive scheme he proposed in accordance with his theory of 'scientific management' was rejected by both management and labour in the US soon afterwards due to its impracticality and flagrant disregard for workers' welfare.[34] Such a reward system enabled control over workers, seriously inhibiting their freedom to explore ingenious ideas conceived on the job. Although Amabile does not state it explicitly, her theory may typically apply to such a reward plan as Taylor's.

B. Opposing View by Eisenberger

In stark contrast to Amabile's view, Eisenberger and colleagues have consistently claimed that monetary reward can unlock people's creativity, albeit under certain conditions. Below are findings from their laboratory or field studies; 'creativity' of the participants in these studies was all assessed objectively by independent judges:

(i) Subjects (school children in Delaware) who had been given large monetary rewards for novel performance in preliminary tasks (which involved generating novel uses for objects) exhibited higher degree of creativity in subsequent tasks

---

[27] Edward L Deci and Richard M Ryan, *Intrinsic Motivation and Self-Determination in Human Behavior* (New York, Plenum Press, 1985) 38.

[28] Frederick Winslow Taylor, *The Principles of Scientific Management* (New York, Harper & Brothers, 1911) 29.

[29] Fred W Taylor, 'A Piece-Rate System' (1896) 1 *Economic Studies* 89, 112.

[30] ibid 112.

[31] ibid 115.

[32] ibid 115–17.

[33] ibid 115.

[34] David F Noble, *America by Design: Science, Technology, and the Rise of Corporate Capitalism* (Oxford, Oxford University Press, 1979) 271–73.

(which involved drawing pictures or suggesting titles for short stories) than those who had been given no or small monetary rewards in the first tasks.[35]

(ii)   When all the subjects (school children in Delaware) had been verbally instructed to be creative in preliminary tasks, rewarded subjects in subsequent tasks exhibited higher degree of creativity than unrewarded subjects.[36]

(iii)   Even when no preliminary tasks had been done, rewarded subjects (school children or college students in the US) showed higher degree of creativity than unrewarded subjects especially when instructions specifically demanded novel performance of them.[37]

(iv)   The offer of monetary reward to subjects (school children or college students in the US) enhanced their intrinsic interest in tasks without damaging their sense of autonomy.[38] Surveys of general employees (salespeople/support staff mainly paid on an hourly basis, or employed alumni of a US university) replicated this finding,[39] further suggesting that their enhanced interest in tasks and 'self-determination' would in turn have a positive influence on their creativity in their approach to the tasks.[40]

Eisenberger's 'learned industriousness theory' posits that when individuals learn that a reward value is conditional on a certain dimension of performance in one task, their effort is guided toward the same performance dimension even in different tasks.[41] Findings (i) and (ii) suggest that past experience gives rise to their learning whilst finding (iii) suggests that even current task instructions on a single occasion suffice.[42] In other words, Eisenberger's theory posits that an individual is

[35] Robert Eisenberger and Stephen Armeli, 'Can Salient Reward Increase Creative Performance Without Reducing Intrinsic Creative Interest?' (1997) 72 *Journal of Personality and Social Psychology* 652, 655–57 Fig 1; Robert Eisenberger and Linda Rhoades, 'Incremental Effects of Reward on Creativity' (2001) 81 *Journal of Personality and Social Psychology* 728, 731–33.

[36] Robert Eisenberger, Stephen Armeli and Jean Pretz, 'Can the Promise of Reward Increase Creativity?' (1998) 74 *Journal of Personality and Social Psychology* 704, 707–09 Fig 1; Robert Eisenberger, Frances Haskins and Paul Gambleton, 'Promised Reward and Creativity: Effects of Prior Experience' (1999) 35 *Journal of Experimental Social Psychology* 308, 314–18 Fig 1.

[37] Eisenberger, Armeli and Pretz (n 36) 709–11 Table 1; Eisenberger and Rhoades (n 35) 733–34.

[38] Eisenberger and Armeli (n 35) 658–59 Figure 2; Robert Eisenberger, Linda Rhoades and Judy Cameron, 'Does Pay for Performance Increase or Decrease Perceived Self-Determination and Intrinsic Motivation?' (1999) 77 *Journal of Personality and Social Psychology* 1026, 1029–30 Fig 1; Robert Eisenberger and Justin Aselage, 'Incremental Effects of Reward on Experienced Performance Pressure: Positive Outcomes for Intrinsic Interest and Creativity' (2009) 30 *Journal of Organizational Behavior* 95, 107–11 Fig 4.

[39] Eisenberger, Rhoades and Cameron (n 38) 1032–33 Table 3, 1034–35 Table 6; Eisenberger and Aselage (n 38) 99–102 Figure 2.

[40] Eisenberger and Rhoades (n 35) 734–35 Fig 1, 735–36 Fig 2; Eisenberger and Aselage (n 38) 103–05 Fig 3.

[41] Robert Eisenberger, 'Learned Industriousness' (1992) 99 *Psychological Review* 248, 250.

[42] Eisenberger and Rhoades (n 35) 729, 737.

likely to display a high degree of creativity 'simply because the task was defined as requiring novel performance by experiment instructions, by comments accompanying the reward, or by information supplied by the reward contingency itself'.[43] On the contrary, it follows from the theory that monetary reward can also stifle people's creativity when individuals learn that conventional performance is rewarded. As laboratory studies by Eisenberger and colleagues confirmed, when subjects in preliminary tasks had been either rewarded for conventional performance or just verbally instructed to perform them in an ordinary way, rewarded subjects in subsequent tasks displayed a lower degree of creativity than unrewarded subjects (finding (v)).[44]

II. General Discussion

Amabile and Eisenberger disagree as to how monetary rewards affect people's creativity. Whilst the former argues that the rewards stifle it by diminishing their intrinsic interest in tasks, the latter contends that the rewards can bring out their creativity irrespective of their effect on 'intrinsic motivation'. Apart from their arguments, an experimental study suggests that the effect of monetary rewards on creativity depends on both people's cognitive style and job complexity.[45] However, it can be safely said that today the dispute between Amabile and Eisenberger provides a basic framework for understanding the topic at issue. In sum, their views differ on the following points: (1) whether the rewards diminish 'intrinsic motivation', or people's intrinsic interest in creative tasks, hindering the application of creative-thinking skills to such tasks, as argued by Amabile; and (2) whether the offer of monetary rewards can induce people to display their creativity, as argued by Eisenberger.

Above all Eisenberger opposes the theory advanced by Amabile (and Deci) that monetary rewards 'crowd out' people's 'intrinsic motivation'. It should be noted, however, that 'intrinsic motivation' is a narrowly-defined concept and thus must be distinguished from general motivation to work discussed in Herzberg's motivation-hygiene theory mentioned earlier. According to his theory, the effect of monetary rewards is neutral: they do not motivate workers to a high level of

---

[43] Robert Eisenberger and Linda Shanock, 'Rewards, Intrinsic Motivation, and Creativity: A Case Study of Conceptual and Methodological Isolation' (2003) 15 *Creativity Research Journal* 121, 124.

[44] Robert Eisenberger and Michael Selbst, 'Does Reward Increase or Decrease Creativity?' (1994) 66 *Journal of Personality and Social Psychology* 1116, 1121; Eisenberger and Armeli (n 35) 657 Fig 1, 659 Fig 3; Eisenberger, Armeli and Pretz (n 36) 709 Fig 1; Eisenberger, Haskins and Gambleton (n 36) 318 Fig 1.

[45] Markus Baer, Greg R Oldham and Anne Cummings, 'Rewarding Creativity: When Does It Really Matter?' (2003) 14 *The Leadership Quarterly* 569, 572, 574, 580 Fig 2. Concerning 'complex jobs', namely 'those characterized by high levels of autonomy, skill, variety, identity, significance and feedback', the study found no significant effect of the rewards on the creativity of 'innovators', who 'tend to be willing to take the risk of violating the agreed-upon way of doing things to develop problem solutions that are qualitatively different from previous ones'. Meanwhile, it found a negative effect on that of 'adapters', who 'tend to operate within given paradigms and procedures without questioning their validity'.

job performance as long as they are guaranteed a satisfactory standard of living.[46] I showed that his model of motivation applies to employee inventors in general who have consistently demonstrated an overwhelmingly high level of interest in *achievement* and *work itself* in the recent empirical surveys.[47] Yet his theory acknowledges that monetary rewards can increase workers' interest in tasks which are unattractive in nature.[48]

Whilst Herzberg discussed the motivation to work in general, the term 'intrinsic motivation' used by Deci and Amabile has a specific meaning. Thus it can be a valid argument in abstract terms, for example, that offering monetary rewards diminishes intrinsic motivation as much as it strengthens pecuniary motives, so that overall the level of the motivation to work remains the same, as Herzberg's theory suggests. Meanwhile, Eisenberger and colleagues claim that monetary rewards can in fact boost intrinsic motivation on the basis of the finding (iv) above.[49] However, that finding is not inconsistent with Herzberg's theory, because according to that theory monetary rewards may have increased the motivation of the subjects in the researchers' experimental studies, who were asked to perform arguably uninteresting tasks such as drawing insignificant pictures and suggesting titles for short stories. In addition, since the other studies relevant to that finding surveyed either students or general employees, notably hourly-paid salespersons,[50] it does not follow from the finding that monetary rewards can enhance the motivation of inventors who generally appreciate the intrinsic value of their work even in the absence of monetary rewards.

Amabile's theory may be compatible with Eisenberger's as far as their theories are applied to the case of employee inventions. Duncker's candle problem cited by Amabile is comparable to inventing in that there was a specific solution to the problem. Thus offering monetary rewards may similarly have a negative effect on the creativity of employee inventors whose job is to find a solution to a given technical problem. By contrast, in the experimental studies of Eisenberger and colleagues there were no specific solutions to the tasks performed by the subjects, such as picture drawing where they freely chose what to draw. It may be inferred from these studies that monetary rewards may have a positive effect on the creativity of the supervisors of rank-and-file inventors or middle-level managers who undertake the planning of a new product or more generally determine technical problems to be solved by the inventors. Yet it should be recalled here that short-term incentives offered to heads of R&D departments, such as bonuses, are less likely to result in pioneering inventions than long-term incentives such as share options according to the recent econometrics study mentioned earlier.[51]

---

[46] See text to ch 2, nn 41–46.
[47] See ch 2, s IV.
[48] See text to ch 2, nn 88, 154.
[49] Eisenberger, Rhoades and Cameron (n 38) 1038; Eisenberger and Rhoades (n 35) 738.
[50] See text to nn 38, 39.
[51] See text to ch 3, nn 16–20.

Nevertheless, the general validity of Amabile's theory is yet to be proven. Although a comprehensive meta-analysis of relevant studies by Deci and colleagues claimed to confirm the theory that monetary rewards generally 'crowd out' people's intrinsic interest in tasks,[52] another meta-analysis by Eisenberger and colleagues showed that rewards did not always have a negative effect on an individual's intrinsic motivation depending on the way they were presented.[53] The latter researchers pointed out that the inconsistency between the results of these meta-analyses was simply due to the difference in the scope of studies included in each.[54] The latest meta-analysis of 52 experimental studies by impartial researchers has also endorsed Eisenberger's theory rather than Amabile's.[55] All things considered, at present it is too early to accept Amabile's theory unconditionally,[56] despite its apparent popularity among general readers.

Incidentally, the controversy among psychologists has inspired many economists to discuss whether rewards crowd out intrinsic motivation of individuals. This can lead to the reconsideration of the major proposition in economics that individuals respond to financial incentives positively. At a theoretical level, for example, Bénabou and Tirole have demonstrated in their principal-agent model that motivation crowding-out can happen on the assumption that higher rewards offered by the principal send a bad signal to the agent concerning the difficulty of the task or the agent's suitability for performing it.[57] A couple of recent field studies yielded different conclusions as to whether there is a trade-off between intrinsic and extrinsic motivation.[58] Overall, there have been few field studies that have investigated the validity of motivation crowding-out theory, whether in economics[59] or psychology.[60] Accordingly, neither psychologists nor economists

---

[52] Edward L Deci, Richard Koestner and Richard M Ryan, 'A Meta-Analytic Review of Experiments Examining the Effects of Extrinsic Rewards on Intrinsic Motivation' (1999) 125 *Psychological Bulletin* 627, 640, 647 Fig 1, 648 Fig 2.

[53] Robert Eisenberger, W David Pierce and Judy Cameron, 'Effects of Reward on Intrinsic Motivation – Negative, Neutral, and Positive: Comment on Deci, Koestner, and Ryan (1999)' (1999) 125 *Psychological Bulletin* 677, 682, 684 Fig 1, 685 Fig 2.

[54] ibid 682.

[55] Kris Byron and Shalini Khazanchi, 'Rewards and Creative Performance: A Meta-Analytic Test of Theoretically Derived Hypotheses' (2012) 138 *Psychological Bulletin* 809, 816, 822 Table 4.

[56] Jing Zhou and Christina E Shalley, 'Expanding the Scope and Impact of Organizational Creativity Research' in Jing Zhou and Christina E Shalley (eds), *Handbook of Organizational Creativity* (New York, Lawrence Erlbaum Associates, 2008) 356.

[57] Roland Bénabou and Jean Tirole, 'Intrinsic and Extrinsic Motivation' (2003) 70 *The Review of Economic Studies* 489, 496–98.

[58] Meiyu Fang and Barry Gerhart, 'Does Pay for Performance Diminish Intrinsic Interest?' (2012) 23 *International Journal of Human Resource Management* 1176, 1188 Table 2 (did not find a trade-off); Amy Wrzesniewski and others, 'Multiple Types of Motives Don't Multiply the Motivation of West Point Cadets' (2014) 111 *Proceedings of the National Academy of Sciences of the United States of America* 10990, 10994, Figs 1, 2, 3 (found a trade-off).

[59] Bruno S Frey and Reto Jegen, 'Motivation Crowding Theory' (2001) 15 *Journal of Economic Surveys* 589, 599 Table 1; Samuel Bowles and Sandra Polanía Reyes, 'Economic Incentives and Social Preferences: A Preference-Based Lucas Critique of Public Policy' (2009) *CESifo Working Paper Series No 2734*, 28-29 Table 4, ssrn.com/abstract=1443865.

[60] Byron and Khazanchi (n 55) 819 Table 2.

have reached an agreement on whether financial incentives actually diminish intrinsic motivation, which affects creativity in organisational contexts according to the assumption shared by Amabile and Eisenberger.[61] Now that some psychologists have begun to question the robustness of the assumption that an individual's intrinsic motivation determines his creativity,[62] the relationship between financial incentives and creativity is all the more equivocal.

With respect to the second point at issue, Eisenberger argues that the effect of monetary rewards depends on the information they convey explicitly or implicitly. As the above findings ((i), (ii), (iii), and (v)) indicate, they can function either as a catalyst or as an inhibitor of people's creativity depending on the information conveyed to subjects as to what is required of them. He points out that the subjects in the studies cited by Amabile were all ill-informed of what was required to obtain rewards so that they failed to display their creativity.[63] He argues that if the promise of rewards is not accompanied by instructions on the required performance standard, it 'often increases conventional performance at the expense of creativity' because such kind of performance 'is most often rewarded in everyday life'.[64] According to his theory, one cannot induce others to display creativity unless there are instructions to that effect. Thus those working on the aforementioned Duncker's candle problem may have failed to perform well because the application of their creative-thinking skills was hindered by the instructions simply to solve it as quickly as possible.[65] In fact, Amabile appears to partly accept Eisenberger's theory because she acknowledges that when people perceive monetary rewards 'as informational (ie, providing information about their competence) or enabling (ie, enabling them to do something exciting)',[66] the offer of rewards may effectively bring out their creativity as long as it does not connote control over them.[67]

III. Analysis of Legal Schemes for Inventor Remuneration

Given the proposition that patent law provides incentives to make inventions, the law should also encourage, or at least not hinder, creativity required for making

---

[61] Not only Amabile but Eisenberger assumes that an individual's intrinsic motivation influences his creativity: Eisenberger and Aselage (n 38) 113. Both disagree as to whether or not monetary rewards crowd out the intrinsic motivation.

[62] Christina E Shalley, Jing Zhou and Greg R. Oldham, 'The Effects of Personal and Contextual Characteristics on Creativity: Where Should We Go from Here?' (2004) 30 *Journal of Management* 933, 945; Jennifer M George, 'Creativity in Organizations' in James P Walsh and Arthur P Brief (eds), *The Academy of Management Annals*, vol 1 (Abingdon, Routledge, 2007) 444.

[63] Eisenberger and Shanock (n 43) 125.

[64] ibid 127.

[65] They were shown boxes filled with tacks and matches in the experiment: see text to n 19. On the contrary, it requires only conventional-thinking skills to solve the problem when the boxes are presented empty. Under such conditions, rewarded subjects could solve it faster than unrewarded subjects: Glucksberg (n 18) 37 Table 1. Eisenberger's theory can give a good account of this result.

[66] Amabile (n 14) 117.

[67] ibid 118–19.

inventions.[68] In view of the controversy among social psychologists about the effect of monetary rewards on creativity, do the current laws on employee inventions encourage or hinder the creativity of employee inventors? First, such legal schemes are unlikely to encourage employee inventors to display their creativity according to not only Amabile's theory but also Eisenberger's because those schemes often link the amount of compensation to the profits employers gain from employee inventions without conveying any information about the creativity of the inventors.[69] Since such profits do not always represent the level of creativity embodied in inventions made by them, highly creative inventors do not necessarily receive compensation commensurate with their creative contribution in theory. For example, compensation to inventor(s) of a pioneering invention will be substantially reduced if it is replaced in the marketplace later by subsequent inventions which improve the quality of the original invention.[70] The subsequent inventors can take the portion realised by the contribution of the original inventor(s) without trouble unless compensation to the subsequent inventors is limited to the increase in the revenue achieved by the improvements.[71] Such outcomes are irrational as the subsequent contribution is usually less significant than the initial one. As the aforementioned data from the PatVal-EU survey (PatVal-I) suggest, this may make the original inventors act unproductively to hinder the creation of subsequent inventions for fear that such inventions will reduce the amount of compensation they receive.[72] Similarly, employee inventors will get nothing when the invention is incorporated into an intermediate product which needs further processing to yield a profitable (final) product.[73]

Fundamentally, even if an employee invention is potentially profitable, no profits will be earned by the employer and hence no compensation will be awarded to its inventor(s) when the employer decides not to exploit it economically. PatVal-I revealed that about 36 per cent of patents surveyed in EU6 countries were not being exploited economically, with nearly half of them being blocking

---

[68] Gregory N Mandel, 'To Promote the Creative Process: Intellectual Property Law and the Psychology of Creativity' (2011) 86 *Notre Dame Law Review* 1999, 1999.

[69] Apart from the legal compensation schemes, some companies offer nominal amount of compensation when an invention is completed. However, this is generally aimed at prompting disclosure of inventions to employers, and thus has no bearing on the issue of inventors' creativity: see text to ch 2, n 9.

[70] Dietmar Harhoff and Karin Hoisl, 'Institutionalized Incentives for Ingenuity – Patent Value and the German Employees' Inventions Act' (2007) 36 *Research Policy* 1143, 1145.

[71] Hans-Gerhard Heine and Helmut Rebitzki, *Die Vergütung für Erfindungen von Arbeitnehmern im privaten Dienst* [The Remuneration for Inventions of Employees in Private Employment] (Weinheim, Chemie, 1960) 91; Ralf Kesten, 'Innovationen durch eigene Mitarbeiter: Betriebswirtschaftliche Aspekte zur monetären Beurteilung von Diensterfindungen nach dem Gesetz über Arbeitnehmererfindungen' [Innovations by Individual Employees: Economic Aspects of Monetary Evaluation of Employee Inventions under the Law on Employee Inventions] (1996) 66 *Zeitschrift für Betriebswirtschaft* (*ZfB*) 651, 655.

[72] See text to ch 3, n 96.

[73] Heine and Rebitzki (n 71) 89.

patents.[74] Apart from truly dormant patents, some blocking patents may potentially boost the market value of their owners by keeping competitors off the market effectively even if they are not actually exploited. A recent study has found that patents which receive 'blocking citations', namely those cited to 'challenge the novelty or inventive step of the patent under examination', contribute to the market value of companies more significantly than those cited simply to 'define the state of the art in a technology field'.[75] It is arguable that, if invention compensation schemes are intended to encourage the creativity of employee inventors, inventors who created such blocking patents should also be remunerated for their creative contribution which accounts for the unrealised economic value added to their employers.[76] This shows that the value of creativity embodied in a patent should be better represented by other indicators than revenue actually achieved, such as 'the number of citations received' and 'patent renewal data', as several economists have suggested.[77] In sum, the current legal compensation schemes cannot have a positive effect on the creativity of employee inventors because they fail to take account of the degree of creativity needed to make an invention.

Next, it needs to be discussed whether the legal schemes hinder the creativity of employee inventors. According to Amabile's 'intuitively appealing premise',[78] monetary rewards undermine an individual's creativity. She argues that if rewards are recognised as 'social constraints', 'external pressures', or 'obligation',[79] this will prevent the generation of novel ideas unfettered by conventional ways of thinking. I took Taylor's differential incentive scheme as an example to which Amabile's theory may typically apply.[80] However, it is unlikely that the current legal compensation schemes fatally undermine the autonomy of employee inventors as Taylor's reward plan may have done. Unlike Taylor's, these legal schemes do not involve punishment when employees cannot complete inventions. Inventors under the legal schemes cannot expect immediate payment of compensation, which Taylor stressed in devising his reward plan,[81] since there is usually an interval of

---

[74] Paola Giuri and others, 'Inventors and Invention Processes in Europe: Results from the PatVal-EU Survey' (2007) 36 *Research Policy* 1107, 1118–19 Table 6. Blocking patents refer to those applied to prevent others from patenting related inventions, and yet 'used neither internally nor for licensing': ibid 1118.

[75] Dirk Czarnitzki, Katrin Hussinger and Bart Leten, 'The Market Value of Blocking Patent Citations' (2011) ZEW Discussion Paper No 11-021, 2, 15, 24 Table 3, papers.ssrn.com/sol3/papers.cfm?abstract_id=1803315.

[76] Guidelines for the Remuneration of Employees' Inventions in Private Employment in Germany lay down general rules for assessing the value of blocking patents for the purpose of calculating compensation to their inventors: see Guidelines, no 18. However, there have been few reported cases of compensation for blocking patents in Germany: Jesse Giummo, 'German Employee Inventors' Compensation Records: A Window into the Returns to Patented Inventions' (2010) 39 *Research Policy* 969, 972.

[77] Harhoff and Hoisl (n 70) 1145 (citations omitted).

[78] George (n 62) 444.

[79] See text to nn 22–27.

[80] See text to nn 28–33.

[81] See text to n 33.

several years between the time of conception of an invention and the payment.[82] If employee inventors feel as if there were 'social constraints', 'external pressures', or 'obligation', it is not because of the compensation offered by the law but various restrictions the management may impose on resources that they can use when they make inventions. It is unreasonable to read more into the legal compensation schemes than they literally mean and assume that employee inventors 'are being bribed or controlled' by them.

Even if rewards do not go as far as to suppress the free will of potential recipients, Duncker's candle problem cited by Amabile may suggest offering monetary rewards to employee inventors adversely affects their problem-solving as I pointed out earlier. Whether or not one adopts her theory that monetary rewards generally crowd out intrinsic motivation, sometimes single-minded pursuit of rewards does cause 'short-term thinking' as well as 'cheating, shortcuts, and unethical behavior' at the sacrifice of the quality of performance.[83] For example, the result of the aforementioned study by Japanese researchers suggests that those inventors who regard monetary rewards as important may choose to tackle 'a safe and easily commercialized research project rather than a more challenging but potentially more valuable project' to enjoy the rewards.[84] In addition, I discussed prospective inventors' 'secrecy', in which they refuse to share information with others in order to monopolise compensation to be awarded.[85] These are examples of inventors' 'short-term thinking' and 'unethical behavior' which are likely to sacrifice the creativity to be embodied in inventions.

If one is genuinely motivated by intrinsic interest in a job and focuses on the task, such evil practices are unlikely to occur.[86] And it is unlikely that the incentives offered by the current invention compensation schemes cause most employee inventors to lose their intrinsic interest in inventing, thereby extensively triggering their behaviour detrimental to creative thinking. It should be recalled here that the data in the PatVal-I, PatVal EU-US/JP II (PatVal-II) and the Research Institute of Economy, Trade and Industry (RIETI) surveys consistently show that the overwhelming majority of respondents in 23 countries surveyed (20 countries in Europe, Israel, the US and Japan) are far more highly motivated by values intrinsic in making inventions than by monetary rewards[87] even though there is some kind of statutory scheme that requires employers to pay compensation for inventions made in the course of employees' duties in all of these countries,

---

[82] See text to ch 2, nn 182–84.

[83] Daniel H Pink, *Drive: The Surprising Truth about What Motivates Us*, pbk edn (Edinburgh, Canongate, 2011) 49–52, 56–59.

[84] See text to ch 2, n 166.

[85] See text to ch 3, nn 90–92.

[86] Pink (n 83) 51, 58.

[87] See ch 2, Figs 8–11.

apart from Belgium,[88] Switzerland,[89] Ireland[90] and the US.[91] However, it may be argued that their intrinsic interest in inventing is unaffected by these statutory schemes in general simply because they do not know the relevant legal provisions. Although there has been no direct evidence that their intrinsic interest in inventing diminishes when they become conscious of these provisions,[92] it may hinder many employee inventors from focusing on creative thinking if governments strengthen invention compensation schemes and implement them vigorously.

Yet at least it is clear from the above discussion that the current legal compensation schemes do not encourage the creativity of employee inventors. The legislature in many countries may expect that employee inventors will produce many valuable inventions which embody highly creative ideas if they are offered large monetary rewards. However, the above discussion suggests that the legal schemes are unlikely to boost the creation of such inventions. Whilst the discussion in chapters two and three suggests that compensation to employee inventors is unlikely to boost the quantity of inventions made in companies,[93] the conclusion here indicates that invention compensation schemes are unlikely to enhance the quality of inventions, so to speak. These observations cast doubt on the reasonableness of the relevant legislation in every jurisdiction.

It must be noticed here that the discussion so far only concerns 'motivation', one of the three components of 'creativity' in Amabile's phraseology, and thus monetary rewards cannot influence the other two, namely 'creative-thinking skills' and 'expertise' directly.[94] It has been observed statistically that some people can achieve considerably higher scientific/inventive productivity than others. Based on his study of articles in scientific journals, Lotka observed that the number of scientists who contributed n articles was about $1/n^2$ of those who made only

[88] Marie-Christine Janssens, 'Belgium' in Toshiyuki Kono (ed), *Intellectual Property and Private International Law: Comparative Perspectives* (Oxford, Hart, 2012) 408.

[89] Alexandre Berenstein, Pascal Mahon and Jean-Philippe Dunand, *Labour Law in Switzerland* (Alphen aan den Rijn, Kluwer Law International, 2011) para 504. Meanwhile, Swiss employers are still required to pay additional compensation if they claim inventions made by their employees while they were at work, yet not in the course of their duties: Code of Obligations of 30 March 1911, art 332(4).

[90] Robert Clark, Shane Smyth and Niamh Hall, *Intellectual Property Law in Ireland*, 3rd edn (Haywards Heath, Bloomsbury Professional, 2010) para 4.11.

[91] See ch 6.

[92] In PatVal-II, German respondents on average gave somewhat modest ratings on values intrinsic in making inventions (the fifth lowest on '[d]esire to solve practical problems', the fifth lowest on '[i]ntellectual challenge', and the third lowest on '[s]atisfaction from showing that something is technically possible' among 20 European countries and Israel): InnoS&T, 'Final Report of PatVal-EU II Survey: Methods and Results' (2010) 40–41 Table 4.11a, bcmmnty-qp.unibocconi.it/QuickPlace/innovativest/Main.nsf/$defaultview/74EA6A33919C1E4BC125775800683221/$File/D_2_5.pdf?OpenElement. However, these data must be interpreted cautiously since German samples in this survey substantially outnumbered those in the other countries: ibid 17 Table 3.1. Thus, it is too rash to assume from these data that German respondents showed less interest in job-intrinsic factors because they became familiar with their legal compensation scheme as a result of frequent award of compensation.

[93] See ch 2, s V and ch 3, s III.

[94] See text to n 2.

one contribution each,[95] and recent studies have found similar, or even more skewed, distribution of patents produced by inventors working in a company.[96] Their varying degree of productivity has a lot to do with their 'creative-thinking skills' which may have been determined conclusively in their childhood, and 'expertise' which is acquired through tertiary education and training throughout their careers. For example, findings in psychology have consistently suggested that children are likely to develop 'creative-thinking skills' when their parents have a feeling of security, diverse interests, confidence in the ability of their children, and allow them to enjoy freedom and autonomy, but these skills are unlikely to develop when the parent-child relationship is characterised as hostility, rejection, detachment, restrictiveness and authoritarian control.[97] With respect to education which allows potential inventors to gain 'expertise', recent studies have found a positive correlation between their possession of a PhD degree and either the quantity or the quality of patents produced by them.[98] Amabile warns, however, that 'an excessively extended formal education' can impair creativity when it 'leads to an over-reliance on established algorithms, or … a slavish imitation of models'.[99] Some successful inventors of the day stress the importance of reading journal articles, attending seminars, conferences and poster sessions, so that they will get acquainted with multiple disciplines whose knowledge is often the key to successful inventions.[100] If 'creative-thinking skills' and 'expertise' acquired by potential inventors have already accounted for their highly skewed creativity, as indicated by research subsequent to Lotka's, there is no overestimating the effect of monetary rewards, if any, on their creativity.

Above all, it should be recalled here that most inventions are created in companies through effective teamwork rather than by the resourcefulness of individual inventors alone. Although some talented inventors may be able to present the central ideas of inventions more frequently than others, they do not usually form these ideas by keeping themselves apart from people around them. Their ideas often rest on a stack of ideas generated by other members of a project team without which its conception would never be possible.[101] The successful creation of

[95] Alfred J Lotka, 'The Frequency Distribution of Scientific Productivity' (1926) 16 *Journal of the Washington Academy of Sciences* 317, 323. According to his theory, if there are 100 scientists who contribute just one article each, there are about, or 25, who produce two papers each, about, or 11, who produce three papers each, and only one scientist who produces ten papers.

[96] Francis Narin and Anthony Breitzman, 'Inventive Productivity' (1995) 24 *Research Policy* 507, 511–15 Fig 3-6; Holger Ernst, Christopher Leptien and Jan Vitt, 'Inventors Are Not Alike: The Distribution of Patenting Output among Industrial R&D Personnel' (2000) 47 *IEEE Transactions on Engineering Management* 184, 190 Fig 3.

[97] Brent C Miller and Diana Gerard, 'Family Influence on the Development of Creativity in Children: An Integrative Review' (1979) 28 *The Family Coordinator* 295, 310.

[98] Myriam Mariani and Marzia Romanelli, '"Stacking" and "Picking" Inventions: The Patenting Behavior of European Inventors' (2007) 36 *Research Policy* 1128, 1137 Table 5; Francesco Schettino, Alessandro Sterlacchini and Francesco Venturini, 'Inventive Productivity and Patent Quality: Evidence from Italian Inventors' (2013) 35 *Journal of Policy Modeling* 1043, 1050 Table 5, 1052.

[99] Amabile (n 14) 251.

[100] Brett Stern, *Inventors at Work: The Minds and Motivation behind Modern Inventions* (Berkeley, Apress, 2012) 78, 160, 233.

[101] Olivier Toubia, 'Idea Generation, Creativity, and Incentives' (2006) 25 *Marketing Science* 411, 412.

inventions in companies depends on whether each project team can bring its members' creativity into play under ideal conditions created by their employers. Nevertheless, I have only discussed so far the creativity of individual inventors independently of organisational contexts. Referring to the conditions necessary for harnessing creativity in organisations, it will be shown in the next section that monetary rewards are no longer considered to be of prime importance as a means of encouraging creativity in actual work settings.

IV. Factors that Facilitate Workplace Creativity and Innovation

The creativity of employee inventors, however remarkable it may be, is in name alone if it is unexploited in the workplace. According to Amabile, the following social-environmental factors are likely to encourage the creativity of individuals in organisational contexts: (1) strategic direction and encouragement toward innovation, whether by management or by immediate supervisors; (2) cooperation among co-workers with diverse skills who are open to new ideas and willing to give constructive feedback on them; and (3) '[r]ecognition that failure in work can provide valuable information'.[102] The last factor, as opposed to '[e]mphasis on the status quo',[103] is particularly crucial to the creation of inventions since, as employed inventors of the day unanimously say, failure is an essential part of inventing which gives inventors valuable opportunities to learn what works and what does not.[104] In essence, to bring the creativity of employee inventors into play in the workplace, employers need to foster an organisational culture in which workers from various backgrounds can express their unique ideas without hesitation and take risks in implementing promising ones with the material and moral support of both management and co-workers.

Although what is described above is confined to generalities, researchers in organisational psychology have studied the influence of specific job dimensions on creative performance in organisations quantitatively. The results of a couple of recent meta-analyses below have revealed that some of these dimensions greatly affect 'workplace creativity' and 'innovation' which subsumes it.[105] One analysis deals with factors which affect general climate in the workplace. It identified 14 workplace dimensions in 42 relevant studies conducted over a decade from 1997 and assessed the effect of each dimension on the level of workplace creativity and innovation by computing its magnitude averaged across these studies.[106]

---

[102] Amabile (n 14) 120 Table C.

[103] ibid.

[104] Stern (n 100) 24, 62, 88, 105, 162, 222, 270, 271.

[105] 'Workplace creativity' concerns 'the generation of new ideas', whilst 'innovation' concerns 'the translation of these ideas into useful new products': Samuel T Hunter, Katrina E Bedell and Michael D Mumford, 'Climate for Creativity: A Quantitative Review' (2007) 19 *Creativity Research Journal* 69, 69.

[106] ibid 73.

According to its results presented in Figure 18 below,[107] 'positive interpersonal exchange', 'intellectual stimulation' and 'challenge' were among the strongest predictors of workplace creativity and innovation. The results suggest that 'an intellectually stimulating environment in which people have challenging work, and colleagues with whom they can exchange ideas, is critical to creativity and innovation'.[108] 'Flexibility and risk-taking', 'top management support', 'positive supervisor relations' and 'positive peer group' had no less effect on workplace creativity and innovation than the above three. These results generally replicate Amabile's observation above. On the other hand, the effect of 'reward orientation', or '[p]erception that creative performance is tied to rewards in the organization', on creativity in work contexts was only the third weakest among 14 dimensions examined.[109] The researchers commented that 'though it is desirable, and perhaps necessary, to ... recognize creative work, ... [it is] not as important as providing challenging work in an intellectually stimulating environment'.[110]

Another meta-analysis focuses on several variables associated with the composition and structure of teams in organisations involved in innovation (team input variables) and those with team process which can promote innovation in organisations (team process variables).[111] It sampled 104 studies that were available by early 2007 and computed mean coefficients of overall correlation between each variable and the level of 'innovation', which subsumes workplace creativity,[112] observed in studies that had investigated that variable.[113] It can be seen from its

Figure 18 Average Effect of Workplace Dimensions on Creative Achievement

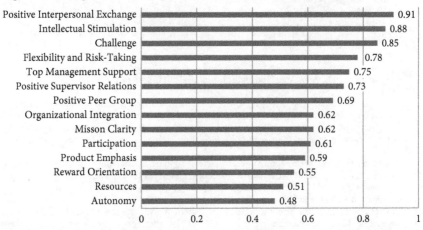

[107] Adapted from Hunter, Bedell and Mumford (n 105) 76 Table 2.
[108] ibid 77.
[109] ibid 74 Table 1, 76 Table 2.
[110] ibid 77.
[111] Ute R Hülsheger, Neil Anderson and Jesus F Salgado, 'Team-Level Predictors of Innovation at Work: A Comprehensive Meta-Analysis Spanning Three Decades of Research' (2009) 94 *Journal of Applied Psychology* 1128, 1129–32.
[112] ibid 1129.
[113] ibid 1133–34.

results presented in Figure 19 below[114] that team process variables contribute to innovation in organisations more significantly than team input variables.[115] Those team process variables that indicated strong correlation with innovation include 'vision',[116] 'external/internal communication',[117] 'support for innovation'[118] and 'task orientation'.[119] Although less influential than these, some team input variables such as 'goal interdependence',[120] 'team size'[121] and 'job-relevant diversity'[122] also account for innovation in organisations to some extent.

Figure 19 Mean Coefficients of Correlation between Team Input/Process Variables and Innovation

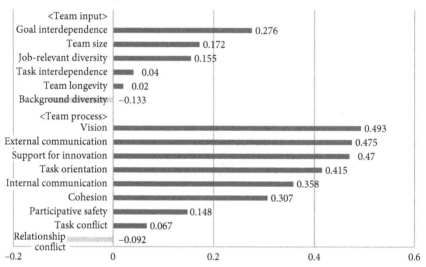

[114] Adapted from Hülsheger, Anderson and Salgado (n 111) 1138 Table 3.

[115] ibid 1137.

[116] This variable assesses 'the extent to which team members have a common understanding of objectives and display high commitment to those team goals': ibid 1131.

[117] Communication with people inside or outside one's own team or organisation is important for innovation because it 'enables the sharing of information and ideas', mutual feedback and support: ibid 1132.

[118] This refers to 'expectation, approval and practical support of attempts to introduce new and improved ways of doing things in the work environment': ibid 1131 (citation omitted).

[119] This means 'a shared concern with excellence of quality of task performance in relation to shared vision or outcomes': ibid (citation omitted).

[120] This variable assesses 'the extent to which team members' goals and rewards are related in such a way that an individual team member can only reach his or her goal if the other team members achieve their goals as well': ibid 1129–30 (citations omitted).

[121] It has been argued that '[o]nly teams with sufficient members might be able to provide a wide array of resources, expertise, skills, and knowledge to complete complex tasks' that innovation usually involves: ibid 1130.

[122] This 'refers to the heterogeneity of team members with respect to job- or task-related attributes, such as function, profession, education, tenure, knowledge, skills, or expertise': ibid 1129 (citations omitted). Meanwhile, it has been said that background diversity, or 'non-task-related differences such as age, gender, or ethnicity' can be detrimental to innovation because it may cause 'communication problems and difficulties in resolving opposing ideas and reaching consensus within the team': ibid.

Although comprehensive, these two meta-analyses only reviewed the research on workplace creativity in the past three decades and thus should not be regarded as conclusive. Nevertheless, the past studies examined in these meta-analyses at least suggest that there are many factors other than monetary rewards that encourage workplace creativity and innovation. Given that most inventions are created through teamwork in organisations today, general environment in an organisation, including material and human resources offered to workers, and interpersonal relationship inside a project team greatly affect workplace creativity.

This does not necessarily mean that monetary rewards have no positive effect on workplace creativity in themselves. The researchers in the first meta-analysis warned against dismissing 'reward orientation' that indicated seemingly a weak correlation with workplace creativity because all the 14 'dimensions ... produced nontrivial, actually sizable, relationships with regard to indices of creative achievement'.[123] However, the offer of rewards is likely to lead to competition inside a project team to the detriment of the creation of inventions through teamwork. As is apparent in the case of the secrecy of employee inventors,[124] prizes create goal conflict among team members, so that they would refuse to share with others information useful for creating inventions.[125] Moreover, prizes may involve members in 'unnecessary activities, such as monitoring the performance of a competitor or contemplating the potential negative consequences of failing to beat the competition', which would prevent them from applying all their efforts to inventive activities.[126] Although prizes offered to teams may have some positive effect on workplace creativity by fostering cooperation among members in each team and thus enhancing their engagement in the task,[127] prizes offered to individuals are likely to have a negative effect on it because such rewards undermine 'internal communication' and 'goal interdependence', both of which are strong predictors of innovation in organisations.[128]

A couple of factors that social psychologists have traditionally considered to be effective for workplace creativity deserve notice. One is 'cohesion', namely 'the extent to which group members have a strong social bond or sense of attraction'.[129] Social psychologists have suggested that this is beneficial to workplace creativity because '[t]eams that have strong interpersonal bonds, a strong shared commitment to the task, and pride in their group would be expected to be more motivated than teams without such features'.[130] Yet cohesion is likely to be undermined if each member pursues personal interests that are incompatible with group goals.

---

[123] Hunter, Bedell and Mumford (n 105) 86.
[124] See ch 3, s II.
[125] Greg R Oldham and Markus Baer, 'Creativity and the Work Context' in Mumford (n 1) 393.
[126] ibid.
[127] ibid.
[128] See text to nn 117, 120.
[129] Paul B Paulus, Mary Dzindolet and Nicholas W Kohn, 'Collaborative Creativity – Group Creativity and Team Innovation' in Mumford (n 1) 340–41 (citation omitted).
[130] ibid 341.

The other is 'psychological or participative safety', namely the feeling of workers 'that the organization or the team is receptive to and supportive of the expression of new ideas'.[131] This is also important for workplace creativity since without it 'individuals will not risk the potential ridicule or negative reactions that may accompany new ideas, especially radical ones'.[132] Offering prizes to individual team members can compromise their psychological safety since it is likely to make each member intensely conscious of intra-group competition and hesitate to share his original ideas with others for fear that their negative reactions could place him in an unfavourable position in the team. In the second meta-analysis these factors showed no less significant correlation with innovation in organisations than those already mentioned in the text.[133] It is crucial not to assess the effect of monetary rewards independently of other factors that affect workplace creativity. Overall, monetary rewards are unlikely to enhance workplace creativity because they will cancel out the positive effect of some team process variables, namely 'internal communication', 'cohesion' and 'psychological (participative) safety'.

In sum, it has been shown in this section that various organisational and/or interpersonal factors rather than monetary rewards for individual workers greatly influence workplace creativity. The legislature lose touch with the reality if they assume that employee inventors will create more inventions when they are offered inventor remuneration. To illustrate this point more clearly, the next section will briefly overview the organisational practices at the 3M Company, one of the leading multinational companies that has been successful in encouraging innovation without offering monetary rewards to employee inventors.

V. Case Study: 3M

3M is a multinational conglomerate whose products include household articles and office supplies sold under the brand names of 'Post-it®, Scotch®, Scotch-Brite®, Filtrete™, O-Cel-O™, Nexcare™, and Command™'.[134] It also provides industrial goods, health care and safety products, and is now branching out into the fields of electronics and energy.[135] As of the end of 2014, it had 89,800 employees operating in more than 70 countries and its global sales stood at $31.8 billion.[136]

3M is a patent-intensive company. Receiving 4,853 US patents in the 1990s, it ranked twenty-seventh among top recipients of US patents in that period.[137]

---

[131] ibid 337.
[132] ibid.
[133] See Fig 19 and text to nn 114–19.
[134] 3M, '3M Business Groups', solutions.3m.com/wps/portal/3M/en_US/3M-Company/Information/AboutUs/Businesses/.
[135] ibid.
[136] 3M, '3M Performance', solutions.3m.com/wps/portal/3M/en_US/3M-Company/Information/Profile/Performance/.
[137] 3M, *A Century of Innovation: The 3M Story* (Saint Paul, 3M Company, 2002) 95.

Although its ranking has dropped ever since, it received 625 patents in the US and 3,342 worldwide in 2014.[138] In 2016 its subsidiary company made the twenty-seventh largest number (653) of published PCT (the Patent Cooperation Treaty) applications among all the business applicants worldwide.[139] The total number of patents obtained in the company history has now exceeded 100,000.[140]

Despite its policy which stresses efficient use of patents,[141] the company has offered no monetary rewards for a patent filed by its employees.[142] The question is what makes 3M prolific of patents without special pecuniary inducements for its employee inventors. (1) Corporate culture and structure and (2) several organisational practices give the key to understanding its high technical productivity.

A. Corporate Culture and Structure

Above all, 3M's highly successful inventions have been made thanks to the company's traditional culture which tolerates employees' failures. The company was originally founded as Minnesota Mining and Manufacturing Company in 1902 to mine corundum which it intended to sell to companies that produced sandpaper.[143] However, when it found that the mineral dug out from mines was worthless, it decided to shift its business to the manufacturing of abrasives which could be developed from the low-grade grit taken from the mines.[144] It introduced a highly successful cloth abrasive called 'Three-M-ite' in 1914, which allowed it to get out of the difficulty suffered by its initial failure in the mining business.[145] The Post-it® note adhesive, one of its key products today, is another example in which the company took advantage of a mistake to create a highly successful invention. What inventors initially made was an 'aberrant' or 'weird' adhesive,[146] which was consistently weak without being harder or softer over time and thus could be put to good use as a stationery.[147]

McKnight, a long-serving chairman of 3M, stated in 1944 that '[t]he best and hardest work is done … in the spirit of adventure and challenge', whilst '[m]anagement that is destructively critical when mistakes are made can kill the initiative' of

---

[138] 3M, '3M Performance' (n 136).

[139] WIPO, *Patent Cooperation Treaty Yearly Review 2017: The International Patent System* (WIPO 2017) 31 Table A15, www.wipo.int/edocs/pubdocs/en/wipo_pub_901_2017.pdf.

[140] 3M, '3M Performance' (n 136).

[141] 3M, *A Century of Innovation* (n 137) 106–07.

[142] Stern (n 100) 234.

[143] Geoffrey C Nicholson, 'Keeping Innovation Alive' (1998) 41(3) *Research-Technology Management* 34, 34.

[144] James C Collins and Jerry I Porras, *Built to Last: Successful Habits of Visionary Companies*, 3rd edn (London, Random House Business, 2000) 150.

[145] ibid 151.

[146] ibid 159.

[147] Adam Brand, 'Knowledge Management and Innovation at 3M' (1998) 2(1) *Journal of Knowledge Management* 17, 19.

employees to the detriment of innovation.[148] Another recent chairman at 3M also commented that '[a]s befits a company that was founded on a mistake, we have continued to accept mistakes as a normal part of running a business'.[149] In addition, its 'flat organizational structure ... [which] allow[s] important decisions to be made at all [divisions]'[150] enables employees to concentrate on new ideas, reducing bureaucracy.[151] 3M's corporate culture and structure thus allow 'flexibility and risk-taking', one of the factors which facilitates workplace creativity mentioned in the meta-analysis above.[152]

B. Organisational Practices

3M has adopted several practices to encourage innovation in the company. First, it tries to recruit the right people who fit its innovative culture. The company interviewed its 25 prolific inventors and found that they were characterised not only by 'their capacity for divergent thinking' but also by 'their breadth of interests beyond their disciplines, their eagerness to experiment and tackle the unusual, their passion for what they did, their tenacity and resourcefulness'.[153] In particular, 'people with broad interests' are regarded as important because they 'are eager to learn, willing to explore ideas with others, have a multi-disciplinary approach, and are happy networking'.[154] It is a fundamental premise for innovation that the company hires and retains creative employees who show great potential as inventors.

The creation of inventions requires resources such as (i) time, (ii) money and (iii) information. Concerning (i) time, 3M's '15% rule' allows employees to spend 15 per cent of their time in pursuing projects of their own choices.[155] The target of '15%' is not sharply defined: some may use more than 15 per cent, whilst others no time whatsoever.[156] Yet this rule is intended to 'create an environment in which creativity flourishes' and trigger 'serendipity', or 'the gift of finding something for which you are not looking', as in the case of Post-it® note which emerged from the 15 per cent time of the inventors.[157] Where they need (ii) money to develop

---

[148] 3M, *A Century of Innovation* (n 137) 17.

[149] Brand (n 147) 19.

[150] ibid.

[151] Pedro Conceição, Dennis Hamill and Pedro Pinheiro, 'Innovative Science and Technology Commercialization Strategies at 3M: A Case Study' (2002) 19 *Journal of Engineering and Technology Management* 25, 33.

[152] See Fig 18.

[153] Brian Leavy, 'A Leader's Guide to Creating an Innovation Culture' (2005) 33(4) *Strategy & Leadership* 38, 41.

[154] Brand (n 147) 21.

[155] Nicholson (n 143) 37.

[156] ibid.

[157] ibid.

their own ideas, inventors can apply for 'Genesis Grants' which allow them 'to buy equipment to assist them in the development of their "15% ideas"' or 'to pay for temporary labour to do some of their existing work while they spend their own time developing their "15% project"'.[158] Sharing (iii) technical information among employees can also boost the creation of inventions in the company. To encourage employees to 'bootleg', a 3M term meaning 'the utilization of company-wide resources ... to explore creative ideas',[159] every division at 3M is allowed to access the technology resources of the company.[160] In addition, 3M's internal organisation called Technical Forum 'enables technical interaction at the grassroots level'.[161] The Forum not only holds 'lectures and problem-solving sessions' but also 'sponsors an annual event where all the divisions show their latest products and technologies'.[162] Thus employees at 3M can obtain up-to-date technical information necessary for creating inventions through 'external/internal communication', which is considered to be one of the strongest predictors of innovation according to the meta-analysis mentioned above.[163]

Although 3M does not offer special pecuniary inducements for individual employee inventors,[164] it attaches great importance to the recognition of their technical contribution. Salary increase and promotion will implicitly accrue to productive inventors,[165] and their achievements will be recognised across the company through articles, presentations or senior management's unofficial visits to them.[166] In addition, it implements official recognition programmes for scientists and engineers working in the company. Based on nominations made by professional colleagues, the Technical Circle of Excellence recognises newer employees who have made excellent technical contribution.[167] They may eventually be admitted to the Carlton Society, a circle of 'highest scientific honour' named after 3M's first head of research and fifth president, if they make 'continuous, outstanding technical contribution over time'.[168]

Of course, the example of 3M cannot be generalised. For example, the International Business Machines Corporation (IBM) offers some remuneration for patent applications and issuances.[169] However, as I pointed out earlier, these

[158] Brand (n 147) 21.
[159] Raghu Garud, Joel Gehman and Arun Kumaraswamy, 'Complexity Arrangements for Sustained Innovation: Lessons from 3M Corporation' (2011) 32 *Organization Studies* 737, 747.
[160] Conceição, Hamill and Pinheiro (n 151) 31; Garud, Gehman and Kumaraswamy (n 159) 747.
[161] Stern (n 100) 233 fn 1.
[162] Conceição, Hamill and Pinheiro (n 151) 33.
[163] See Fig 19.
[164] See text to n 142.
[165] Conceição, Hamill and Pinheiro (n 151) 33.
[166] Brand (n 147) 21; Nicholson (n 143) 38.
[167] Nicholson (n 143) 38.
[168] ibid.
[169] Martin A Bader, *Intellectual Property Management in R&D Collaborations: The Case of the Service Industry Sector* (Heidelberg, Physica, 2006) 67.

kinds of rewards are usually aimed at the disclosure of inventions rather than their creation.[170] Apart from these, IBM gives awards for employees' 'breakthrough thinking, technical leadership, outstanding teamwork, knowledge sharing ... and other achievements'[171] to stimulate workplace creativity. Since these awards do not always accompany cash rewards,[172] the significance of monetary rewards offered to individual employees is presumably small even at IBM. The episode of 3M shows that corporate culture, staff who have the talent to create inventions, company resources and communication among colleagues play an important role in encouraging workplace creativity. Companies may offer monetary rewards in recognition of inventors, yet such rewards are likely to end up intensifying internal competition to the detriment of workplace creativity and innovation.

According to the incentive theory about the patent system it is understood that the law on employee inventions intends to increase inventions made in the country. However, the legislature loses sight of various factors mentioned in Figures 18 and 19 that determine workplace creativity. Employers can take various measures to create an environment ideal for innovation, whilst it is unrealistic to expect the law to intervene to foster workplace creativity on behalf of employers. Rather the current law is likely to hinder the creation of inventions because awarding compensation to employee inventors will stifle workplace creativity. Accordingly, it is irrational to enforce its payment by law on the assumption that it will encourage employee inventors to create inventions.

VI. Summary of Part I

By referring to studies in social psychology and econometrics, it was discussed whether financial incentives offered to employee inventors have a positive effect on their motivation, productivity and creativity. First, such incentives are unlikely to boost the motivation of employee inventors in general because the vast majority of them feel motivated by values intrinsic in inventing rather than by material rewards according to the recent surveys of inventors in Europe, the US and Japan. Second, such incentives are unlikely to boost the productivity of employee inventors immediately because successful inventions depend on various factors beyond the capacity of individual employees such as serendipity, corporate hierarchy and teamwork. Offering inventor remuneration is likely to cause the secrecy of inventors who want to monopolise it and trigger negative reactions of those who do not receive it, so that it will adversely affect the teamwork of employee inventors whether in individualist or collectivist societies. Team-based incentives are also

---

[170] See ch 2, s I.
[171] Bader (n 169) 67.
[172] ibid.

unlikely to be effective because of the line-of-sight problem and social-loafing. Finally, monetary rewards are unlikely to stimulate the creativity of employee inventors. Even if monetary rewards may bring out the creativity of prospective recipients depending on the information the rewards convey as theorists in social psychology argue, the current law on employee inventions is unlikely to induce employee inventors to be more creative because the amount of compensation awarded to them by the law does not usually reflect the level of creativity embodied in inventions made by them. In fact, workplace creativity depends on non-pecuniary factors such as interpersonal relationships among colleagues and the vision of supervisors and top management and the law can do little to encourage workplace creativity on behalf of employers. Overall, the current law on employee inventions is unlikely to encourage the creation of inventions as the legislature intends.

PART II

Ownership of Employee Inventions and the Validity of the Inventor Principle

5

Legitimacy of Employer Ownership

I. Rationale

The incentive theory regarding the patent system holds that incentives are given to enable 'innovation', not just the creation of inventions.[1] Yet incentives provided by the patent system are highly precarious in nature. As long as an inventor behaves in a rational way to maximise his profits, he will not set about inventing unless (i) he can estimate the costs of innovation and the gross profits to be brought by a patent on the invention and (ii) is convinced that the estimated gross profits will be sufficient to derive *net* profits, recouping the estimated costs of innovation. However, each condition inevitably entails highly hypothetical arguments. In the first place, an innovation process can demand enormous costs, often higher than anticipated. The costs to be recouped by a patent must include those of failures unable to be identified beforehand.[2] It is no less difficult to estimate the gross profits to be brought by the patent. Fundamentally, even if a patent is formally granted, it may become void afterwards or the patentee may not be able to practise it where it is granted on an improvement of a process or a device patented prior to his patent unless the preceding patent expires or he obtains the consent of its holder.[3] In addition, a patentee generally faces the risk of litigations by his competitors which not only make the patent protection uncertain but also cost him often considerable expenses for lawsuits.[4]

Even if an inventor has obtained a valid patent and practises it, the patentee is not allowed to do whatever it takes to make immense profits in the market of the patented item. He must not engage in any act which is against competition law, such as price-fixing and predatory pricing, in the name of the practice of the patent.[5] Moreover, monopoly profits brought by a patent are vulnerable to the uncertainty in the market. A patented item may sometimes bring windfall profits to the patentee, but he must always be conscious of the risk that it may not be as profitable as anticipated. Accordingly, there is no guarantee that a patent will bring gross profits enough to recoup the costs of innovation already incurred by the patentee and bring satisfactory *net* profits to him.

---

[1] See ch 1, s II.
[2] Suzanne Scotchmer, *Innovation and Incentives* (Cambridge, Massachusetts, The MIT Press, 2004) 40.
[3] Michael Polanyi, 'Patent Reform' (1944) 11 *The Review of Economic Studies* 61, 69–70.
[4] ibid.
[5] Louis Kaplow, 'The Patent-Antitrust Intersection: A Reappraisal' (1984) 97 *Harvard Law Review* 1815, 1817–18.

Employers can typically make a better use of patents than employee inventors, overcoming the precarious nature of incentives provided by the patent system mentioned above. Companies may have accumulated expertise enough to estimate profits and costs through their experience in R&D and marketing, so that they can diversify their portfolio against the risk of failure which can cause them considerable losses. However, employee inventors lack funds and expertise to undergo the whole process of innovation in today's economic world unless they happen to be unusual venture capitalists. Given the '"business" aspect of the matter which is responsible for the actual delivery of the invention into the hands of the public',[6] it 'is a great mistake' to assume that an individual inventor is the sole actor in the patent system.[7] Accordingly, the traditional assumption that inventors originally retain economic rights in patents needs to be reconsidered.

In theory, as between employers and employees employee inventions should belong to employers in theory for a couple of reasons. First, employer ownership is likely to promote innovation today whilst employee ownership is not. Given the premise of the incentive theory that the patent system should necessarily encourage innovation, as I have just mentioned employers who generally accumulate sufficient funds and expertise are generally in a better position to facilitate innovation than individual employees who usually lack the will and resources to be entrepreneurs. Meanwhile, today many companies invest substantial funds in R&D and patents on the resultant inventions are an effective means for them to recoup the investment. Without patents, which should guarantee them monopoly profits for 20 years, companies are unlikely to create inventions which require sizable R&D investment, such as pharmaceuticals, because they cannot expect to recoup the investment. Apart from patents, many companies rely on lead-time or first-mover advantage, which often enables the first developer of an innovative product to reap massive profits before competitors can put similar products onto the market.[8] Nevertheless, they are likely to become reluctant to invest in R&D without the prospect of obtaining patents which would prevent their competitors from exploiting the technology developed by themselves. If it is laid down as a rule that employers own patents on employee inventions, useful inventions are more likely to be made and delivered to the society.

As Merges points out, employee ownership is likely to involve 'the possibility of holdups by employee-inventors'.[9] In most cases, employee inventions 'are one component of a complex, multi-component product whose total market value

[6] Giles S Rich, 'The Relation between Patent Practices and the Anti-Monopoly Laws' (1942) 24 *Journal of the Patent Office Society* 159, 177.

[7] ibid 175.

[8] Wesley M Cohen, Richard R Nelson and John P Walsh, 'Protecting Their Intellectual Assets: Appropriability Conditions and Why U.S. Manufacturing Firms Patent (or Not)' (2000) *NBER Working Paper 7552*, 10 Figs 1 and 2, www.nber.org/papers/w7552.pdf; Stuart JH Graham and others, 'High Technology Entrepreneurs and the Patent System: Results of the 2008 Berkeley Patent Survey' (2009) 24 *Berkeley Technology Law Journal* 1255, 1290 Fig 1.

[9] Robert P Merges, 'The Law and Economics of Employee Inventions' (1999) 13 *Harvard Journal of Law and Technology* 1, 12.

often by far exceeds the value of the component standing alone'.[10] Accordingly, employee ownership would allow employee inventors to adopt a holdup strategy, so that they can 'extract much of the value of the final product by waiting until all the other rights-holders have granted licenses to the manufacturer' who 'wants to develop a new product'.[11] Employers may give up performing R&D if the transaction costs are manipulated upwards by the employees.[12] In addition, given that many inventions have more than one named inventor today,[13] employee ownership would in many cases result in the co-ownership of the inventions by individual inventors which would make it difficult to exploit them where all the co-inventors do not agree to do so.[14] If employers own employee inventions there will be no fear that the conflicts among co-inventors over the exploitation might stifle innovation.

Next, employee ownership, as opposed to employer ownership, could bring unreasonable profits to inventors in disregard of the interests of employers who have invested in the creation of the invention as well as the contribution made by other employees besides named inventors. According to the 'no risk, no return' principle widely accepted in the business world,[15] those who do not run financial risks should not take profits gained from the investment. Thus it is unreasonable to allow employees, who receive their salary whether or not inventions are made successfully, to claim their ownership only when they are profitable.[16] Whilst employers who invest in highly uncertain R&D need to recoup the investment by exploiting successful inventions, employee inventors who reveal a preference for stable salary over risk-taking by the fact that they choose not to be entrepreneurs are in no position to count on the ownership of the inventions.[17] In addition, given that not all the employees who have contributed to the creation of an invention are named as (co-)inventors in law,[18] it would give named inventors preferential treatment if they enjoy the ownership of the invention to the exclusion of other members of a project team. Such a problem will not arise if their employer exploits the economic rights in the invention on behalf of 'everyone' who made it jointly in the company.

In short, as between employers and employees employee inventions should belong to employers because of (i) the purpose of the patent system to encourage innovation and (ii) the unreasonable profits employee ownership would bring to named inventors. Meanwhile, if employers become the licensees of employee inventions with their ownership vested in employee inventors, employers may not be able to recoup the funds invested in R&D where they are granted only

[10] ibid 13.
[11] ibid.
[12] ibid.
[13] See text to ch 3, nn 33, 34.
[14] See, eg, the UK Patents Act 1977, s 36(3).
[15] James Lam, *Enterprise Risk Management: From Incentives to Controls* (Hoboken, John Wiley & Sons, 2003) 4.
[16] Merges (n 9) 30–31.
[17] ibid 31.
[18] See ch 3, s II.

non-exclusive licences.[19] In addition, employers cannot transfer the inventions to other companies which would be able to exploit them more effectively. Furthermore, the issues of the holdup strategy by inventors, the conflicts among co-inventors over the licensing and their preferential treatment over other contributors will remain unsettled if the licences involve the payment of royalties to the inventors. Accordingly, this solution is not superior to employer ownership in terms of encouraging innovation.

Although it may be argued that the law should provide that employee inventors are the initial owners of employee inventions to improve their status as workers, this book adopts the view that the protection of workers is not relevant to the issue of the ownership of employee inventions.[20] The relevance of the US Constitution and the 'inventor principle' in some civil law countries to the issue in question will be discussed later.

II. Treatment of Academic and Incidental Inventions

The above argument for employer ownership is based on the premise that employers exploit inventions to pursue profits and that employees are expected to act in the economic interests of their employers. By contrast, universities fulfil a different social function from for-profit companies and thus academics do not usually owe a duty to invent under the contract of employment. Stressing this point, Australian courts have recently held that universities do not own inventions made by academics in principle, where no proper arrangements about their ownership have been made in advance. The treatment of such academic inventions will be discussed in detail in chapter eight.

The argument in this chapter does not concern incidental inventions, or those employees have made not in the course of their duties, yet using employers' resources, which accounted for nearly 10 per cent of all the inventions made by the employee inventors sampled in the PatVal-EU (PatVal-I) and Research Institute of Economy, Trade and Industry (RIETI) surveys.[21] Although employers do not acquire the ownership of incidental inventions according to the employment contract in theory,[22] they may want to own or exploit such inventions because their resources are used in the course of inventing.

---

[19] Although Japanese employers are automatically entitled to a non-exclusive licence to exploit employee inventions according to the Japanese Patent Act, the industry argued that it was not enough for them. See ch 9, s II for more details.

[20] See also ch 1, s I.

[21] See ch 3, Fig 14.

[22] According to an English court, employees' normal duties specified in the employment contract may expand in the course of time so as to include inventive tasks: *LIFFE Administration and Management v Pinkava* [2007] EWCA Civ 217, [2007] RPC 30 [58]. However, it is still uncertain whether employers in common law countries become the owner of incidental inventions where there are no express contract terms to that effect.

Many countries do not have a statutory rule on the treatment of incidental inventions. In such countries the treatment shall be determined by negotiation between employers and employees who initially own the inventions, though this is often likely to yield results disadvantageous to employees because of their general lack of bargaining power. Meanwhile, as discussed later the shop right rule in the US only allows employers to obtain a non-exclusive royalty-free licence to use incidental inventions. However, employers may want to secure the ownership of such inventions rather than the mere right to use them if they embody employers' trade secrets. German employers can claim inventions which employees have made during the term of employment using 'technical knowledge available within the company'[23] in return for 'reasonable compensation' since 'service inventions' under the Act on Employees' Inventions include those which 'are essentially based upon experience or activities of the company'.[24]

The ownership of incidental inventions shall be split between employers and employees according to the laws in Greece and Brazil.[25] However, such a rule will make it difficult for both parties to exploit the inventions in case they cannot reach agreement on it. Laws in other countries allow employers to acquire full ownership of incidental inventions. For example, French law provides that employers can acquire incidental inventions ('inventions beyond mission') from employees in return for a 'fair price', which is to be determined in consideration of 'the initial contributions of either of them and the industrial and commercial utility of the invention'.[26] According to the statutes in Austria,[27] Italy,[28] Spain,[29] Portugal,[30] Poland,[31] Slovenia[32] and Argentina,[33] employers may either acquire or exploit incidental inventions in return for proper remuneration. In Scandinavian countries (Norway, Sweden, Finland and Denmark), employers may acquire incidental inventions for proper remuneration, though those in Norway and Sweden are also entitled to the option to exploit such inventions.[34]

---

[23] Michael Trimborn, *Employees' Inventions in Germany: A Handbook for International Businesses* (Alphen aan den Rijn, Kluwer Law International, 2009) para 84.

[24] See text to ch 1, n 5.

[25] Yet employers in both countries shall have the right to exploit these inventions preferentially in return for remuneration: Law No 1733/1987 on Technology Transfer, Inventions, Technological Innovation and the Establishment of the Atomic Energy Committee (Greece), art 6(4)(6); Law No 9279 of 14 May 1996 (Brazilian Industrial Property Law), art 91, (2).

[26] Intellectual Property Code, art L611-7(2).

[27] Patent Act (Federal Law Gazette 259/1970), ss 7(1)(3)b)c), 8(1), 9.

[28] Industrial Property Code (Legislative Decree No 30 of 10 February 2005), art 64(3).

[29] Law No 24/2015 of 24 July on Patents, art 17.

[30] Industrial Property Code (as amended up to Law No 46/2011 of 24 June 2011), art 59(3).

[31] Act of 30 June 2000 Industrial Property Law (as amended up to Act of 24 July 2015), arts 11(5), 22(1).

[32] Job-Related Inventions Act of 25 July 1995, arts 3(2)(b), 6(1), 8, 15, 16.

[33] Law on Patents and Utility Models (Law No 24,481 of 30 March 1995, as amended by Law No 24,572 of 28 September 1995), art 10b)c).

[34] Law on Employees' Inventions (Act No 21 of 17 April 1970, Norway), ss 4(2), 7(1)(2); Act on the Right to Inventions by Employees (1949:345, Sweden), ss 3(2), 6; Act on the Right in Employee Inventions 29.12.1967/656 (Finland), ss 4(1), 7(1)(2); Consolidated Act on Employees' Inventions (Consolidated Act No 131 of 18 March 1986, Denmark), ss 5, 8.

To protect the interests of employees who retain the initial ownership of incidental inventions, it is desirable to have legislation which requires employers who acquire their ownership to pay a fair amount of remuneration to their inventors as statutes in some countries do. However, the amount does not need to be equal to their commercial value because it should be determined on a case-by-case basis in consideration of various factors, including employers' resources used in inventing, such as trade secrets, funds, staff, materials and facilities.

According to the fundamental principle in employment law, employers are naturally entitled to the fruits of labour expended by employees. The conclusion in this chapter that employee inventions should belong to employers is consistent with this principle. Nonetheless, laws in some jurisdictions presume that the ownership of such inventions is initially vested in employees on the assumption that employee ownership would guarantee them an incentive to invent (eg, the US), or that only natural persons capable of intellectual activity are eligible for inventorship under the patent law (eg, Germany). Since in these jurisdictions inventions made by employees do not naturally belong to employers on the basis of employment contract, there still remains a question about whether employers who want to secure their ownership are required to offer something, or what is referred to as 'consideration' in common law countries, to employee inventors from whom the inventions are transferred to employers, regardless of the discussion about the incentives for employee inventors in Part I of this book.

In Part II of the book it will be shown first that despite the US Constitution which vests the ownership of inventions in their inventors, US courts have developed various legal theories in view of the reality of inventive activities taking place in companies today, so that in most cases US employers can own or exploit inventions made by employees without paying additional compensation. Next, it will be seen that case laws on employee inventions in other common law countries such as England and Wales, Australia and Canada are generally consistent with that principle in employment law although inventions made by university researchers cannot be treated in the same way because they do not owe a 'duty to invent' according to their employment contract. Observations on the relevant statutory rules in civil law countries such as Germany and Japan will follow thereafter.

6

The United States

In the US 'an invention presumptively belongs to its creator'.[1] This principle is derived from Article I Section 8 Clause 8 of the US Constitution which will be referred to as 'the Patent and Copyright Clause'. It provides that 'The Congress shall have Power ... To promote the Progress of Science and useful Arts, by securing for limited Times to Authors and Inventors the exclusive Right to their respective Writings and Discoveries'.[2] Pursuant to the Clause 'patent laws reward individuals for contributing to the progress of science and the useful arts'[3] and 'the inventor owns his invention ... as part of that reward'.[4] Thus it is presumed that an individual employee owns his invention even if he made it in the course of his duties.[5]

Equally, 'the law recognizes that employers may have an interest in the creative products of their employees'.[6] Although employers can safeguard their interest by requiring their employees to assign the invention to them,[7] no explicit contract is concluded 'in an appreciable number of cases'.[8] In order to settle disputes in which there is no such express contract, the default rules on allocation of rights between employers and employees were formed at US common law over 90 years from the nineteenth to the early twentieth century.[9]

These default rules comprise the 'hired to invent' and 'shop right' rule.[10] The former rule stipulates that '[o]ne employed to make an invention, who succeeds,

---

[1] *Teets v Chromalloy Gas Turbine Corp*, 83 F3d 403, 407 (Fed Cir 1996).

[2] US Constitution, art I, § 8, cl 8.

[3] *Teets* (n 1) 407.

[4] ibid.

[5] ibid, citing *Hapgood v Hewitt*, 119 US 226, 233–34 (1886).

[6] *Teets* (n 1) 407, citing *Solomons v United States*, 137 US 342, 346 (1890).

[7] According to the US patent law, 'patents ... have the attributes of personal property' and thus are 'assignable in law': 35 USC § 261 (2012).

[8] Robert P Merges, 'The Law and Economics of Employee Inventions' (1999) 13 *Harvard Journal of Law and Technology* 1, 5.

[9] Steven Cherensky, 'A Penny for Their Thoughts: Employee-Inventors, Preinvention Assignment Agreements, Property, and Personhood' (1993) 81 *California Law Review* 595, 616 fn 93. These default rules have developed since the mid-nineteenth century when the US Supreme Court dealt with this issue in *McClurg v Kingsland*, 42 US (1 How) 202 (1843) and culminated in *United States v Dubilier Condenser Corp*, 289 US 178 (1933).

[10] Merges (n 8) 5–6. The provenance of the phrase 'shop right' is uncertain: Christopher M Mislow, 'Necessity May Be the Mother of Invention, but Who Gets Custody?: The Ownership of Intellectual Property Created by an Employed Inventor' (1985) 1 *Santa Clara Computer & High-technology Law Journal* 59, 69 fn 59.

during his term of service, in accomplishing that task, is bound to assign to his employer any patent obtained'.[11] The latter rule means that 'where [an employee], during his hours of employment, working with his [employer's] materials and appliances, conceives and perfects an invention for which he obtains a patent, he must accord his [employer] a non-exclusive right to practice the invention'.[12] However, neither of these rules applies to 'independent inventions', or '[i]nventions unrelated to job function or [those] made away from the job site using employee resources', which 'often belong exclusively to the employee'.[13] Summarised below in Table 1 are the consequences of the application of American common law rules regarding the ownership of inventions made by employees.

Table 1 Summary of the US Common Law Default Rules[14]

'Hired to Invent' Rule	Employer owns outright
Shop Right Rule	Split entitlement: employer has a non-exclusive license to use invention owned by employee
Independent Inventions	Employee owns outright

In addition, inventors who assume the position of the employer's *alter ego* owe the fiduciary duty to assign the ownership of the inventions to their employers, even in the absence of express contracts to that effect.[15] Regardless of these default rules, most employers in the US, in order to secure the ownership of inventions made by their employees, require the employees to sign a pre-invention assignment agreement which supersedes the common law allocation rules.[16] This kind of agreement is 'a clause of an employment contract that obligates the employee to assign to the employer all interests in any future inventions conceived during … the employment term'[17] and US courts generally affirm its enforceability.[18]

Although the default rules are less significant nowadays because of the prevalence of pre-invention assignment agreements, the default rules are still 'instructive in that they provide an indication of norms, policies, and usages as understood by the courts over a period of time'.[19] After examining the historical context of the presumption of inventors' ownership of inventions stipulated in the US Constitution, it will be shown in this chapter that US courts have developed various legal theories to reconcile the constitutional principle with the reality of R&D performed in companies today.

---

[11] *Dubilier* (n 9) 187.
[12] ibid 188, citing *McClurg* (n 9) and *Solomons* (n 6).
[13] Merges (n 8) 6.
[14] Adapted from Merges (n 8) 7 Table 1.
[15] *Dowse v Federal Rubber Co*, 254 F 308, 310 (ND Ill 1918).
[16] Cherensky (n 9) 617–18.
[17] ibid 598 fn 2.
[18] ibid 597.
[19] ibid 617.

I. Significance of the Patent and Copyright Clause: Adding the Fuel of Interest to the Fire of Genius

It is presumed from the Patent and Copyright Clause that an invention belongs to its inventor(s) *ab initio* even when it is conceived in the course of duties that they owe as employees. Hence US patent law requires in principle that actual inventor(s) file an application for a patent.[20] It should be noted here, however, that inventorship and the ownership of inventions are theoretically separate issues[21] and thus the constitutional principle concerning inventorship does not automatically determine who ultimately retains the ownership right to an invention.[22] Nevertheless, in the absence of express assignment agreements, there is a strong presumption pursuant to the Clause that inventorship accords with the ownership of the invention. Accordingly, it is presumed that the ownership of inventions made by employees first rests with them, though their employers may acquire a shop right over them based on the principles of 'equity and fairness'.

To understand why the Constitution established the principle that inventors secure the exclusive right to their discoveries, it is necessary to consider the view of those who framed the Constitution, who '[f]or the first time in the world … laid the entire stress of their effort on the recognition and reward of inventive thought'.[23] They adopted a new theory that the most effective way of securing new industries or improving old industries was 'to encourage intellectual effort by way of invention and discovery' 'by the certainty of reward' gained from the exclusive right secured to inventors.[24] As Abraham Lincoln succinctly put it, '[t]he [US] patent system … *added the fuel of interest to the fire of genius*, in the discovery and production of new and useful things'.[25]

---

[20] 35 USC §§ 102(f), 111(a)(1) (2012). This principle has been unchanged since the first US patent act was legislated in 1790: see Patent Act of 1790 § 6. However, after the relevant provisions in the Leahy-Smith America Invents Act came into force on 16 September 2012, 'a person to whom the inventor has assigned or agreed in writing to assign the invention' is allowed to file an application for a patent: Public Law 112-29 § 4(b)(e); 35 USC § 118 (2012). Thanks to this provision, an employer can now file for a patent as an exception to the constitutional principle.

[21] '[I]nventorship is a question of who actually invented the subject matter claimed in a patent. Ownership, however, is a question of who owns legal title to the subject matter claimed in a patent': *Beech Aircraft Corp v EDO Corp*, 990 F2d 1237, 1248 (Fed Cir 1993).

[22] '[T]he patent right initially vests in the inventor' and, 'patents having the attributes of personal property' pursuant to 35 USC § 261 (2012), '[the inventor] may then, barring any restrictions to the contrary, transfer that right to another, and so forth. However, who ultimately possesses ownership rights in that subject matter has no bearing whatsoever on the question of who actually invented that subject matter': *Beech Aircraft* (n 21) 1248.

[23] Frederick P Fish, 'The Patent System in its Relation to Industrial Development' (1909) 28 *Transactions of the American Institute of Electrical Engineers* 315, 322.

[24] ibid 322–23.

[25] Abraham Lincoln, 'Second Lecture on Discoveries and Inventions' in Roy P Basler (ed), *The Collected Works of Abraham Lincoln*, vol 3 (New Brunswick, Rutgers University Press, 1953) 363 (emphasis added).

It is generally agreed that the inclusion of the Patent and Copyright Clause in the Constitution was inspired by the operation of the patent system in England, which had already been successful when the Constitutional Convention approved the draft of the Constitution in 1787.[26] In England, at least as far back as the reign of Edward III in the fourteenth century, what corresponds to today's industrial patent was also 'granted for the purpose of inducing foreign workmen', such as 'Flemish cloth-makers, German armourers, Italian grass-workers and French iron-founders', 'to introduce new arts into England'.[27] When Elizabeth I was on the throne in the sixteenth century, she began to grant patents which were of an almost modern type not only 'as a reward to the inventor' but also 'for the intro-duction of a new art into England'.[28] Since these patents 'gave the opportunity to establish monopolies ... hostile to the public good', Elizabeth I and her successor, James I, tended to abuse the patent system by granting patents to their favourites, so that they could not only control industries but also increase revenue by extract-ing large compensation for the grants.[29] This led to the legislation of the 'Statute of Monopolies' in 1624, the first patent statute which was aimed at barring Kings from creating monopolies at their discretion.[30] However, all through these periods, there was a consensus among the royal authorities that 'the introduction of new industries' as well as 'the encouragement of invention' was 'of prime importance'.[31] Hence patents were granted not only to inventors but also to those who brought an industry and/or an improvement into England from foreign countries.[32] The rewards were awarded 'for giving to the community the knowledge of an art that it did not have before' rather than 'for inventive achievement'.[33]

Under the English system, patents tended to be a privilege, or 'a product of the prerogative' for monopolists.[34] The American colonists, who emigrated from England to achieve freedom from the monopolistic economic practices in their mother country,[35] drafted the Patent and Copyright Clause on their belief that 'every man should have the right to exploit his own talents without arbitrary

---

[26] George Ramsey, 'The Historical Background of Patents' (1936) 18 *Journal of the Patent Office Society* 6, 6. The following statement on the significance of this constitutional provision by James Madison, one of the framers of the Constitution, provides evidence for this view: 'The utility of this power [of the Congress] will scarcely be questioned. The copyright of authors has been solemnly adjudged, in Great Britain, to be a right of common law. The right to useful inventions seems with equal reason to belong to the inventors.' James Madison, 'Federalist Paper No 43' in Alexander Hamilton, James Madison and John Jay, *The Federalist Papers* (originally published 1788, New York, Cosimo Classics, 2006) 279.

[27] Fish (n 23) 317.

[28] ibid 318.

[29] ibid 319.

[30] ibid 319–20.

[31] ibid 319.

[32] ibid 322.

[33] ibid.

[34] Edward C Walterscheid, 'To Promote the Progress of Science and Useful Arts: The Anatomy of a Congressional Power' (2003) 43 *IDEA: The Journal of Law and Technology* 1, 36.

[35] Edward S Irons and Mary H Sears, 'The Constitutional Standard of Invention–The Touchstone for Patent Reform' [1973] *Utah Law Review* 653, 663.

interference' by monopolistic powers.[36] Neither the word 'patent' nor 'grant' occurs in the Clause;[37] the framers intended that the Congress should be prevented from creating 'arbitrary, exclusive privileges akin to those afforded by English absolute sovereigns'.[38] The Clause meant that the Congress secured inventors' exclusive rights 'that were inherent and were not created by any Monarch or Sovereign'.[39] Thus it is said that the Clause became 'the first substantive ... law in history which affirmatively recognizes property rights in the result of the type of mind work productive of inventions'.[40]

Citing the Patent and Copyright Clause, the Supreme Court in *Dubilier* also pointed out that 'a patent is not, accurately speaking, a monopoly ... which connotes the giving of an exclusive privilege [to the patentee]'[41] and that '[a] patent is granted' to '[a]n inventor ... [who] gives something of value to the community by adding to the sum of human knowledge ... [i]n consideration of ... the consequent benefit to the community'.[42] An inventor retains the title to his own idea, so that it will encourage his intellectual effort which may eventually bring 'benefit to the community' 'by adding to the sum of human knowledge'. As Dratler put it, the Court stressed here that 'the idea belongs inalienably to the inventor' as 'a sort of "moral right"' in principle.[43] The Court has cited the Clause in its judgments over 200 times since its first citation in 1810[44] and again in 2011 in *Board of Trustees of the Leland Stanford Junior University v Roche Molecular System Inc*,[45] in which the Court ruled on the ownership of an invention arising from US government-funded research under the Bayh-Dole Act.[46] Stanford University contended that it had acquired 'superior rights in the invention',[47] citing a provision in the Act that each federal contractor 'may ... elect to retain title to any subject invention'.[48]

---

[36] ibid 663–64.

[37] Ramsey (n 26) 15.

[38] Mary H Sears, 'The Corporate Patent: Reform or Retrogression' (1979) 61 *Journal of the Patent Office Society* 380, 405.

[39] Ramsey (n 26) 15.

[40] ibid.

[41] *Dubilier* (n 9) 186.

[42] ibid.

[43] Jay Dratler Jr, 'Incentive for People: The Forgotten Purpose of the Patent System' (1979) 16 *Harvard Journal on Legislation* 129, 140.

[44] Walterscheid (n 34) 2 fn 4.

[45] 563 US _ (2011). In this case, Dr Holodniy, a research fellow at Stanford University, developed an HIV (Human Immunodeficiency Virus) measurement technique while conducting a part of the research at Cetus, a company which was later acquired by Roche. He had signed agreements with both Stanford and Cetus in advance that he would assign inventions he might create to each. Roche commercialised HIV test kits based on that technique, whilst Stanford claimed that the kits infringed its patents on the technique.

[46] The Act, or the Patent and Trademark Act Amendments of 1980 (Public Law 96-517), is codified in 35 USC §§ 200-12 (2012). It allocates patent rights in inventions made with federal funds between the federal government and contractors that perform federally funded research: 35 USC § 202(a) (2012). See ch 8, s II for details. Since the research project in the *Stanford* case was partly funded by the federal government, the invention in question was subject to the Act.

[47] *Stanford* (n 45).

[48] 35 USC § 202(a) (2012).

Notwithstanding, the Court held that, since the Act did not mean to replace the constitutional principle that inventors enjoy their inherent ownership rights in their inventions, the university never acquired the title to the invention which had already been assigned in effect to a third party by the inventor.[49] The Court noted that '[a]lthough much in intellectual property law has changed in the 220 years since the first Patent Act, the basic idea that inventors have the right to patent their inventions has not'.[50] The Court has firmly attached great importance to recognising inventive thoughts of individuals to this day, respecting the spirit of the Patent and Copyright Clause.

When the draft of this constitutional clause was approved in 1787, the drafters had in their minds the image of generalist hero inventors who did not mind facing the financial risk that the process of inventing might inevitably involve.[51] When they successfully created inventions, they often became innovators themselves so that they could reap the benefit of their hard work by exploiting their inventions. Edison, who established the Edison Illuminating Company in 1880, and Bell, who became one of co-founders of the Bell Telephone Company in 1877, provide good examples on popularising great inventions. However, the drafters of the Clause in the late eighteenth century did not live to witness the emergence of employee inventors in the late nineteenth century, about a century after the drafting, who worked in laboratories set up by companies, avoiding the burden of financial risk.[52] Now that over 200 years have passed since the establishment of the Constitution, it is open to question whether it really encourages the creation of inventions if their ownership is secured to employee inventors, who are mostly unwilling to exploit the inventions by themselves. Rather, in today's fast-changing business world, inventions owned by employee inventors are unlikely to be exploited profitably because of the aforementioned transaction costs potential developers would need to bear.[53] Meanwhile, if employers own and exploit employee inventions that may generate handsome profits, it will not reduce incentives for employee inventors since, generally speaking, '[e]nhanced prospects for the employer ... can translate into enhanced earnings for the creative employee'.[54] The principle of inventor ownership laid down in the Clause has been virtually undermined in relation to employee inventors, as distinct from independent inventors, since US courts have considered the interests of employers in forming the 'hired to invent' and shop right rule and ruling on the validity of pre-invention assignment agreements. These will be explained in turn below.

---

[49] *Stanford* (n 45). The Court pointed out that the Act only 'serves to clarify the order of priority of rights between the Federal Government and a federal contractor in a federally funded invention *that already belongs to the contractor*' (emphasis added).

[50] ibid.

[51] See text to ch 3, n 23.

[52] See text to ch 3, nn 24–26.

[53] See text to ch 5, nn 9–12.

[54] Robert P Merges, *Justifying Intellectual Property* (Cambridge, Massachusetts, Harvard University Press, 2011) 198.

II. The 'Hired to Invent' Rule

Regardless of the principle under the Patent and Copyright Clause that an inventor secures the exclusive right in his invention, his employer owns an invention made by him even in the absence of an express contract to that effect where he 'is employed to devise or perfect an instrument, or a means for accomplishing a prescribed result'.[55] In this case the employer can acquire the created invention without paying additional compensation to the employee.[56] This is called the 'hired to invent' rule.

Courts reason that '[w]hen the purpose for employment ... focuses on invention,[57] '[an employee] has sold in advance to his employer' what he was paid to create,[58] whilst he 'has received full compensation for his ... inventive work'.[59] The employer is not obliged to pay him more than that when he has created an invention because 'he has only produced' what is to be owned by the employer as 'the precise subject of the contract of employment'.[60]

Where this rule applies, employers do not automatically acquire the right to inventions made by employees; they only 'obtain equitable title, allowing them to specifically enforce the employees' implied contractual obligations to assign the patents to the employers'.[61] To apply the rule 'a court must examine the employment relationship at the time of the inventive work to determine if the parties entered an implied-in-fact contract to assign patent rights',[62] which 'is inferred, as a fact, from conduct of the parties showing, in the light of the surrounding circumstances, their tacit understanding'.[63] Factors that courts consider to find such an implied-in-fact contract include the following:

(1) previous assignments of patents on other inventions by the employee; (2) a customary practice within the company for other similarly situated employees to assign; (3) whether the invention was conceived during the period of employment; (4) who originally posed the problem solved by the invention; (5) the employee's authority within the company to determine to whom to give a problem for solution; (6) the relative importance of the idea to the employer's business; (7) a previous inconsistent position on inventorship by the employer; (8) an agreement by the employer to pay

---

[55] *Solomons* (n 6) 346.
[56] Richard C Witte and Eric W Guttag, 'Employee Inventions' (1989) 71 *Journal of the Patent and Trademark Office Society* 467, 472.
[57] *Teets* (n 1) 407.
[58] *Solomons* (n 6) 346.
[59] *Teets* (n 1) 407.
[60] *Dubilier* (n 9) 187.
[61] Henrik D Parker, 'Reform for Rights of Employed Inventors' (1984) 57 *Southern California Law Review* 603, 606 (citation omitted). See also Thomas R Savitsky, 'Compensation for Employee Inventions' (1991) 73 *Journal of the Patent and Trademark Office Society* 645, 647; Cherensky (n 9) 617 fn 97.
[62] *Banks v Unisys Corp*, 228 F3d 1357, 1359 (Fed Cir 2000) (citations omitted).
[63] ibid.

royalties to the employee; (9) payment of patent procurement expenses by the employer or employee; and (10) the absence of initial interest by the employer when the employee first exposed the idea.[64]

Meanwhile, an employee who conducts research, improves and/or designs products is not 'hired to invent' even if he has the title of 'chief engineer'.[65] Where an express term in an employment contract requires an employee 'to exercise his inventive faculties with reference to the specific inventions in question for the sole benefit of his employer',[66] courts are generally reluctant to find an implied-in-fact contract to assign an invention even if the employment contract covers a field of labour and effort the employee expended to conceive the invention.[67] A scholar comments that since his primary task is not inventing something, it does not necessarily meet the reasonable expectations of both parties if the invention is assigned to the employer who did not give him any specific instructions to make it.[68]

Nevertheless, some courts have applied the 'hired to invent' rule to general employees[69] so as to find implied-in-fact contracts to assign inventions made by them to their employers.[70] In principle, a contract to assign an invention does '[not] need ... [to] be expressed any more than any other contract'[71] and a justice of the Supreme Court opined that the Court did not intend to make 'the distinction between specific employment or assignment and general employment to invent' on this point.[72] Another court also acknowledged that if an employer proves that 'the inventor was employed to exercise his inventive faculties for the employer's benefit', his employer acquires the patent on the invention.[73] Thus in theory general employees, who are not specifically 'hired to invent', are also required to assign inventions made by them to their employers as long as courts find an implied contract to that effect.

[64] *Chisum on Patents*, vol 8 (New York, LexisNexis Matthew Bender, 2012) § 22.03[2] (citations omitted).

[65] ibid.

[66] *American Circular Loom Co v Wilson*, 84 NE 133, 135 (Mass 1908).

[67] *Dubilier* (n 9) 187–88.

[68] William P Hovell, 'Patent Ownership: An Employer's Right to His Employee's Invention' (1983) 58 *Notre Dame Law Review* 863, 869–70.

[69] ibid 868; Mislow (n 10) 62; Paul M Rivard, 'Protection of Business Investments in Human Capital: Shop Right and Related Doctrines' (1997) 79 *Journal of the Patent and Trademark Office Society* 753, 756.

[70] See, eg, *E F Drew & Co Inc v Reinhard*, 170 F2d 679, 683 (2nd Cir 1948) (holding that an employee who was 'chief chemist' of the company implicitly understood that his company would become the owner of the invention).

[71] ibid 682.

[72] *Dubilier* (n 9) 213 (Stone J, dissenting).

[73] *Wommack v Durham Pecan Co*, 219 USPQ (BNA) 1153, 1156 (5th Cir 1983).

III. The Shop Right Rule

Where an employee is neither 'hired to invent' nor in a fiduciary relationship with his company,[74] he retains the exclusive right in an invention he has made in principle as the Patent and Copyright Clause provides. Nevertheless, where 'an employee … uses his employer's resources to conceive an invention or to reduce it to practice', the employer obtains a 'shop right', or 'a non-exclusive, royalty-free, non-transferable license to make use of the invention'.[75] As a 'shop right' does not amount to ownership interest in the patent, an employer who acquires it can neither join in an infringement action[76] nor grant licences.[77] Yet the employer can invoke it as a defence to a patent infringement claim by the employee.[78]

Courts have not agreed on the doctrinal basis of the 'shop right' rule and the circumstances necessary to establish a shop right.[79] As a rationale for the rule, the Supreme Court historically advanced (1) the 'implied license theory', (2) 'equitable estoppel theory' and (3) 'equity and fairness theory' in turn, before the Court of Appeals for the Federal Circuit recently combined these theories to adopt (4) the 'totality of the circumstances' test to determine whether an employer has acquired a shop right.[80]

In the nineteenth century, the Supreme Court advanced (1) the 'implied license theory' in such cases as *McClurg v Kingsland*[81] and *Solomons v United States*.[82] According to this theory, an employer acquires a shop right because '[t]he actions of both the employee and the employer … warrant the assumption that the employee had consented to allow limited use of his invention in return for assistance in development of the idea'.[83] For example, the Court in *Solomons* inferred an implied licence for the employer from the fact that the employer had specifically asked the employee to devise the instrument in question.[84]

Shortly after *Solomons*, the Supreme Court in *Gill v United States*[85] adopted (2) the 'equitable estoppel theory'. The idea underlying this theory, as summarised later by another court, is that

> if an employee encourages his employer to use an invention, and then stands by and allows him to construct and operate the new device without making any claim for

---

[74] See text to n 15.
[75] *Chisum on Patents* (n 64) § 22.03[3].
[76] *Kurtzon v Sterling Industries, Inc*, 228 F Supp 696, 697 (ED Pa 1964).
[77] *Ushakoff v United States*, 327 F2d 669, 673 (Ct Cl 1964).
[78] *Chisum on Patents* (n 64) § 22.03[3].
[79] *McElmurry v Arkansas Power & Light Co*, 995 F2d 1576, 1580–81 (Fed Cir 1993).
[80] Rivard (n 69) 758–61.
[81] *McClurg* (n 9).
[82] *Solomons* (n 6).
[83] *Chisum on Patents* (n 64) § 22.03[3].
[84] *Solomons* (n 6) 348.
[85] *Gill v United States*, 160 US 426 (1896).

compensation or royalties, it would not be equitable to allow the employee later to assert a claim for royalties or other compensation.[86]

According to the Court, the employer's acquisition of a shop right was 'not a question of [the inventor's] intention ... but of legal inference ... resulting from the conduct of the inventor'.[87] Holding that '[t]he ultimate fact to be proved [was] the estoppel', the Court inferred that the employee had consented to the employer's use of the invention, from which the estoppel on the part of the employee arose, from the fact that the employee had used the employer's property in inventing.[88] That fact also had important implications for the 'risk bearing' analysis which 'appears to have been determinative in the Court's ruling'.[89] After reviewing the facts in *McClurg* and *Solomons*, the Court seriously considered the financial risk that the employer bore even though the employee might fail in inventing or the created invention might turn out to be of little practical use:

> The material fact is that ... the patentee made use of the labor and property of the [employer] in putting his invention into the form of an operative machine ... In neither case [*McClurg* and *Solomons*] did the [employee] risk anything but the loss of his personal exertions in conceiving the invention. In both cases, there was a question whether machines made after his idea would be successful or not, and if such machines had proven to be impracticable, the loss would have fallen upon the [employer].[90]

Following *Gill*, the Supreme Court in *United States v Dubilier Condenser Corp* relied on (3) the 'equity and fairness theory' and held that what the employer had to show to claim a shop right was not estoppel but only the fact that the employee had used the employer's time and/or property.[91] According to another court, this theory considers 'it ... fair that when an employee has used his employer's time and equipment to make an invention, the employer should be able to use the device without paying a royalty'.[92] It is arguable that the theory implicitly followed the risk-bearing analysis of the Court in *Gill*, which had suggested that employers should acquire a shop right because they bore all the financial risk involved in inventing.

The Court of Appeals for the Federal Circuit recently pointed out that the fact analysis based on 'implied license theory' and 'equitable estoppel theory' would eventually be 'driven by principles of equity and fairness' and thus 'the end result under either is often the same'.[93] Without specifying the legal character of a shop right, the Court adopted (4) the 'totality of the circumstances' test

---

[86] *Hobbs v United States*, 376 F2d 488, 495 (5th Cir 1967).
[87] *Gill* (n 85) 430 (citation omitted).
[88] ibid 435.
[89] Scott P Sandrock, 'The Evolution and Modern Application of the Shop Right Rule' (1983) 38 *The Business Lawyer* 953, 960.
[90] *Gill* (n 85) 434.
[91] *Dubilier* (n 9) 188–89.
[92] *Hobbs* (n 86) 495.
[93] *McElmurry* (n 79) 1581.

to determine whether an employer had acquired it under the principles of equity and fairness:

> [W]e believe that the proper methodology for determining whether an employer has acquired a 'shop right' in a patented invention is to look to the totality of the circumstances on a case by case basis and determine whether the facts of a particular case demand, under principles of equity and fairness, a finding that a 'shop right' exists. In such an analysis, one should look to such factors as the circumstances surrounding the development of the patented invention and the inventor's activities respecting that invention, once developed, to determine whether equity and fairness demand that the employer be allowed to use that invention in his business.[94]

In sum, the Supreme Court, which at first advanced (1) the 'implied license theory' to find a shop right for the employer in *McClurg* and *Solomons*, later adopted (2) the 'equitable estoppel theory' in *Gill* so as to acknowledge that the employer's shop right would result from 'legal inference' rather than from the intention of the inventor. Whilst the Court relied on (3) the 'equity and fairness theory' in *Dubilier*, recent courts have taken a modern approach in which they look to (4) 'totality of the circumstances' surrounding the creation of the invention to determine whether 'equity and fairness' demand that an employer acquire a shop right irrespective of the intention of the inventor. This approach contrasts with the application of the 'hired to invent' rule which calls the implied intention of both parties into question.[95]

IV. Pre-invention Assignment Agreements

It is uncertain whether employers can acquire the ownership of inventions made by employees, not just a shop right. For example, the Court of Appeals for the Federal Circuit in *Teets v Chromalloy Gas Turbine Corp* found an employee's implied agreement to assign the right in his invention to his employer where the inventor had 'spent 70% of his time on the [employer's] project' and '[the employee had] repeatedly acknowledged [the employer's] role in the development of the [invention]'.[96] On the contrary, the Court in *Banks v Unisys Corp* did not find an implied agreement to that effect where the inventor had refused to sign standard forms drafted by the employer who had included clauses on the employee's obligation to assign the rights in inventions made by him to the employer.[97]

Whether or not courts find such an implied-in-fact contract 'is a question to be decided upon all the facts of the individual case'.[98] Accordingly, where there

---

[94] ibid 1581–82.
[95] See text to nn 62, 63.
[96] *Teets* (n 1) 408.
[97] *Banks* (n 62) 1358.
[98] *E F Drew* (n 70) 682.

is no explicit agreement on the assignment of inventions between an employer and an employee, the employer may not be able to secure the ownership right in the invention.[99] To avoid this uncertainty employers in the US normally require potential employees to sign a pre-invention assignment agreement which supersedes the common law principles as a condition of employment.[100] The core clause in the agreement, for example, reads as follows:

> The employee agrees … that all inventions and improvements made, developed, perfected, devised, or conceived by the Employee either solely or in collaboration with others during the Employee's employment by [corporate name], whether or not during regular working hours, relating to the business, developments, products, or activities of [corporate name], or its subsidiaries, shall be and are the sole and absolute property of [corporate name] …[101]

The above clause allows the employer to claim all the inventions made by the employee, including those created in his private activity.[102] Depending on the wording in the clause, however, an employee may be allowed to engage in inventive activities without using his employer's resources as long as he does not neglect his duty.[103] The agreement may contain ancillary provisions which require an employee to assist his employer in securing the rights in the invention so that the employer can keep records of the invention and preserve its confidential information.[104]

Nonetheless, these measures are not necessarily enough for employers to secure the ownership of inventions made by their employees. For example, the court in *Jamesbury Corp v Worcester Valve Co*[105] held that the employer did not acquire the ownership of the invention where the employee had agreed 'without further consideration to give to [the company] the full benefit and enjoyment of any and all inventions or improvements which he may make *while in the employ of* [the company]'.[106] The court reasoned that even though the employee had conceived the invention in the course of employment,[107] he 'had not made an invention, within the meaning of the employment contract when he left [the company], because he had not put any of his ideas down in any tangible form'.[108] For fear that

---

[99] Where an employer does not claim the ownership of the invention, courts only examine whether the employer acquires a shop right: see, eg, *McElmurry* (n 79).

[100] Cherensky (n 9) 617–18.

[101] Orin E Laney, 'Intellectual Property and the Employee Engineer' (IEEE-USA Professional Guideline Series, The Institute of Electrical and Electronics Engineers 2001) 13, www.ieeeusa.org/members/IPandtheengineer.pdf.

[102] ibid.

[103] ibid.

[104] ibid 13–15.

[105] *Jamesbury Corp v Worcester Valve Co* 443 F2d 205 (1st Cir 1971).

[106] ibid 207 (emphasis added), 214.

[107] ibid 208.

[108] ibid 213. The court followed a precedent in Massachusetts according to which 'an idea did not become an invention until it was put into practice or embodied in some tangible form' because 'before an idea became a workable reality, "there often lie severe and long continued labor and repeated

employees may circumvent the contractual obligation to assign an invention,[109] some employers include a provision that requires employees to assign any invention made even '*after termination of employment*'.[110] This is called a 'trailer' or 'hold-over' clause,[111] which provides an exception to the principle established by courts that inventors can transfer 'the general skills and knowledge gained through their former employers' to other employers without restraint.[112]

Courts have ruled that a trailer clause without a limitation on time and/or subject matter is void as an unreasonable restraint on an employee's freedom to 'engag[e] in the gainful occupation for which he is particularly fitted for all time, anywhere in the United States'.[113] They examine the enforceability of a trailer clause by analogy with a non-competition clause.[114] Concerning time, a clause which lasts for months has been found to be enforceable whilst one for five years, 10 years or of a permanent duration is unenforceable.[115] Concerning subject matter, a clause has not been found unreasonable where it only covers inventions relating to areas an employee works in,[116] whilst this is likely to be found unreasonable if it covers 'an entire industry or field of inventions'.[117]

A pre-invention assignment agreement is generally offered on a 'take-it-or-leave-it' basis.[118] Because of the overwhelming bargaining power of employers, employees are generally compelled to accept it.[119] A trailer clause, which is 'analogous to covenants not to compete',[120] may not only unjustly limit an employee's opportunity to work elsewhere after his employment ends but also violate the antitrust law.[121] With all these potential legal issues, courts generally

---

failures, and … success is not always achieved by the one who first strikes out the idea'": ibid 211, citing *Lamson v Martin*, 35 NE 78, 80 (Mass 1893).

[109] The court in *Jamesbury* found that while employed the employee had 'deliberately refrained from making any drawings' to circumvent his contractual obligation: *Jamesbury* (n 105) 213.

[110] ibid (emphasis added).

[111] Parker (n 61) 609.

[112] Peter Caldwell, 'Employment Agreements for the Inventing Worker: A Proposal for Reforming Trailer Clause Enforceability Guidelines' (2006) 13 *Journal of Intellectual Property Law* 279, 292–93 (citation omitted).

[113] *Guth v Minnesota Mining & Mfg Co*, 72 F2d 385, 389 (7th Cir 1934).

[114] Caldwell (n 112) 288. However, Caldwell argues that a trailer clause is more analogous to a confidentiality clause than a non-competition clause since an invention is made with an employer's confidential information: ibid 302.

[115] Marc B Hershovitz, 'Unhitching the Trailer Clause: The Rights of Inventive Employees and Their Employers' (1995) 3 *Journal of Intellectual Property Law* 187, 200 (citations omitted). However, opinions of courts have been divided on a clause which lasts for one year.

[116] ibid 200–01.

[117] Caldwell (n 112) 290.

[118] Cherensky (n 9) 621.

[119] Franklin D Ubell, 'Assignor Estoppel: A Wrong Turn from *Lear*' (1989) 71 *Journal of the Patent and Trademark Office Society* 26, 27.

[120] Rivard (n 69) 754. 'A covenant not to compete', or 'noncompetition covenant', is '[a] promise, usu. in a sale-of-business, partnership, or employment contract, not to engage in the same type of business for a stated time in the same market as the buyer, partner, or employer': *Black's Law Dictionary*, 9th edn (Saint Paul, West, 2009).

[121] Parker (n 61) 609–10.

uphold assignment agreements as valid and thus enforceable,[122] and nowadays, '[a]cceptance of such agreements is a nearly universal requirement of employment for engineers, research scientists and others hired primarily to design, create, invent, or discover'.[123]

A. Enforceability

It is possible under the US patent law to assign rights in future inventions even by an oral agreement.[124] Nevertheless, until the late nineteenth century, courts limited the scope of a pre-invention assignment agreement, or even denied the existence of an agreement itself where there was no clear and written contract.[125] They were cautious about enforcing pre-invention assignment agreements as the opinion of a court in 1887 suggests:

> A naked assignment or agreement to assign, in gross, a man's future labors as an author or inventor,—in other words, a mortgage on a man's brain, to bind all its future products,—does not address itself favorably to our consideration.[126]

However, courts soon came to affirm the reasonableness of pre-invention assignment agreements in the late nineteenth century. For example, in 1895, the court in *Hulse v Bonsack Machine Co*[127] held that the employer had reason to acquire the ownership of the invention because the employer had offered the employee the opportunity to invent using the time and resources of the employer:

> If any improvement suggested itself to [the employee's] mind, he could, by using the machine and the time and material of the company, experiment upon it, and ascertain its value. The improvement would be his idea. But it owed its suggestion and origin, its progressive development and perfection, to the business, the practical working, the opportunity afforded by the company. When, therefore, the company, taught by costly experience, determined to protect itself ... by a covenant in advance of any employment with those seeking its service, it did a fair thing.[128]

The court also confirmed the reasonableness of the trailer clause in the agreement.[129] Furthermore, it was held that the assignment was by no means void as against public policy because the public benefited from the invention once the

---

[122] Cherensky (n 9) 619.

[123] Laney (n 101) 5.

[124] According to 35 USC § 261 (2012), a patent on a perfected invention is assignable 'by an instrument in writing'. Nevertheless, an inchoate invention is not within this principle and thus assignable by an oral agreement: *Burr v De La Vergne*, 7 NE 366, 369 (NY 1886).

[125] Catherine L Fisk, 'Removing the "Fuel of Interest" from the "Fire of Genius": Law and the Employee-Inventor, 1830–1930' (1998) 65 *The University of Chicago Law Review* 1127, 1185–87.

[126] *Aspinwall Mfg Co v Gill*, 32 F 697, 700 (CCDNJ 1887).

[127] *Hulse v Bonsack Machine Co*, 65 F 864 (4th Cir 1895).

[128] ibid 867–68.

[129] ibid 868.

employer secured its ownership and exploited it.[130] However, courts do not affirm the enforceability of pre-invention assignment agreements without qualification. First, an employee's promise to assign future inventions must be supported by consideration in accordance with the general principle of the US contract law.[131] If courts do not find 'adequacy of consideration' in the agreement, they may deem it as unconscionable and thus unenforceable.[132] Second, a trailer clause is subject to some legal limitations for fear that it may unduly limit opportunities for an employee to find a new job.[133]

B. Adequacy of Consideration

With a pre-invention assignment agreement an employer can acquire future inventions made by an employee without paying additional compensation for them. Here a question arises as to whether such an agreement is essentially unenforceable because the employer offers no consideration in exchange for the employee's future inventions. However, courts generally hold that a pre-invention assignment agreement made as a condition of employment is enforceable because employment itself constitutes an adequate consideration and thus an employee is considered to be adequately compensated according to the term of the employment.[134] Courts rule the same way even where an agreement requires an employee to assign all the inventions he makes without a limitation on subject matter.[135] Hence pre-invention assignment agreements allow employers to acquire the ownership of independent inventions, namely those 'unrelated to the employers' businesses, conceived outside the scope of employment, and developed without the employers' resources',[136] which would belong to employees according to the common law default rule.[137]

It appears that an employer needs to offer a separate consideration where a pre-invention assignment agreement is made *after* an employee took up employment since the employer's past offer of employment cannot be a consideration for

---

[130] ibid 870.

[131] Robert A Hillman, *Principles of Contract Law* (Saint Paul, West, 2004) 16.

[132] Cherensky (n 9) 622. Courts do not generally weigh the adequacy of consideration on the assumption that the contracting parties should decide on it for themselves. However, if the imbalance is severe, the contract is deemed as unconscionable and thus void: Hillman (n 131) 26–27. Courts generally 'look at whether the bargaining process is deficient (called "procedural unconscionability") and whether the substantive terms are oppressive ("substantive unconscionability")': ibid 213. Both types of unconscionability may be found in a pre-invention assignment agreement since there is generally an imbalance in bargaining power between employers and employees: Cherensky (n 9) 621–22.

[133] *Guth* (n 113) 387–89.

[134] *Cubic Corp v Marty*, 229 Cal Rptr 828, 833–34 (Ct App 1986).

[135] *Palcy v Du Pont Rayon Co*, 71 F2d 856, 858 (7th Cir 1934); *Patent & Licensing Corp v Olsen*, 188 F2d 522, 525 (2d Cir 1951).

[136] Parker (n 61) 608.

[137] See text to n 13.

the employee's present assignment of future inventions in theory.[138] However, the majority of courts have held that a mere offer of continued employment constitutes an adequate consideration since it confers a real benefit on employees given the doctrine of 'employment at will' generally accepted in the US.[139] According to a court, the policy behind the at-will employment lies in 'the stability of the business community' which can be achieved when 'employers' and employees' decisions remain subject only to the express or implied contracts into which they have voluntarily entered or subject to statute'.[140] Thanks to this doctrine, employers in the US can dismiss employees at will with or without reason,[141] unless the dismissal falls within some judicially created exceptions.[142] Although some courts reject formalism and hold that the continuation of employment for a substantial length of time is necessary to constitute adequate consideration,[143] the Court of Appeals for the Federal Circuit has recently confirmed that an assignment agreement is 'enforceable with only continued employment as consideration'.[144] Overall, it is unlikely that an employee can claim additional compensation for an invention he has made even where he signed a pre-invention assignment agreement after he took up employment.

C. Attempts to Regulate Assignment Agreements by Federal and State Legislation

Job-seeking employees are virtually forced to sign a pre-invention assignment agreement which is offered on a 'take-it-or-leave-it' basis.[145] The uncertain nature of a future invention, or 'something which does not exist and which may never exist', also makes it difficult for employees to bargain with employers over compensation for the invention.[146] Whilst employees may be able to plead their

---

[138] '[A] promise to perform an existing legal or contractual obligation is, without more, insufficient consideration to support a new contract': *International Paper Co v Suwyn*, 951 F Supp 445, 448 (SDNY 1997) (citations omitted).

[139] Mislow (n 10) 100. Evolved from the English common law on employment relationship, this doctrine was formulated by a dogmatic declaration made by Horace Wood, a treatise writer, in 1877 and assimilated into American law without question by 1930: Clyde W Summers, 'Employment at Will in the United States: The Divine Right of Employers' (2000) 3 *University of Pennsylvania Journal of Labor and Employment Law* 65, 66–68.

[140] *Preston v Marathon Oil Co*, 277 P3d 81, 87–88 (Wyo 2012).

[141] *Payne v Western & Atlantic Railroad Co*, 81 Tenn 507, 518 (1884).

[142] Summers (n 139) 70–72. Apart from these judiciary exceptions, Montana passed the Wrongful Discharge From Employment Act in 1987, by which it became the only state in the US where an employer is required to have 'good cause' to discharge an employee: Montana Code Annotated, § 39-2-904(1) (2011).

[143] Mislow (n 10) 101.

[144] *Preston v Marathon Oil Co*, 684 F3d 1276, 1285 (Fed Cir 2012).

[145] See text to nn 118, 119.

[146] Cherensky (n 9) 622–23.

employers' fraud to make the agreement void under exceptional circumstances,[147] five federal Bills have been proposed since 1963 to protect employee inventors, who have only the weak bargaining power against employers.[148] These Bills proposed to limit the scope of inventions employers could claim[149] or to make it mandatory for employers to pay a certain amount of compensation for inventions they would claim from employees.[150] However, all these Bills did not pass because of the strong lobbyist efforts of corporate employers and the lack of a union to represent employee inventors.[151] Most engineers and scientists view themselves as creative and professional individualists[152] and their diverse citizenship, resident status, cultural and ethnic backgrounds make coordinated political involvement almost impossible.[153] Meanwhile, eight states so far have passed laws which bar employers from requiring employees to assign inventions made in their own time without using employers' resources.[154] However, their effect is limited because of the exceptions made in these laws which allow an employer to acquire 'inventions that relate to the employer's business, or actual or demonstrably anticipated research or development, or result from work performed by the employee for the employer'.[155] Overall, these state laws have not greatly changed the situation of employee inventors.[156]

---

[147] Hovell (n 68) 877.

[148] These Bills are: Brown Bill, HR 4932, 88th Cong (1963), reintroduced as HR 5918, 89th Cong (1965); Moss Bill, HR 15512, 91st Cong (1970), reintroduced as HR 1483, 92nd Cong (1971), HR 2370, 93rd Cong (1973), HR 5605, 94th Cong (1975), HR 2101, 95th Cong (1977); Hart-Owens Bill, S 1321, 93rd Cong (1973), HR 7111, 93rd Cong (1973); Kastenmeier Bill (I), HR 4732, 97th Cong (1981); and Kastenmeier Bill (II), HR 6635, 97th Cong (1982), reintroduced as HR 3285, 98th Cong (1983).

[149] See Brown Bill and Kastenmeier Bill (I) (n 148). These Bills proposed to bar employers from acquiring by contracts the rights in inventions made by employees not hired to invent (Brown Bill) or from forcing employees to sign pre-invention assignment agreements except those concerning 'employment invention' (defined as 'one made by an employee during his term of employment') (Kastenmeier Bill (I)): Parker (n 61) 618; Hovell (n 68) 883, 885. The net effect of these Bills would have been 'a return to the common law allocation of patent rights': Parker (n 61) 617–18, fn 119.

[150] See Moss Bill, Hart-Owens Bill and Kastenmeier Bill (II) (n 148). These Bills proposed to require employers to pay employee inventors 'a minimum of two percent of the profits or savings to employers resulting from the employees' inventions' (Hart-Owens Bill) or their 'fair market value' 'adjusted to reflect the position and duties of the employees and the degree to which the operations of the employers contributed to the inventions' (Moss Bill and Kastenmeier Bill (II)): Parker (n 61) 618, 620 (citation omitted).

[151] Cherensky (n 9) 626; Richard A Kamprath, 'Patent Reversion: An Employee-Inventor's Second Bite at the Apple' (2012) 11 *Chicago Kent Journal of Intellectual Property* 186, 189.

[152] Witte and Guttag (n 56) 467.

[153] Kamprath (n 151) 189.

[154] See Minnesota Statutes Annotated, § 181.78 (2012) (enacted 1977); Washington Revised Code Annotated, §§ 49.44.140, 49.44.150 (2012) (enacted 1979); California Labor Code, §§ 2870-72 (2012) (enacted 1979); North Carolina General Statutes, §§ 66-57.1, 66-57.2 (2012) (enacted 1981); 765 Illinois Compiled Statutes, 1060/2 (2012) (enacted 1983); Delaware Code Annotated, Title 19, § 805 (2013) (enacted 1984); Kansas Statutes Annotated, § 44-130 (2012) (enacted 1986); Utah Code Annotated, §§ 34-39-2, 34-39-3 (2012) (enacted 1989).

[155] Laney (n 101) 16.

[156] Unlike the eight states mentioned in the text, Nevada passed a law which was unfavourable to employee inventors in 2001. Totally replacing the common law default rules, the state has adopted a statutory rule whereby a patentable invention made by an employee 'that relates directly to work

In sum, today the Patent and Copyright Clause, which should secure inventors the exclusive right in their inventions to 'add the fuel of interest to the fire of genius', 'basically plays no role in governing the ownership of employee inventions'[157] because of the common law default rules and pre-invention assignment agreements. Under the default rules employers can own or exploit inventions made by employees without paying them additional compensation in many cases. Regarding pre-invention assignment agreements courts generally hold that employers do not need to pay additional compensation for inventions to be transferred from employees since employment itself constitutes an adequate consideration. Fisk observes that courts became willing to hold that employee inventions would belong to employers after around 1910 when employers' lawyers began to emphasise that inventing is a 'collective and corporate-sponsored enterprise'[158] and that 'judicial solicitude toward employee-inventors' ended in the mid-1920s.[159] Thus it is arguable that courts have virtually made the Clause a dead letter and now accept that for the sake of innovation employers own or exploit inventions made by employees without paying additional compensation in principle.

performed during the course and scope of the employment' belongs to his employer unless there is an express written agreement to the contrary: Nevada Revised Statutes, § 600.500 (2013). Now Nevada is 'the only state that allows ownership of patentable inventions to be transferred from one party to another in the complete absence of an assignment agreement, and without any form of actual notice to the transferor': Mary LaFrance, 'Nevada's Employee Inventions Statute: Novel, Nonobvious, and Patently Wrong' (2002) 3 *Nevada Law Journal* 88, 88. Although the purpose of the legislation was 'to attract more high-technology businesses to Nevada', the legislature did not critically examine whether such legislation would really serve its intended purpose: ibid 90, 110.

[157] Witte and Guttag (n 56) 467.
[158] Fisk (n 125) 1174–76.
[159] ibid 1179.

7

Other Common Law Countries

I. England and Wales

In the nineteenth century, 'true and first inventors' were presumed to be the first owners of inventions in England and Wales, meaning in the employment context that there was a presumption of employee ownership.[1] For example, in *Bloxam v Elsee*,[2] Bayley J stated that 'if a servant make an improvement, his master is not entitled to take out a patent for it' on the premise that the inventor in question had not been 'employed ... for the express purpose of devising improvement'.[3] Nevertheless, it came to be recognised that employment contracts imported 'the rights of an employer to the products of his employees' labour and the duties of an employee not to harm his employer's trade',[4] both of which could be at odds with 'the rights of an employee as "true and first inventor"'.[5] Thus early in the twentieth century, English courts began to imply that 'a particular employer was entitled to the fruits of invention produced by a particular employee'.[6] In *Edisonia Ltd v Forse*,[7] Warrington J referred to the relevant law, citing the following passage from an influential commentary on patent law at that time:

> In the absence of special contract the invention of a servant, even though made in the employer's time and with the use of the employer's materials and at the expense of the employer, does not become the property of the employer ... It may very well be that, in the circumstances of a particular case, it is inconsistent with the good faith which ought properly to be inferred or implied as an obligation arising from the contract of service that the servant should hold the Patent otherwise than as a trustee for his employer.[8]

---

[1] Justine Pila, '"Sewing the Fly Buttons on the Statute": Employee Inventions and the Employment Context' (2012) 32 *Oxford Journal of Legal Studies* 265, 269.

[2] *Bloxam v Elsee* (1825) 1 C & P 558.

[3] ibid 568 (Bayley J).

[4] Pila (n 1) 269–70.

[5] ibid 270.

[6] Jeremy Phillips and Michael J Hoolahan, *Employees' Inventions in the United Kingdom: Law and Practice* (Oxford, ESC, 1982) 18.

[7] *Edisonia Ltd v Forse* (1908) 25 RPC 546.

[8] ibid 549 (Warrington J).

English courts affirmed by the mid-twentieth century that inventions made by employees were assignable to employers as property by an express term in an employment contract.[9] However, such a term could be held unenforceable as unfair restraint of trade where it covered inventions irrelevant to the employer's business.[10] This contrasts with the case of pre-invention assignment agreements in the US, which have generally been held enforceable even if they allow employers to claim the ownership of such inventions.[11]

Furthermore, English courts accepted that an invention made in the course of an employee's duties was presumed to belong to the employer even where there was no express term to that effect, regardless of 'the specific nature of the individual employee's duties'.[12] This is a further development of the implied term theory established in early nineteenth-century cases such as *Edisonia*, in which the court held that an employee retained his invention as trustee for his employer only 'in the circumstances of a particular case'.[13] In *Sterling Engineering and Co v Patchett*,[14] Lord Simonds declared:

> It appears to me ... that it is an implied term, though not written at large, in the contract of service of any workman that what he produces by the strength of his arm or the skill of his hand or the exercise of his inventive faculty shall become the property of the employer.[15]

Although before this judgment 'emphasis tended to be placed on the need to show either a positive contract in the employer's favour or an implied duty of trust',[16] it is said that '[t]he tendency to increase the presumption in favour of his employer probably grew as cases arose in which employees were trying to stop their employer from using the invention in his own business'.[17] In accordance with the report issued by the Banks Committee in 1970,[18] the UK government confirmed in its White Paper that at English common law 'if an invention is made by an employee in the course of his employment, the right to patent the invention belongs to the employer',[19] whilst 'an employer may not require his employees to assign to him any inventions which they may make in the future outside the course of their employment'.[20] When the Patents Act 1977 was later introduced,

---

[9] Pila (n 1) 285–86.

[10] *Electrolux v Hudson* [1977] FSR 312, 321–23.

[11] See text to ch 6, nn 135–37.

[12] Phillips and Hoolahan (n 6) 19.

[13] See text to n 8.

[14] *Sterling Engineering and Co v Patchett* [1955] AC 534.

[15] ibid 544 (Lord Simonds).

[16] William Cornish, David Llewelyn and Tanya Aplin, *Intellectual Property: Patents, Copyright, Trade Marks and Allied Rights*, 8th edn (London, Sweet & Maxwell, 2013) para 7-03.

[17] ibid.

[18] *The British Patent System: Report of the Committee to Examine the Patent System and Patent Law* (Banks Report, Cmnd 4407, 1970) ch 16.

[19] Board of Trade, *Patent Law Reform* (White Paper, Cmnd 6000, 1975) para 34.

[20] ibid para 35.

these common law principles were codified in its section 39 and 42(2) respectively, which read as follows:

> [Section 39] (1) Notwithstanding anything in any rule of law, an invention made by an employee shall, as between him and his employer, be taken to belong to his employer for the purposes of this Act and all other purposes if—
>
> (a) it was made in the course of the normal duties of the employee or in the course of duties falling outside his normal duties, but specifically assigned to him, and the circumstances in either case were such that an invention might reasonably be expected to result from the carrying out of his duties....
>
> (2) Any other invention made by an employee shall, as between him and his employer, be taken for those purposes to belong to the employee.

> [Section 42] (2) Any term in a contract ... which diminishes the employee's rights in inventions of any description made by him after the appointed day and the date of the contract, or in or under patents for those inventions or applications for such patents, shall be unenforceable against him to the extent that it diminishes his rights in an invention of that description so made, or in or under a patent for such an invention or an application for any such patent.

It is observed that '[t]he law relating to the ownership of inventions evolved so as to accommodate the newly-revealed demands for what the courts perceived to be industrial necessity'.[21] Whilst English courts at first held that the ownership was vested in an employee as 'true and first inventor' in the eighteenth century, they came to adopt the principle that an employee invention *ab initio* belongs to an employer in the first half of the twentieth century, which is codified in the current Patents Act 1977. Since the English law has followed an 'all-or-nothing' approach,[22] where either an employer or an employee enjoys the ownership to the exclusion of the other, no legal theory which corresponds to the American shop right rule has been formed there. Where an employee who is normally engaged in non-inventive tasks made an invention incidental to the employment, English courts in the early twentieth century tended to hold that in the absence of an agreement his employer owned it exclusively since his duties had come to include producing the best solutions for the employer by making the most of his skill, ingenuity and inventive ability.[23] An American scholar observed that '[t]he English law on this subject was fabricated in cases involving employees hired to invent'.[24]

The report issued by the Swan Committee in 1947 recognised 'a third possibility' that 'both employer and employee can fairly be said to be entitled to a share in

---

[21] Phillips and Hoolahan (n 6) 43–44.

[22] Pila (n 1) 275.

[23] *British Reinforced Concrete Engineering Co Ltd v Lind* (1917) 34 RPC 101, 109; *Adamson v Kenworthy* (1932) 49 RPC 57, 68. Though in *Adamson*, the court also found that there had been an employer's special instruction to make an invention: ibid 69.

[24] C Robert Morris Jr, 'Patent Rights in an Employee's Invention: the American Shop Right Rule and the English View' (1960) 39 *Texas Law Review* 41, 55.

the benefits of an invention.[25] In accordance with the report, section 56(2) of the Patents Act 1949 provided that 'unless satisfied that one or other of the parties is entitled, to the exclusion of the other, to the benefit of an invention made by the employee', 'the court … may … by order provide for the apportionment between them of the benefit of the invention … in such manner as the court … considers just'. Nevertheless, in *Sterling Engineering*, Lord Reid, who presumably failed to turn his attention to the 'third possibility' mentioned in the Swan Report,[26] stated in *obiter* that '[i]n the absence of agreement I do not see how there can be a case where the one party is not entitled to the whole benefit to the exclusion of the other'.[27] On the basis of his opinion which made the provision 'virtually a dead letter',[28] the aforementioned Banks Committee recommended that it should be repealed in introducing the current Patents Act 1977.[29] Unless fresh legislation akin to that provision in the 1949 Act takes place, there is no adopting the American shop right rule under the English law.[30]

Independently of the previous cases, where courts tended to find that an incidental invention made by an employee belonged to his employer,[31] the rights in an invention made by an employee after the 1977 Act came into force 'are to be governed by, and only by, the provisions of section 39'.[32] For example, it was held that a manager of a company department in *Harris' Patent* initially owned an invention he had made neither in the course of his normal duties nor at his employer's special instruction.[33] Nonetheless, an employer may still become the initial owner of an incidental invention made by an employee who usually engages in non-inventive tasks, for the scope of his 'normal duties' specified in the initial contract of employment may expand in the course of time.[34]

II. Australia, Canada and Other Common Law Jurisdictions

Pursuant to section 15(1) of the Patents Act 1990 in Australia, 'a patent for an invention' made in the course of an employee's duties may be granted to his

---

[25] Board of Trade, *Patents and Designs Acts: Final Report of the Departmental Committee* (Swan Report, Cmd 7206, 1947) paras 25, 27.

[26] Kenneth R Swan, 'Patent Rights in an Employee's Invention' (1959) 75 *The Law Quarterly Review* 77, 88.

[27] *Sterling Engineering* (n 14) 546 (Lord Reid).

[28] Banks Report (n 18) para 447.

[29] ibid para 467.

[30] Morris (n 24) 57.

[31] See text to nn 23, 24.

[32] *Harris' Patent* [1985] RPC 19, 28 (Falconer J).

[33] ibid 34, 37.

[34] *LIFFE Administration and Management v Pinkava* [2007] EWCA Civ 217, [2007] RPC 30 [58].

employer as 'a person who … would, on the grant of a patent for the invention, be entitled to have the patent assigned to the person' or who 'derives title to the invention from the inventor'.[35] However, since this provision does not define who initially owns an invention created in the employment context, one must refer to cases decided by Australian courts to discover whether the initial owner is an employer or an employee.

French J in *University of Western Australia v Gray (No 20)*[36] pointed out that there had been 'two principal reported Australian cases on employee inventors' before his court.[37] In *Spencer Industries Pty Ltd v Collins*,[38] one of these cases, the parties agreed that the relevant law on this issue in Australia derived from the opinion of Lord Reid in the aforementioned English *Sterling Engineering* case. In this case, his lordship had opined that 'it is, in my judgment, inherent in the legal relationship of master and servant that any product of the work which the servant is paid to do belongs to the master' unless it is modified 'by express agreement or by an agreement which can be implied from the facts of the case'.[39] In *Victoria University of Technology v Wilson*,[40] another case cited by French J, Nettle J summarised the general law in Australia as follows:

> It is an implied term of employment that any invention or discovery made in the course of the employment of the employee in doing that which he is engaged and instructed to do during the time of his employment, and during working hours, and using the materials of his employers, is the property of the employer and not of the employee. Having made a discovery or invention in course of such work, the employee becomes a trustee for the employer of that invention or discovery, and he is therefore as a trustee bound to give the benefit of any such discovery or invention to his employer.[41]

Similarly, a court in New Zealand has confirmed that an employer's ownership of employee inventions is implied in the contract of employment.[42] Despite the lack of a legal provision, courts in Australia and New Zealand have thus followed the English approach concerning the ownership of employee inventions. Meanwhile, section 39 of the Patents Act 1977 in the UK has been transplanted into patent statutes in Singapore[43] and Hong Kong.[44] It follows that employers in these jurisdictions acquire the ownership of employee inventions without offering consideration for them in principle. However, courts may refer not only to the

---

[35] Patents Act 1990, s 15(1)(b)(c).
[36] *University of Western Australia v Gray (No 20)* (2008) 246 ALR 603.
[37] ibid [144].
[38] *Spencer Industries Pty Ltd v Collins* (2003) 58 IPR 425.
[39] ibid [69], citing *Sterling Engineering* (n 14) 547 (Lord Reid).
[40] *Victoria University of Technology v Wilson* (2004) 60 IPR 392.
[41] ibid [104].
[42] *Empress Abalone Ltd v Langdon* [2000] 2 ERNZ 53, [7-004].
[43] Patents Act (Cap 221), s 49(1).
[44] Patents Ordinance (Cap 514), s 57.

provisions in an employment contract but also to the circumstances in which it was created to determine whether an employee's duty included making the invention.[45] Where an employee's normal duty does not involve creating inventions, 'the mere existence of the employer/employee relationship will not give the employer ownership of inventions made by the employee during the term of the relationship'[46] unless there are special circumstances which suggest otherwise. For example, it was held that a sales manager in *Spencer Industries* owned an invention made by him since he had not been directed to make it by his employer.[47] Similarly, an employer is not *ipso facto* entitled to own an invention which an employee hired to invent in one area of his employer's business created outside that area.[48]

By contrast, Canadian courts have made it clear that they do not to follow the current English approach on the subject. In *Comstock Canada v Electec Ltd*,[49] the Federal Court of Canada confirmed the principle that employees initially own inventions made by them, citing the opinion of Lord Tenterdon in the English *Bloxam* case that 'if a servant, while in the employ of his master, makes an invention, that invention belongs to the servant, not to the master'.[50] According to the Court, '[t]he only exceptions to the presumptions which favour the inventive employee are: (1) an express contract to the contrary; or (2) where the person was employed for the express purpose of inventing or innovating'.[51] Regarding the latter exception, '[t]he Court should consider the nature and context of the employer-employee relationship,' including the following factors:

(a)   whether the employee was hired for the express purpose of inventing;
(b)   whether the employee at the time he has hired had previously made inventions;
(c)   whether an employer had incentive plans encouraging product development;
(d)   whether the conduct of the employee once the invention had been created suggested ownership was held by employer;
(e)   whether the invention is the product of the problem the employee was *instructed* to solve, ie whether it was duty to make inventions;
(f)   whether the employee's invention arose following his consultation through normal company channels (ie was help sought?);
(g)   whether the employee was dealing with highly confidential information or confidential work;
(h)   whether it was a term of the servant's employment that he could not use the ideas which he developed to his own advantage.[52]

---

[45] *British Reinforced Concrete Engineering* (n 23) 109.
[46] *Victoria University of Technology* (n 40) [104].
[47] *Spencer Industries* (n 38) [83].
[48] *Empress Abalone* (n 42) [8].
[49] *Comstock Canada v Electec Ltd* (1991) 38 CPR (3d) 29.
[50] ibid [72], citing *Bloxam* (n 2) 564 (Lord Tenterdon).
[51] *Comstock Canada* (n 49) [77]–[79].
[52] ibid [79].

In addition, a fiduciary duty that a senior employee may owe to his employer 'alone does not impede the employee from claiming that the invention is his own' under the Canadian law.[53] The Court summarised the Canadian approach as follows:

> There is no such presumption permitting an employer to claw out of an employee's hand, without compensation, the fruits of his labour just by virtue of his employment. If the U.S. and English jurisprudence show such tendencies, so be it. In Canada, the law first looks, of course, to discover if the parties have concluded an objectively provable or reasonably inferred agreement about inventions. If there be no objectively proved agreement, … then the circumstances of the employment could indicate the correct result, by inference. … [H]owever, the presumption in Canada operates in the direction of freedom, not slavery. In the absence of reliable *indicia*, the inventor keeps the benefit of the invention.[54]

Thus it appears that unlike employers in other common law jurisdictions Canadian employers are required to offer additional compensation for inventions they acquire from employees who have made them in the course of their duties. Nevertheless, employment itself usually constitutes an adequate consideration for the assignment of inventions where both parties agree on it when 'the employee is for the first time inducted into the service'.[55] An employer may be required to supply an additional consideration where the employer wants to modify an existing employment contract to request the assignment. However, an Ontario court held that continued employment can suffice as consideration where an employer has made a tacit promise 'to forbear from dismissing the employee for a reasonable period of time thereafter'.[56] This approach contrasts with that of US courts, which generally hold that continued employment itself suffices as consideration even if it does not guarantee an employee further employment for a substantial length of time.[57] Apart from this point, however, the judicial treatment of employee inventions in Canada does not differ much from that in other common law jurisdictions. Accordingly, despite the presumption in favour of employee inventors suggested by the Court in *Comstock Canada*, Canadian courts are likely to acknowledge that employers acquire employee inventions without paying additional compensation to their inventors in most cases.

---

[53] ibid.
[54] ibid [87].
[55] *Techform Products Ltd v Wolda* (2001) 2001 CanLII 8604 (ON CA) [19], citing *Kadis v Britt*, 29 SE 2d 543, 548 (NCSC1944).
[56] *Techform Products* (n 55) [28].
[57] See ch 6, s IV.B.

8

Inventions Made
by University Researchers

I. The *Victoria University of Technology* and *University of Western Australia* Cases

As the names of the parties suggest, Australian courts discussed whether inventions made by university researchers should be exempt from the principle that employers own employee inventions in the aforementioned *Victoria University of Technology* and *University of Western Australia* cases. In the former, two senior academics and a former student at the then Victoria University of Technology (VUT) developed an e-commerce system during their working hours. They initially intended to use the system in online courses to be offered by the university's School of Applied Economics, but later sought to patent it with the intention of offering it to certain industry partners for commercial use. The Supreme Court of Victoria in the first place dismissed VUT's submission that the university acquired the ownership of the invention in question pursuant to its intellectual property policy on the grounds that it had not promulgated the policy effectively.[1] The Court went on to hold that there was no implied term in the academics' contracts of employment which purportedly allowed the university to claim the invention created in the course of their research because inventing internet-based e-commerce systems had never been the activity of the School of Applied Economics.[2] The Court found that, despite their initial intention of designing the system as a university project, the academics had completed it in a private capacity, and thus the university could not acquire the ownership of the system on the grounds of their duties to research at the university.[3] However, the Court found that VUT was entitled to the academics' share of the invention for the reason that they had breached the fiduciary obligations they had owed to the university as head of the School of Applied Economics or director of a research centre established in it.[4] The Court specifically pointed out that by their actions the

---

[1] *Victoria University of Technology v Wilson* (2004) 60 IPR 392 [82], [91].
[2] ibid [107], [110].
[3] ibid [139].
[4] ibid [149], [150], [176], [220].

academics had taken away from VUT the opportunity of developing the system so as to exploit it 'for their own benefit to the exclusion of the university'.[5]

The latter case concerned the ownership of inventions made by Dr Gray, a professor of surgery, during his tenure at the University of Western Australia (UWA). He was obliged under the contract of employment to teach and conduct research in his field of expertise, namely the treatment of liver cancer using microsphere technologies, and sought to patent the technologies which, UWA argued, he had developed during his employment with the university.[6] French J for the Federal Court of Australia found that the university had failed to promulgate its intellectual property regulations so that it could not invoke them to acquire the ownership of the inventions.[7] Furthermore, he dismissed UWA's submission that it was still entitled to the rights in the inventions under a term implied in Dr Gray's contract of employment. The Court found that the following aspects of his employment were at odds with the argument advanced by the university:

1. The absence of any duty to invent anything.

2. The freedom to publish the results of his research and any invention developed during that research notwithstanding that such publication might destroy the patentability of the invention.

3. The extent to which Dr Gray, as a researcher and those working with him, were expected to and did solicit funds for their research, including the development of inventions, from sources outside UWA ...

4. The necessity, consistent with research of the kind he was doing, to enter into collaborative arrangements with external organisations ...[8]

Concerning the first point, French J stated 'as a general proposition' that universities are not entitled to own inventions made by their staff in the course of their research unless they are specifically hired to produce inventions[9] since 'a duty to research does not carry with it a duty to invent'.[10] He found that 'Dr Gray had no duty to invent anything' because he just owed a duty 'to undertake research and to stimulate research amongst staff and students at UWA' under his contract of employment.[11] This aspect of the researcher's employment alone, the appeal court pointed out, 'could well of itself have justified the dismissal of UWA's claim'.[12]

Raising the second, third and fourth points above, French J drew attention to adverse effects on the activities of academics that would be caused if inventions made by them were to belong to their universities. First of all, he pointed out that

---

[5] ibid [150], [155].

[6] However, French J in the trial court found in *obiter* that all but one technology had not been developed in the course of his employment with the university: *University of Western Australia v Gray (No 20)* (2008) 246 ALR 603 [15].

[7] ibid [246].

[8] ibid [1366].

[9] ibid [163], [164].

[10] ibid [12].

[11] ibid [1360].

[12] *University of Western Australia v Gray* (2009) 179 FCR 346 [206].

'the general obligation of secrecy imposed upon the employee who has a duty to invent' would compromise the academic freedom of university researchers.[13] As the appeal court reasoned, UWA's argument that a duty to invent could subsist without such obligation is untenable because an employee owing such a duty could freely 'destroy the potential patentability of an invention by progressively putting research results into the public domain', thus preventing his employer from making the best use of the product of his labour.[14] If an implied duty of confidentiality were imposed upon university researchers, it would inhibit not only academic collaborations and exchanges with those in other institutions,[15] but the mobility of academic staff commonly found in the field of science or technology.[16] In addition, the trial and appeal courts argued, an academic working for a university would face difficulties in seeking not only funding from sources outside the university[17] but also collaborative arrangements with other research institutions if his university could exclusively appropriate the product of the research made possible by these funds and/or collaboration with external organisations.[18]

In contrast to the finding in *Victoria University of Technology*, the university's other claim that the academic had breached fiduciary duties owed to the university as his employer was also dismissed. Whilst UWA framed the researcher's fiduciary duties on the premise that he had an obligation not to benefit himself with rights which the university retained, both the trial and appeal courts found that the premise itself broke down since the university could not establish its ownership of the inventions made by Dr Gray.[19] In addition to the way UWA pleaded its claim based on Dr Gray's fiduciary duties,[20] the fact that he was not in a position to manage a department or faculty unit at the university, in contrast to the two senior academics in *Victoria University of Technology*,[21] also warranted the dismissal of the claim.[22]

In sum, both the trial and appeal court in *University of Western Australia* concluded that Dr Gray, as a researcher at UWA, was not subject to an implied term generally found in the contracts of employment that allows employers in industry to claim inventions made by their employees. The courts seriously considered the fact that a university serves public purposes, such as offering higher education courses, providing research facilities and conferring degrees, which is not the case with industrial employers.[23] The courts added that, even

---

[13] *University of Western Australia* (n 6) [159].
[14] *University of Western Australia* (n 12) [191].
[15] ibid [127], [190].
[16] ibid [164], [190].
[17] *University of Western Australia* (n 6) [161].
[18] *University of Western Australia* (n 12) [204].
[19] *University of Western Australia* (n 6) [1567], (n 12) [214].
[20] 'They were not pleaded as misappropriated 'opportunities' claims as was the claim in *Victoria University of Technology*': *University of Western Australia* (n 12) [214]. See also text to n 5.
[21] See text to n 4.
[22] William van Caenegem, 'VUT v Wilson, UWA v Gray and University Intellectual Property Policies' (2010) 21 *Australian Intellectual Property Journal* 148, 155.
[23] *University of Western Australia* (n 6) [160], [1361], (n 12) [183].

though most universities nowadays pursue some commercial activities, there was still a good reason to distinguish UWA from industrial employers since its commercial activities had not yet replaced its traditional functions.[24] Above all, they were concerned that if UWA's claim were to be allowed it would adversely affect the academic freedom of university researchers, their freedom to publish in particular.[25]

The Australian courts' arguments in *University of Western Australia* about the university's public purposes, commercial activities, and the academic freedom of university researchers apply to universities and academic inventors in general regardless of jurisdiction. In the decisions it was assumed that inventions made in academia would be patented and exploited later, whether they are initially owned by universities or academic inventors themselves. However, there is a strong argument that such inventions should not be monopolised by the relevant parties since universities have traditionally promoted 'open science' where researchers are supposed to disseminate their research results to the public freely without aiming to profit financially. In the section below I will elaborate on this point before discussing the above decisions of the Australian courts.

II. Open Science and the Issue of Patenting Academic Inventions

A. Open/Proprietary Science and its Relation to Basic/ Applied Research

Open science is the mode of science in which complete disclosure and open inquiry of research findings contribute to the effective generation of scientific knowledge.[26] Openness, it is said, 'abets rapid validation of findings, reduces excess duplication of research effort, [and] enlarges the domain of complementarities and beneficial "spill-overs" among research programs'.[27] According to David, this mode of scientific enquiry originated in 'the patronage system in post-Renaissance Europe' where kings and nobles sought to sponsor natural philosophers whose achievements would enhance the prestige of the patrons themselves.[28] Later, the communities of scientists took over the aristocratic patrons' role to evaluate the works of their peers during the sixteenth century.[29] The foundation of the Royal

---

[24] *University of Western Australia* (n 6) [1362], (n 12) [133], [184].

[25] *University of Western Australia* (n 6) [159], (n 12) [186].

[26] Paul A David, 'Understanding the Emergence of "Open Science" Institutions: Functionalist Economics in Historical Context' (2004) 13 *Industrial and Corporate Change* 571, 576.

[27] ibid.

[28] ibid 578–79.

[29] ibid 580.

Society in London in 1660 and subsequent formation of many societies of modern science paved the way for the institutionalisation of open science in Europe under the auspices of state-sponsored academies in the later seventeenth and eighteenth centuries.[30]

In open science it is supposed that research findings are shared by peer scientists freely, so that they can enquire into the findings and develop further scientific knowledge. The primary reward for scientists that affects their research career is honorific recognition of originality by their fellows.[31] This reward system, in which scientists compete to be the first to make a discovery, serves to hasten both discoveries and their disclosure.[32] Open science contrasts with proprietary science, where those who have produced scientific knowledge try to appropriate that information as intellectual property to gain financial profits which provide an incentive to invest in research activities.[33] These two domains of science 'serve different and potentially complementary societal purposes'.[34] Proprietary science typically concerns applied research[35] conducted in industrial contexts, where companies aim to maximise economic rents gained from commercially exploiting inventions their research is likely to produce.[36] Meanwhile, basic research[37] is undertaken mainly in the domain of open science, ie government laboratories and universities, where emphasis is placed on maximising the stock of public knowledge.[38] Basic research would not be possible without substantial public funding because companies seeking short-term profits tend to underinvest in the kind of research which does not result in patentable technologies immediately.[39] However, from society's perspective, it is important to maintain the sufficient level of basic research because

---

[30] ibid 582–83.

[31] Robert K Merton, *The Sociology of Science: Theoretical and Empirical Investigations* (Chicago, The University of Chicago Press, 1973) 297–302.

[32] Partha Dasgupta and Paul A David, 'Toward a New Economics of Science' (1994) 23 *Research Policy* 487, 498–500. However, despite the ideology of open science, until the final results are published researchers may tend to keep the relevant information and ideas secret for fear that competitors may claim to be the first to discover them: Ann Monotti and Sam Ricketson, *Universities and Intellectual Property: Ownership and Exploitation* (Oxford, Oxford University Press, 2003) paras 6.72, 6.177.

[33] Diana Rhoten and Walter W Powell, 'The Frontiers of Intellectual Property: Expanded Protection versus New Models of Open Science' (2007) 3 *Annual Review of Law and Social Science* 345, 347–48.

[34] David (n 26) 576.

[35] According to the Frascati Manual on R&D statistics in OECD member states, '[a]pplied research is original investigation undertaken in order to acquire new knowledge. It is, however, directed primarily towards a specific, practical aim or objective': OECD, *Frascati Manual 2015: Guidelines for Collecting and Reporting Data on Research and Experimental Development* (Paris, OECD, 2015) para 2.29.

[36] Dasgupta and David (n 32) 498; David (n 26) 576.

[37] In the Frascati Manual basic research is defined as 'experimental or theoretical work undertaken primarily to acquire new knowledge of the underlying foundations of phenomena and observable facts, without any particular application or use in view': OECD, *Frascati Manual 2015* (n 35) para 2.25.

[38] Dasgupta and David (n 32) 498; David (n 26) 576.

[39] Richard R Nelson, 'The Simple Economics of Basic Scientific Research' (1959) 67 *Journal of Political Economy* 297, 302–04; Kenneth J Arrow, 'Economic Welfare and the Allocation of Resources for Invention' in National Bureau of Economic Research, *The Rate and Direction of Inventive Activity: Economic and Social Factors* (Princeton, Princeton University Press, 1962) 618–19.

this kind of research is more likely to bring significant breakthroughs in scientific knowledge than applied research.[40]

In 2015 the spending on basic research accounted for 17 per cent of gross domestic expenditure on R&D in Organisation for Economic Co-operation and Development (OECD) member countries,[41] where on average more than three quarters of basic research was performed in the higher education and government sectors.[42] Academic freedom guaranteed in universities has created an ideal environment for open science and basic research closely associated with it. Academic freedom regarding research activities means (i) '[t]he … freedom to choose the subject or line of research and the manner of its pursuit' and (ii) 'the freedom to decide when and how to publish the products of one's research to the extent that these subsist'.[43] It is entirely fair to say that 'the unfettered exchange of ideas and intellectual debate' ensured by the academic freedom are 'the most effective means of promoting production and dissemination of the kinds of knowledge that the wider community needs'.[44] It should also be noticed here that the freedom to publish, the latter aspect of academic freedom, is a necessary condition for the effective operation of the reward system of open science mentioned above, where those who first disclose new discoveries win honorific recognition.[45]

B. Proprietary Science at Universities and the Effect of the Bayh-Dole Act

Since basic research is performed without any particular use or application in view, most basic research conducted in universities does not usually result in patentable inventions. However, some patentable inventions may be created incidentally in the course of basic research when it 'is carried out with the expectation that it will produce a broad base of knowledge likely to form the basis of the solution to recognised or expected current or future problems' ('oriented basic research')[46] even though it is still regarded as basic research because it does not envisage any *particular* use or application.

---

[40] Nelson (n 39) 301.

[41] OECD, *OECD Science, Technology and Industry Scoreboard 2017: The Digital Transformation* (Paris, OECD, 2017) 27.

[42] ibid 100. Note, however, that the business sector was the principal contributor to basic research in Japan, South Korea and Slovenia: ibid 101.

[43] *University of Western Australia* (n 12) [186].

[44] Monotti and Ricketson (n 32) para 2.47.

[45] See text to nn 31, 32.

[46] OECD, *Frascati Manual 2015* (n 35) para 2.28. This concept is distinguished from 'pure basic research', which 'is carried out for the advancement of knowledge, without seeking economic or social benefits or making an active effort to apply the results to practical problems or to transfer the results to sectors responsible for their application': ibid.

Meanwhile, US universities have actively institutionalised applied research from which patentable inventions are fairly likely to result since the mid-nineteenth century, when land-grant colleges, whose original mission was to serve the practical needs of local industry, agriculture in particular, were established with the grant of public land after the passage of the Morrill Act in 1862.[47] These colleges also trained professional engineers who subsequently worked in corporate laboratories, which began to emerge in great numbers in the same period.[48] Being expected to play an important role in enhancing the country's economic prosperity,[49] American universities have assumed more practical character than their European counterparts and by the time World War II broke out applied research such as engineering discipline 'had established firm places in the American university system'.[50] Yet basic research has always been the main arena of university research even in the US: the spending on basic research in the US higher education sector accounted for 64 per cent of gross expenditure on R&D in the sector in 2014, when the corresponding figure for applied research was 27 per cent.[51]

In his report which discussed the science policies the US federal government should adopt after World War II, Dr Vannevar Bush, who served as director of the war-time Office of Scientific Research and Development, stressed the need to strengthen basic research in colleges, universities and research institutes in the country,[52] arguing that it would 'bring higher standards of living, [would] lead to the prevention or cure of diseases … and [would] assure means of defence against aggression'.[53] Consistent with his recommendation, in the post-war period the National Institutes of Health (NIH) and the Department of Defense (DoD) became the source of more than half of federal research funds used in US universities, sponsoring basic research programmes which were in fact motivated by practical problems arising in the field of health and national defence.[54] Whilst such research programmes often produced patentable inventions, there was a criticism that they were for the most part not licensed to developers, thereby hindering effective exploitation of the results of government-sponsored research, because of the bureaucracy in federal agencies which lacked a uniform policy on the ownership of patents originating from such research.[55] Universities claimed

---

[47] Nathan Rosenberg and Richard R Nelson, 'American Universities and Technical Advance in Industry' (1994) 23 *Research Policy* 323, 324–26.

[48] See text to ch 3, n 24.

[49] Corynne McSherry, *Who Owns Academic Work? Battling for Control of Intellectual Property* (Cambridge, Massachusetts, Harvard University Press, 2001) 55.

[50] Rosenberg and Nelson (n 47) 333.

[51] National Science Board, *Science and Engineering Indicators 2018* (National Science Foundation 2018) 5-13–5-14 Table 5-2.

[52] Vannevar Bush, *Science, The Endless Frontier: Report to the President on a Program for Postwar Scientific Research* (Washington DC, United States Government Printing Office, 1945) 13–15.

[53] ibid 5.

[54] Rosenberg and Nelson (n 47) 335 Table 3; National Science Board (n 51) 5-21 Table 5-4.

[55] Monotti and Ricketson (n 32) paras 6.37–6.41.

that they could be more efficient licensers if they were allowed to retain the title to such patents because they were more familiar with the inventions and their inventors, who would interact directly with potential licensees.[56] Meanwhile, there was a general consensus among commentators that inventions resulting from government-sponsored research should not be left unpatented because no one else should be allowed to claim patent rights in such inventions,[57] which needed to be commercialised domestically so that federal taxpayers could capture the benefits of the research.[58]

The Bayh-Dole Act,[59] which took effect in 1980, established a set of rules on the ownership of inventions arising from federally funded research with the aim of promoting the utilisation of such inventions.[60] According to the Act, a university[61] that performs research funded in whole or in part by the federal government is allowed to 'elect to retain title to' any invention made in the course of the research in principle.[62] In this case a relevant federal agency retains 'a nonexclusive, nontransferrable, irrevocable, paid-up license' to practise the invention or have it practised 'for or on behalf of the United States'.[63] To promote the exploitation of the invention the agency may also exercise its march-in rights to require the university to grant a licence to a responsible licensee or to grant a licence itself where the university refuses to do so.[64] Meanwhile, where the university does not elect to retain the title to the invention, the federal agency may receive it[65] or allow the inventor to acquire it.[66]

Whether the Act has actually encouraged the commercial exploitation of the results of federally funded research is open to question. To begin with, it is arguable that the legislation was in fact unnecessary because the federal government might be no less capable of licensing inventions that are truly valuable to industry than are universities. Although before the passage of the Act the proponents of the legislation claimed that '[o]nly a small percentage of [the federal government's] estimated 28,000–30,000 patents had been successfully licensed and exploited commercially',[67] they overlooked the fact that the majority of these patents

---

[56] Rebecca S Eisenberg, 'Public Research and Private Development: Patents and Technology Transfer in Government-Sponsored Research' (1996) 82 *Virginia Law Review* 1663, 1700.

[57] ibid 1675–76.

[58] David C Mowery and Bhaven N Sampat, 'University Patents and Patent Policy Debates in the USA, 1925-1980' (2001) 10 *Industrial and Corporate Change* 781, 796–97.

[59] The Patent and Trademark Act Amendments of 1980 (Public Law 96-517): see ch 6, n 46.

[60] 35 USC § 200(b)(e) (2012).

[61] The Act applies to small business firms and non-profit organisations, including universities, which conduct federal-sponsored research: 35 USC § 200(c) (2012). Meanwhile, large businesses were not included in the Act because it would raise antitrust concern if those with sufficient market power could acquire the title to inventions arising from such research: Eisenberg (n 56) 1691, 1695.

[62] 35 USC §§ 201, 202(a) (2012).

[63] 35 USC § 202(c)(4) (2012).

[64] 35 USC § 203 (2012).

[65] 35 USC § 202(c)(2) (2012).

[66] 35 USC § 202(d) (2012).

[67] Eisenberg (n 56) 1702.

had resulted from the research funded by the DoD and thus had only a limited commercial applicability.[68] Where other government agencies funded research, a far larger portion of the resultant patents, albeit few, had been licensed success-fully by the federal government presumably because they were commercially valuable.[69]

The rapid increase in the number of patents issued to US universities since 1980 may seem to demonstrate the success of the Act in encouraging technology transfer from universities. The number of utility patents granted by the United State Patent and Trademark Office (USPTO) to US universities grew from 394 in 1980 (0.64 per cent of total utility patents issued by the same federal agency in the same year) to 4797 in 2012 (1.89 per cent).[70] However, university patenting had already started to grow in the 1970s prior to the legislation due to such factors as increased public funding for academic research, universities' reduced dependence on the inefficient Research Corporation, a private foundation to which they had outsourced the management of academic patents, and their growing involvement in patenting biomedical technologies.[71] Thus it is an exaggeration to say that tech-nology transfer has been encouraged by the change in the intellectual property regime alone.[72]

Some may refer to patent revenue received by Technology Transfer Offices (TTOs) at universities, which manage and license inventions made by academ-ics, to measure the success of the Act. Data from the Association of University Technology Managers (AUTM) show a rising trend in royalties received by US universities up to the present, but only around 40 per cent of active licences actually make profits.[73] Their revenue is small compared to the total research expenditure: in the fiscal year 2012 the 194 academic and non-profit research institutions in the US that responded to the AUTM survey reported a total revenue of $2.6 billion, only 4.1 per cent of their total research expenditure ($63.7 billion).[74] Moreover, the revenue distribution was highly skewed as '50% of the nationwide returns were received by only 12 institutions, with each of these "winning" institutions having 80-90% of their revenue due to only a single technology', notably a pharmaceutical

---

[68] ibid 1702–03 fn 161.

[69] ibid 1703.

[70] USPTO Patent Technology Monitoring Team, 'U.S. Colleges and Universities – Utility Patent Grants 1969-2012: Ownership Category Breakout', www.uspto.gov/web/offices/ac/ido/oeip/taf/univ/asgn/table_1_2012.htm.

[71] Mowery and Sampat (n 58) 798–808. The last factor greatly contributed to the growth in patenting at the University of California, Columbia and Stanford University in the same decade: David C Mowery and others, 'The Growth of Patenting and Licensing by U.S. Universities: An Assessment of the Effects of the Bayh-Dole Act of 1980' (2001) 30 *Research Policy* 99, 106, 110–12 Figs 7 and 8.

[72] ibid 116–17; Mowery and Sampat (n 58) 811.

[73] National Science Board (n 51) 8-39, Appendix Table 8-26.

[74] Lita Nelsen, 'Technology Transfer in US Universities and Research Institutions' in Shiri M Breznitz and Henry Etzkowitz (eds), *University Technology Transfer: The Globalization of Academic Innovation* (Abingdon, Routledge, 2016) 454–55.

drug.[75] It should be noticed that TTOs' revenue itself does not essentially indicate whether the Act has actually realised its primary goal to encourage commercial exploitation of academic inventions.[76] Thus it is neither appropriate nor realistic for US universities to expect technology licensing to be a reliable source of research funding. The same can be said of universities outside the US. Although many of them, notably those in Europe, have also established TTOs which are modelled after those at US universities, at present their average licensing revenue is far lower than that of US TTOs and only a small number of TTOs with a few profit-making patents enjoy most of the total licensing income earned by TTOs operating in each country.[77]

C. Approach to Patenting Academic Inventions

The courts in *University of Western Australia* held that the inventor's freedom to publish his research results, which could destroy the patentability of the inventions he had made, was at odds with the university's claim that it was entitled to the rights in the inventions in question.[78] Their view is similar to that expressed by Jacob J in *Greater Glasgow Health Board's Application*,[79] the UK case where the Patents Court allowed a doctor's appeal against the Hearing Officer's decision that the rights in the invention he had made while employed by a medical institution belonged to his employer.[80] Although it was not a university that had employed the inventor at the time of the invention in that case,[81] the judge argued that it would be irrational if doctors, who 'frequently devise new and better treatments' while employed, would 'have to get their employer's permission to publish' 'what they have devised' even though they actually did not have to.[82]

Whilst the academic inventor in *University of Western Australia* sought to patent the inventions he had made, the courts in that case are unlikely to have excluded the possibility that inventions made by academics are left unpatented and disclosed to the public in accordance with the idea of open science. Some university researchers argue against patenting academic inventions. In 2009, for example, scholars affiliated with the University of Manchester in the UK published the Manchester Manifesto, which they hoped would 'serve as a starting point for discussion' on

---

[75] ibid 455.
[76] Eisenberg (n 56) 1710–11.
[77] OECD, *Turning Science into Business: Patenting and Licensing at Public Research Organisations* (Paris, OECD, 2003) 70–71 Table 3.13, 7273; Annamaria Conti and Patrick Gaule, 'Is the US Outperforming Europe in University Technology Licensing? A New Perspective on the European Paradox' (2011) 40 *Research Policy* 123, 126–27 Fig 3.
[78] See text to nn 8, 13, 14.
[79] *Greater Glasgow Health Board's Application* [1996] RPC 207.
[80] Yet the doctor had conceived 'the original idea for the invention, not during clinical work, but while he [had been] involved in private study at home': ibid 211.
[81] Yet the employer was closely affiliated with a university.
[82] *Greater Glasgow Health Board's Application* (n 79) 223.

the question of 'Who Owns Science?'[83] On the understanding that 'the current method of managing innovation ... has significant drawbacks in terms of its effects on science and economic efficiency',[84] they argued that it was possible to adopt 'completely open-access models',[85] reforming the current patent system which could hinder the public access to the benefits of research and obstruct the flow of information in the scientific community to the detriment of the progress of science and innovation.[86] Meanwhile, Aarhus University in Denmark has recently launched the 'Open Science platform', where researchers working in academia and industry collaborate to create fundamental knowledge which no parties involved may patent in order to make it freely available to anyone who is interested in using it.[87] With the Danish Industry Foundation providing some funds to the platform, it is expected that researchers take the risk of doing fundamental research without caring about its commercial applicability and costs associated with patenting its results.[88]

Academics who are in favour of open science are unlikely to suggest that universities become a completely 'IP law-free zone'.[89] At English common law, for example, it has been regarded as 'both just and commonsense' that the copyright in lectures belongs to those who have delivered them in the absence of an agreement to the contrary.[90] Whilst intellectual property policies at many UK universities state that universities own copyrighted materials created by academics, including computer programmes and databases, academics are normally allowed to retain the copyright in works they have produced to advance their academic career, such as scholarly books, articles and lectures.[91] With respect to inventions made by academics, at present few universities would subscribe to the view that they should always be left unpatented so that no one can claim the rights in them. Typically, those in developing countries may want to patent and license them to those who will certainly exploit them in the interests of the public where they are made in the fields of agriculture, biomedicine and energy, all of which are vital to the stability of the citizens' lives.[92] In this case patents serve as a means for controlling the use

---

[83] The University of Manchester Institute for Science, Ethics and Innovation, 'Who Owns Science? The Manchester Manifesto' (2009) 7, www.isei.manchester.ac.uk/TheManchesterManifesto.pdf.

[84] ibid 2.

[85] ibid 6.

[86] ibid 3–4. Note, however, that their views did not represent the official position of the University.

[87] Peter F Gammelby, 'Aarhus University and industry open patent-free playground' (24 July 2017), scitech.au.dk/en/about-science-and-technology/current-affairs/news/show/artikel/aarhus-universitet-og-industrien-aabner-patentfri-legeplads/.

[88] ibid.

[89] Monotti and Ricketson (n 32) para 2.45.

[90] *Stephenson Jordan & Harrison Ltd v MacDonald & Evans* (1952) 69 RPC 10, 18.

[91] Andreas Rahmatian, 'Make the Butterflies Fly in Formation? Management of Copyright Created by Academics in UK Universities' (2014) 34 *Legal Studies* 709, 726–28.

[92] Fabio Montobbio, 'Intellectual Property Rights and Knowledge Transfer from Public Research to Industry in the US and Europe: Which Lessons for Innovation Systems in Developing Countries?' in WIPO, *The Economics of Intellectual Property: Suggestions for Further Research in Developing Countries and Countries with Economies in Transition* (2009) 182, www.wipo.int/export/sites/www/ip-development/en/economics/pdf/wo_1012_e_ch_6.pdf.

of the results of university research for the sake of the public good.[93] Meanwhile, universities in developed countries generally aim to encourage the commercial exploitation of academic inventions by industry, with a naive expectation that it will also help to boost their research budget. Yet commercial entities that develop the inventions usually require the patent rights in them so that they can exclude competitors from the market for the relevant products.[94] In the case of joint industry-university research industrial partners may refuse to provide sufficient funds where they cannot expect to retain some rights in the results of the joint research.[95] In addition, if academic inventions are not patented, only large companies with the capacity to develop them on a large scale may take advantage of the results of university research without paying for its cost. Given that in 2015 on average 70 per cent of R&D carried out by the higher education sector in OECD member countries was funded by governments,[96] taxpayers are likely to regard such a free ride as unfair.[97]

As long as universities not only disseminate the results of their research but try to encourage their effective exploitation, it is legitimate to seek to patent inventions made by academics. However, patenting cannot be the principal role of universities, which, as the courts in *University of Western Australia* pointed out, have traditionally served various public functions as institutions of higher education.[98] If universities actively pursue commercialisation of research and focus on producing patentable inventions which will eventually bring them great profits, it will undermine the objectivity of university research and public trust in it.[99] It is also important to maintain the fruitful division of roles between universities, which are mainly responsible for fundamental research, and industry, which usually pursues proprietary science.[100] Although academics may exceptionally owe a *specific* duty 'to produce an invention or to do research directed to producing an invention' 'under a special contract with' their universities,[101] it is arguable that universities cannot impose a *general* duty to invent on academics because they are essentially different to commercial enterprises.

The key point is that universities may be involved in patenting to the extent that it is merely incidental to academic research. Even if academic inventions are patented, in terms of maintaining the openness of science other researchers should not be prevented from doing further research based on the patented technologies. The researchers' use of the technologies should qualify for the experimental

---

[93] Monotti and Ricketson (n 32) paras 2.52, 2.58.

[94] Eisenberg (n 56) 1709; Monotti and Ricketson (n 32) para 2.53.

[95] Monotti and Ricketson (n 32) para 2.54.

[96] OECD, *OECD Science, Technology and Industry Scoreboard 2017* (n 41) 100.

[97] Monotti and Ricketson (n 32) para 2.50. See also text to nn 57, 58.

[98] See text nn 23, 24.

[99] Monotti and Ricketson (n 32) paras 11.14, 11.21.

[100] Rosenberg and Nelson (n 47) 346; Eisenberg (n 56) 1714–15. See also text to nn 34–38.

[101] *University of Western Australia* (n 12) [178]. See also *University of Western Australia* (n 6) [12], [163].

use defence to patent infringement as long as it is not intended for commercial activities.[102] Yet in the US there is concern that the defence is too narrow because courts have held it is only applicable to actions performed solely 'for amusement, to satisfy idle curiosity, or for strictly philosophical inquiry'[103] and that 'the profit or non-profit status of the user is not determinative'.[104] Thus universities and academics are expected to refrain from patenting technologies typically used in subsequent research, such as 'research tools' in life sciences (eg, antibodies, cell lines and transgenic mice) to be used in a drug discovery process,[105] because such materials are not commercially exploited and thus patenting them does not essentially lead to technology transfer.[106]

III. Ownership of Academic Inventions

Where academic inventions are patented according to the proprietary science model, who becomes the owner of the patents as between universities and academic inventors? In chapter five I mentioned a couple of reasons for favouring employer ownership regarding inventions made in industry, namely (i) the purpose of the patent system to encourage innovation and (ii) the unreasonable profits employee ownership would bring to inventors. Concerning the first rationale, I have argued that employer ownership fits the patent law's purpose of encouraging innovation because employers are more likely to have funds and expertise necessary for performing R&D. However, since universities do not perform R&D themselves as commercial enterprises do, it is necessary to examine here independently of the arguments advanced in that chapter whether the ownership of academic inventions should be vested in universities in terms of encouraging technology transfer, which leads to the process of innovation for which industry is mainly responsible.

A. Can Academic Inventors Encourage Technology Transfer?

In Italy a law introduced so-called 'professors' privilege' in 2001, where patentable inventions made by researchers at Italian universities belong to the researchers

---

[102] Monotti and Ricketson (n 32) paras 11.11, 12.14.

[103] *Roche Prods, Inc v Bolar Pharm Co*, 733 F2d 858, 863 (Fed Cir 1984).

[104] *Madey v Duke University*, 307 F3d 1351, 1362 (Fed Cir 2002). The court suggested that research projects conducted at universities would not automatically fall within the experimental use exemption because 'these projects unmistakably further the institution's legitimate business objectives, including educating and enlightening students and faculty participating in these projects[,] ... [and] also serve ... to increase the status of the institution and lure lucrative research grants, students and faculty'.

[105] Mowery and others (n 71) 118.

[106] See text to nn 94, 95.

themselves,[107] on the assumption that they were more likely to encourage technology transfer than universities that 'lacked the competence and the culture to promote patenting.'[108] However, a study revealed that after the legislation there had been a downward trend in the percentage of academic patents in Italy, in which at least one academic holding a post at an Italian university had been designated as an inventor, to the total number of patents held by Italian inventors, suggesting that the law did not have a positive effect on technology transfer.[109] Rather, the study found that Italian universities had increased their share of the ownership of patents on inventions made by their researchers in the same period, contrary to the assumption at the time of the legislation that universities would not be interested in their ownership.[110] In response to the scepticism about its effectiveness the 2001 Law was amended by a legislative decree in 2005, so that now the 'professors' privilege' does not apply where the research is funded even in part by private entities or carried out in the context of specific research projects funded by public entities to which the researchers do not belong.[111] By contrast, Germany abolished the long-established 'professors' privilege' in 2002 for the reason that it had not apparently facilitated scientific progress in German universities.[112] German academics are now required to report inventions they have made to universities in principle, as employees working in industry do to their employers, so that the universities can decide whether they claim their ownership.[113] With Austria, Denmark, Finland and Norway having made a similar change in law at around the same time in imitation of the Bayh-Dole Act in the US,[114] now inventions made in the course of research carried out by academics are generally owned by institutions they belong to, according to the laws in most European countries with the exceptions of Sweden and Italy.[115]

---

[107] Law No 383 of 18 October 2001, art 7(1); Industrial Property Code (Legislative Decree No 30 of 10 February 2005), art 65(1).

[108] Nicola Baldini and others, 'Organisational Change and the Institutionalisation of University Patenting Activity in Italy' (2014) 52 *Minerva* 27, 32.

[109] Francesco Lissoni and others, 'University Autonomy, the Professor Privilege and Academic Patenting: Italy, 1996-2007' (2013) 20 *Industry and Innovation* 399, 407 Fig 2, 418.

[110] ibid 409 Fig 3.

[111] Industrial Property Code (Legislative Decree No 30 of 10 February 2005), art 65(5).

[112] Christian G Stallberg, 'The Legal Status of Academic Employees' Inventions in Britain and Germany and Its Consequences for R&D Agreements' [2007] *Intellectual Property Quarterly* 489, 496.

[113] Act on Employees' Inventions, ss 5(1), 42(1).

[114] Aldo Geuna and Federica Rossi, 'Changes to University IPR Regulations in Europe and the Impact on Academic Patenting' (2011) 40 *Research Policy* 1068, 1068, 1070.

[115] ibid 1069 Table 1. Despite the lack of legislation the UK has virtually adopted the Bayh-Dole-style system since 1987, when the then Prime Minister Margaret Thatcher made a decision to abolish the monopoly enjoyed by the post-war National Research for Development Corporation (now the British Technology Group) on commercialising the fruits of publicly funded research at universities: Graham Richards, 'Bayh-Dole-Thatcher' in Graham Richards (ed), *University Intellectual Property: A Source of Finance and Impact* (Petersfield, Harriman House, 2012) 19–20. Yet legislation similar to the Bayh-Dole Act has not been introduced in the UK ever since on the grounds that it 'would present greater risks to existing collaborations [between companies and British universities]': *Lambert Review of Business-University Collaboration: Final Report* (HM Treasury 2003) para 4.29.

There has been little evidence so far that 'professors' privilege' encourages technology transfer. Even so, it is rash to assume that it will encourage technology transfer if the law provides that universities become the owner of academic inventions. Whilst the above study of academic patents in Italy showed that the *introduction* of 'professors' privilege' did not have a positive effect on technology transfer, another study of inventions patented by biotechnology companies specialising in drug discovery suggested that the *abolition* of that privilege in Denmark had a negative effect on that. It found that university researchers in that country had become less involved in patents filed by drug discovery companies after the abolition of the privilege in 2000, though such a trend was not observed in Sweden where the privilege has been maintained to the present.[116] The researchers who did this study argued that it was because profit-oriented TTOs, which manage the rights in academic inventions retained by Danish universities under the new legal scheme, had discouraged exploratory research conducted jointly by academics and industry which would not generate profits immediately.[117] They added, however, that this might not be the case with joint research close to technological innovation in which the interests of academics, industry and universities would coincide in most cases.[118]

University TTOs are not necessarily competent enough to intermediate effectively between academic inventors and developers, whether spin-offs or established companies to which 'the overwhelming majority of licenses' are granted today.[119] In theory, established companies are unable to decide whether or not they will invest in inventive activities when no information on their profitability is available.[120] TTOs are expected to devote their resources to collecting that information and assessing the ability of potential licensees to make effective use of the inventions so that they can fulfil their intermediary function.[121] For that purpose, however, TTOs must have sufficient staff who have acquired 'competence and skills across a wide range of activities, including technology assessment, patent search, marketing, patent law, and intellectual property issues' as well as 'an appreciation of the specific science and industry associated with each particular invention'.[122] A number of TTOs, especially those outside the US, are relatively new and have

---

[116] Finn Valentin and Rasmus Lund Jensen, 'Effects on Academia-Industry Collaboration of Extending University Property Rights' (2007) 32 *The Journal of Technology Transfer* 251, 263, 264 Table 6, 264–65, 267 Table 9.

[117] ibid 272.

[118] ibid 274.

[119] Erika Färnstrand Damsgaard and Marie C Thursby, 'University Entrepreneurship and Professor Privilege' (2013) 22 *Industrial and Corporate Change* 183, 190.

[120] Heidrun C Hoppe and Emre Ozdenoren, 'Intermediation in Innovation' (2005) 23 *International Journal of Industrial Organization* 483, 487.

[121] ibid.

[122] Martin Kenney and Donald Patton, 'Reconsidering the Bayh-Dole Act and the Current University Invention Ownership Model' (2009) 38 *Research Policy* 1407, 1415.

only a few members of staff and thus lack personnel who have considerable experience in these activities. TTOs tend to suffer bureaucracy, which prevents them from making appropriate decisions in a timely manner,[123] whilst academic inventors usually have a good knowledge of the possible applications of the inventions and potential developers interested in them.[124] As a matter of fact, they can even refuse to disclose inventions to TTOs because the administration has no direct control or supervision over the way they work.[125] Accordingly, academic inventors may be in a better position to encourage technology transfer.

In view of the foregoing it is hard to deduce from patent law's purpose of encouraging innovation whether academic inventions should belong to universities or academic inventors.

B. Conflict of Interest in Scholarly Activities

Yet another rationale for favouring employer ownership of employee inventions made in industry, namely the unreasonable profits employee ownership would bring to inventors, equally applies in the case of academic inventions. The creation of inventions in academia similarly involves teamwork among researchers, the use of research facilities, funds provided by universities, and even external funding in many cases.[126] The mobility of researchers which is common in academia often makes it hard to determine who has contributed to the inventive concept of an invention.[127] Nevertheless, according to some anecdotes from academics in the US, the determination of inventorship can sometimes be rigged due to academic hierarchy whereby a 'powerful' professor who runs a laboratory claims the sole inventorship, often on the erroneous belief that only a laboratory manager is eligible for it 'as a matter of honor', despite the creative contribution of other researchers subordinate to the professor.[128] It is even more likely to cause misconduct among academics if the ownership of inventions is vested in them because it can drive them to engage in lucrative research projects during their working hours at the expense of research funds provided by universities or external funding bodies. If an employed academic researcher is allowed to place the ownership of an invention he has created at his own disposal, as the two senior academics

---

[123] ibid 1412.
[124] ibid 1411.
[125] ibid 1413, 1414.
[126] *University of Western Australia* (n 6) [14], (n 12) [121], [126].
[127] The appeal court in *University of Western Australia* observed that '[k]nowledge/information of varying degrees of significance to a research project of Dr Gray may have been generated before a particular researcher joined his team; may have been generated by a member of the team who was not an employee of … UWA; or may have been provided to a team member by way of scholarly exchange or assistance by a stranger to the project who was employed by another institution': *University of Western Australia* (n 12) [127].
[128] McSherry (n 49) 182–85.

in *Victoria University of Technology* tried to do, it would inevitably raise the following ethical question:

> [W]ould it be right ... for [him] to take advantage of his freedom to set research direction ..., to spend all his time on pursuing commercially valuable inventions, which he then turned to his own account without telling the university a thing about it?[129]

Such unethical behaviour of academics involves the question of 'conflict of interest', which 'exists when the researcher ... has a financial or other interest in an activity or business that may be in conflict with the performance of his university functions or obligations or his activities within the university'.[130] If the law provides that university researchers become the owners of academic inventions, some may compromise their professional judgement about conducting research and disseminating knowledge to protect the commercial value of inventions which they can exploit for financial gain.[131] If they owe fiduciary duties to universities, this will be a groundless concern since they are obliged to hand over the rights in the inventions to universities. However, most academics are unlikely to owe such duties because they do not occupy managerial positions as did the senior academics in *Victoria University of Technology*.

C. Legislation or IP Policies to Establish Universities' Ownership of Academic Inventions

In terms of eliminating such conflict of interest, it seems desirable to vest the ownership of academic inventions in universities rather than academics themselves. However, given French J's opinion in *University of Western Australia* that 'a duty to research does not carry with it a duty to invent',[132] such inventions do not belong to universities according to academics' employment contracts. Nor do those made by postgraduate students unless they enter into a specific contract with their universities to produce them.[133] Furthermore, the appeal court in that case did not favour UWA's submission that a duty to research implies a duty to invent 'at least in the applied sciences', pointing out that 'there are university researchers in the sciences who may carry out research without aiming for or achieving a patentable invention'.[134] Citing the academic freedom of university researchers, the same court held that their

> seeming freedom to choose the subject or line of research and the manner of its pursuit ... sit uneasily with employment notions such as the implied duty of an employee

---

[129] van Caenegem (n 22) 155.
[130] Monotti and Ricketson (n 32) para 9.84.
[131] ibid para 9.88.
[132] See text to n 10.
[133] *University of Western Australia* (n 6) [163].
[134] *University of Western Australia* (n 12) [124].

to obey all lawful and reasonable instructions of the employer within the scope of the employee's employment.[135]

Yet that court added that 'while our conclusion recognises a distinction between the ownership of employee inventions in universities and in private sector business entities, we should not be taken as suggesting that the solution reached ... is necessarily a desirable one in either case'.[136]

Although academics do not owe a general duty to invest since universities essentially differ from companies, it follows from the *University of Western Australia* decision that 'each researcher would be free to take his results with him if he moved to other employment'[137] even though a company employee is usually not allowed to do so. This distinction between university researchers and company employees cannot be justified just because the former enjoy academic freedom. In order to eliminate the conflict of interest academics may face and the inequality in the treatment of the rights in inventions made in academia and industry, it is necessary to adopt a legal framework whereby universities become the owner of inventions made by academics, including students and postdoctoral researchers, 'by or under legislation or ... by an express contractual régime appropriate to the circumstances of the individual case'.[138] In addition, universities should be allowed to promulgate an intellectual property policy to that effect. Although it remains to be proved empirically whether it will really encourage technology transfer if universities become the owner of academic inventions, such a framework would let university TTOs gain necessary expertise and experience in it. However, this is not to say that the framework imposes a general duty to invent on academics, since it is inconsistent with their freedom to choose research areas as well as the non-commercial nature of universities. The framework only allows universities to acquire inventions made incidentally in the course of the research conducted by academics and thus does not threaten such freedom they have.

Meanwhile, the following two points the courts in *University of Western Australia* cited to oppose vesting the ownership of academic inventions in universities do not provide a strong basis for their argument. First, they argued that a duty of confidentiality imposed on academics to protect the patentability of such inventions would inhibit not only academic collaboration between research institutions but the mobility of researchers.[139] Such a duty also arises from a duty of fidelity, or good faith, which employees generally owe to their employers.[140] However, universities should be presumed to implicitly authorise academics to disclose confidential information among those participating in research projects because it is necessary for conducting research, which is the principal mission of

---

[135] ibid [186].

[136] ibid [211].

[137] William Cornish, David Llewelyn and Tanya Aplin, *Intellectual Property: Patents, Copyright, Trade Marks and Allied Rights*, 8th edn (London, Sweet & Maxwell, 2013) para 7-05.

[138] *University of Western Australia* (n 12) [211].

[139] See text to nn 15, 16.

[140] *Faccenda Chicken Ltd v Fowler* [1986] 1 All ER 617, 625. This point was not discussed by the Australian courts: *University of Western Australia* (n 12) [149].

universities. Yet another problem arises when academics publish research results publicly, destroying the patentability of inventions they have made. This point will be discussed later.

Second, the courts also warned that researchers would face difficulties in securing research funding from outside their universities or negotiating collaborative arrangements with other research institutes if it is provided that universities become the owner of inventions made by academics.[141] However, that is no reason to allow researchers to keep the fruits of research to themselves since the courts assumed that those funding bodies and/or external organisations would claim the rights in the inventions. The conclusion on who own academic inventions as between universities and academics is unlikely to affect the possibility of getting external funding and collaboration to a great degree because it is only the default position to be modified by negotiation where there are third parties who have interests in the inventions. Rather the success in getting them should depend chiefly on the resourcefulness of persons who run laboratories and the nature of research projects.

D. Academic Freedom to Publish and the Need for Academic Grace Period

If inventions made by academics belong to universities, the inventors are obliged not to destroy their patentability in theory.[142] However, that obligation imperils their freedom to publish research results. Whilst some econometrics studies found that patenting could boost the number of relevant publications by academics,[143] the majority of academic researchers surveyed in an empirical study reported that they had experienced delays in publication due to patenting.[144] Since the timing of publication matters in the reward system of academia as mentioned earlier,[145] the latter finding is enough to show that academics' freedom to publish is curtailed because of the need to protect the patentability of inventions.

---

[141] See text to nn 17, 18. They found that Dr Gray's team had acted like 'entrepreneurs' in securing funding for their research from outside the university: *University of Western Australia* (n 6) [1366], (n 12) [202].

[142] See text to n 14.

[143] Kira R Fabrizio and Alberto Di Minin, 'Commercializing the Laboratory: Faculty Patenting and the Open Science Environment' (2008) 37 *Research Policy* 914, 924–25 Table 7; Gustavo Crespi and others, 'The Impact of Academic Patenting on University Research and its Transfer' (2011) 40 *Research Policy* 55, 61–62 Fig 1, 65. However, the latter study also suggests that a very high level of patenting (about 10 patents or more) can rather cause a decrease in the number of academic publications because academics who focus on making many patentable inventions may be distracted from publishing their research results.

[144] Aldo Geuna and Lionel JJ Nesta, 'University Patenting and its Effects on Academic Research: The Emerging European Evidence' (2006) 35 *Research Policy* 790, 797 Fig 1.

[145] See text to nn 31, 32.

Patent laws in some countries such as the US,[146] Canada,[147] Australia,[148] China,[149] the Republic of Korea[150] and Japan[151] have a provision for a general grace period that protects the patentability of inventions against publication for a year or less. An econometrics study has shown that such a provision accelerates the disclosure of knowledge by academic inventors.[152] Meanwhile, European countries generally lack a broad grace period provision. Regulations at many UK universities restrict public disclosure of inventions made by the staff for varying periods before filing patent applications.[153] The German Act on Employees' Inventions requires university employees to give their employers at least two months' notice when they publish inventions they have made in the course of teaching and research.[154]

An internationally harmonised academic grace period, whereby the patentability of academic inventions is maintained for a limited time after publication by academics, needs to be introduced to ensure their freedom to publish. However, international frameworks such as the World Intellectual Property Organization (WIPO) and the European Patent Office (EPO) have failed to adopt a harmonised grace period because of the lack of consensus among member states.[155] At present delays in scientific publication are inevitable even in countries where a grace period is put into effect because disclosure in such countries will destroy the patentability of academic inventions in those without a corresponding system.[156]

E. Compensation and Royalties to Be Paid to Academic Inventors

Although employers in common law countries are not required to pay compensation for employee inventions they claim in general, universities are in theory required to pay it to academic inventors. It is because inventions made by academics, who do not owe a duty to invent in general, are not included in the fruits of labour that naturally belong to universities under the contract of employment. Academics receive their basic salaries in return for their commitment to

---

[146] 35 USC § 102(b)(1) (2012).
[147] Patent Act, s 28.2(1)(a).
[148] Patents Act 1990, s 24(1).
[149] Patent Law, art 24.
[150] Patent Act, art 30.
[151] Patent Act (as amended up to Act No 55 of 2015), art 30.
[152] Chiara Franzoni and Giuseppe Scellato, 'The Grace Period in International Patent Law and its Effect on the Timing of Disclosure' (2010) 39 *Research Policy* 200, 206–07 Table 5.
[153] Stallberg (n 112) 521–26.
[154] Act on Employees' Inventions, s 42(1).
[155] Monotti and Ricketson (n 32) paras 6.86–6.91.
[156] ibid para 6.105; Franzoni and Scellato (n 152) 207 Table 6.

research and other relevant tasks, including teaching and administrative duties, whilst inventions that may be produced in the course of their research are usually left out of consideration in the employment contract because they do not usually owe a duty to invent contractually. In theory the amount of additional compensation they receive should be on the same level with that to be paid for the transfer of incidental inventions made by industrial employees, which similarly do not *ab initio* belong to employers according to the employment contracts.[157]

Under the US Bayh-Dole Act universities are required to share with inventors royalties earned from licensing inventions[158] and in most cases academic inventors receive between 25 per cent and 35 per cent of royalties.[159] Intellectual property policies at major UK universities also allow academic inventors to share in revenues gained from inventions made by them in the form of royalties.[160] Universities may want to retain prominent scholars by offering them handsome royalties. Given that most inventions made in academia are only in embryonic stages, such schemes may also serve to secure the cooperation of academic inventors in developing them, which often requires their tacit knowledge on the inventions. According to persons in charge of TTOs at 62 research universities in the US, nearly 70 per cent of inventions licensed by them in fiscal years between 1991 and 1995 required the cooperation of the inventors in further development.[161] However, it is open to question whether academics may earn a lot from royalties because their main duty is to do research, not to develop inventions. Although they may contribute to the development of inventions to the extent that it is beneficial to their research, royalties should not be paid to them in principle because the payment would involve the issue of the conflict of interest.

---

[157] See ch 5.
[158] 35 USC § 202(c)(7)(B) (2012).
[159] Nelsen (n 74) 453.
[160] Stallberg (n 112) 511–19.
[161] Richard Jensen and Marie Thursby, 'Proofs and Prototypes for Sale: The Licensing of University Inventions' (2001) 91 *American Economic Review* 240, 242–43 Table 1.

9

Civil Law Countries

According to the fundamental principle in employment law that employers are naturally entitled to receive the fruits of labour expended by employees, employee inventions, apart from those made in academia, should *ab initio* belong to their employers. Nevertheless, on the assumption that only natural persons can create inventions ('inventor principle'), it is presumed under the law in some civil law countries that independently of employment contracts the ownership of inventions is initially vested in employees who have created them. In theory, employers in these countries do not acquire the ownership of employee inventions unless they claim it in a manner prescribed in a statute or the employees agree to transfer it to the employers. Countries whose current statutes presumably adopt the 'inventor principle' include the following: Austria,[1] Germany,[2] Nordic countries (Norway,[3] Sweden,[4] Finland[5] and Denmark[6]), Hungary,[7] the Czech Republic,[8] Slovakia,[9] Slovenia,[10] Turkey,[11] the Republic of Korea[12] and Japan[13] (yet the principle was modified by the amendment to the Japanese Patent Act in 2015 as discussed below).

The statutes in the above countries provide that under certain conditions those employers must offer additional compensation for employee inventions they acquire as the inventors' legal successor in title. Some Finnish lawyers argue that 'a system according to which the rights originally accrue to an individual … inventor is the best means of guaranteeing a fair balance of interests and bargaining in the context of employment relationships'.[14] The German legislature assumed

---

[1] Patent Act (Federal Law Gazette 259/1970), ss 6(1), 7, 12(1).

[2] Act on Employees' Inventions, ss 5–7.

[3] Law on Employees' Inventions (Act No 21 of 17 April 1970), ss 4(1), 5, 6(1).

[4] Act on the Right to Inventions by Employees (1949:345), ss 3(1), 4, 5(1).

[5] Act on the Right in Employee Inventions 29.12.1967/656, arts 4(1), 5, 6(1).

[6] Consolidated Act on Employees' Inventions (Consolidated Act No 131 of 18 March 1986), ss 5, 6, 7(1).

[7] Act XXXIII of 1995 on the Protection of Inventions by Patents, arts 10(1), 11(1)(2).

[8] Law No 527/1990 of 27 November 1990 on Inventions and Rationalisation Proposals, s 9(1)–(3).

[9] Act No 435/2001 Coll on Patents, Supplementary Protection Certificates and on Amendment of Some Acts, art 11(1)–(3).

[10] Job-Related Inventions Act of 25 July 1995, arts 5, 6, 8(1).

[11] Law on Industrial Property No 6769, art 115.

[12] Invention Promotion Act (Act No 4757 of 24 March 1994), art 10(1)(3).

[13] Patent Act (Act No 121 of 1959, as amended up to Act No 36 of 2014), art 35(1)(2).

[14] Niklas Bruun and others, 'Finland Group Report Q 183: Employers' Rights to Intellectual Property' (39th World Intellectual Property Congress, AIPPI, Geneva, June 2004) 6, aippi.org/wp-content/uploads/committees/183/GR183finland.pdf.

that their Act on Employees' Inventions was 'social legislation intended to protect the inventive employee', not just 'to promote and foster the economic development of Germany by presenting to creative employees incentives to invent'.[15] Despite the conclusion in Part I of this book that inventor remuneration is unlikely to boost the creation of inventions, it appears that employers in the above countries are always required to offer additional compensation to employee inventors in theory when they acquire employee inventions. However, the legal provisions in Austria,[16] Norway,[17] Sweden[18] and Denmark[19] state that additional compensation must be paid only in exceptional cases where inventions transferred to employers turn out to be so valuable that employees' salaries and benefits stipulated in the employment contracts cannot be presumed to cover the payment for such inventions.[20] This suggests that the 'inventor principle' has not been applied rigidly in these countries.

Meanwhile, according to the current statutes in other civil law countries that presumably do not adopt the 'inventor principle', such as France,[21] Italy,[22] the Netherlands,[23] Spain,[24] Portugal,[25] Poland,[26] Russia,[27] China (mainland),[28] Taiwan,[29] Indonesia,[30] Malaysia,[31] Mexico,[32] Brazil[33] and Argentina,[34] employers acquire the ownership of employee inventions *ab initio* without declaring their intent to claim it or making a special agreement to that effect with employee inventors. If there are legal provisions for compensation for employee inventions in these countries, the most plausible explanation may be that they are intended to give employee inventors an incentive to invent. However, at present there is no

---

[15] James W Brennan, 'The Developing Law of German Employee Inventions' (1962) 6 *The Patent, Trademark and Copyright Journal of Research and Education* 41, 42 (citations omitted).

[16] Patent Act (Federal Law Gazette 259/1970), s 8(2).

[17] Law on Employees' Inventions (Act No 21 of 17 April 1970), s 7(1).

[18] Act on the Right to Inventions by Employees (1949:345), s 6(2).

[19] Consolidated Act on Employees' Inventions (Consolidated Act No 131 of 18 March 1986), s 8(1).

[20] Yet according to the latest collective agreement reached in 2015, Swedish unionised employees shall receive a lump sum payment of at least 0.5 statutory price basic amount (kr22,150 ≒ €2,400, as of 2016) for an employee invention acquired by their employers, or 1 statutory price basic amount (kr44,300 ≒ €4,800, as above) where the invention has considerable commercial importance to them: Agreement concerning the Rights to Employee Inventions between Swedish Enterprise and PTK, s 4(2). See also text to ch 1, n 22.

[21] Intellectual Property Code, art L611-7(1).

[22] Industrial Property Code (Legislative Decree No 30 of 10 February 2005), art 64(1).

[23] Patent Act 1995 (Act of 15 December 1994), art 12(1).

[24] Law No 24/2015 of 24 July on Patents, art 15(1).

[25] Industrial Property Code (as amended up to Law No 46/2011 of 24 June 2011), art 59(1).

[26] Act of 30 June 2000 Industrial Property Law (as amended up to Act of 24 July 2015), art 11(3).

[27] Civil Code, art 1370(3).

[28] Patent Law, art 6(1).

[29] Patent Act, art 7(1).

[30] Law on Patents No 13 of 2016, art 12(1).

[31] Patents Act 1983, s 20(1).

[32] Law of Industrial Property, art 14; Federal Labor Law, art 163(2).

[33] Law No 9279 of 14 May 1996 (Industrial Property Law), art 88.

[34] Law on Patents and Utility Models (Law No 24,481 of 30 March 1995, as amended by Law No 24,572 of 28 September 1995), art 10a).

such legal provision in Switzerland.[35] Romania, whose patent law used to require the payment of additional compensation for employee inventions,[36] passed a special law in 2014 so that employers in that country now acquire employee inventions without paying additional compensation.[37] Since it is clear from the analysis in Part I of this book that incentive schemes for employee inventors are unlikely to be effective, there is no need to further examine the relevant laws in these countries.

In this chapter I will discuss the rationale for additional compensation to employee inventors under the German Act on Employees' Inventions, and the latest amendment to the Japanese patent law in 2015 thereafter, to question the validity of the 'inventor principle' which purportedly requires the payment of additional compensation for employee inventions.

I. Germany

The 'inventor principle' (*Erfinderprinzip*) in Germany holds that application for a patent on an invention must be made by either its inventor, a natural person who has made creative contribution to the invention, or one who has derived its ownership from him.[38] It follows from this principle that employers are required to offer additional compensation for the right to patent employee inventions which is initially vested in employee inventors in theory. However, it was not originally axiomatic that the right to patent an invention originates from a natural person who has made it. Instead, the German patent system prior to 1936 was operated on the basis of 'application principle' (*Anmeldeprinzip*) so that a patent 'was granted not only to the inventor but also to the first applicant who offered to the public the fruits of the inventive activity of the inventor'.[39] Although German courts under 'application principle' distinguished the right in an invention from the patent right in the strict sense of the word, an employer who agreed with an employee in advance on the transfer of the former right could obtain it the instant he made an invention, and subsequently file an application for a patent without naming him as its inventor.[40] Furthermore, German courts introduced the concept of 'company inventions' (*Betriebserfindung*) in around 1920, where a company itself was regarded as an inventor on condition that 'so much of the employer's suggestion, know-how, prior work in the field of special tools [we]re used that the completion

[35] Yet employers must pay remuneration for incidental inventions they claim: Code of Obligation of 30 March 1911, art 332.
[36] Patent Law No 64/1991 (as amended up to Law No 28/2007), art 5(1)a.
[37] Yet employers must pay remuneration for incidental inventions they claim: Law No 83/2014 on Employees' Inventions, arts 3, 5–7.
[38] Patentgesetz vom 5 Mai 1936 (RGBl II S 117), s 3 (the current Patent Act, s 6); Brennan (n 15) 46.
[39] Brennan (n 15) 43 (citation omitted).
[40] ibid.

of the invention require[d] no more than the usual professional skill', or that 'it [wa]s impossible to determine which of several employees was the inventor'.[41] Thus, German jurisprudence before 1936 did not fully recognise employees' right in inventions they made.

The German legislature at the turn of the twentieth century already expressed the concern that the indifference toward the rights of employee inventors would lead to the 'disruption of the relations between employer and employee and the loss of invention to Germany'.[42] In line with the recommendation that a patent should be applied for in the name of the true inventor like in the US,[43] the 1936 Patent Act, which replaced 'application principle' with 'inventor principle', guaranteed inventors' moral right to be named as such.[44] Nevertheless, some German courts at that time held that the concept of 'company inventions' still survived.[45] Meanwhile, the Austrian Patent Act as amended in 1925, which came into effect prior to the German occupation of Austria in 1938, contained advanced provisions on compensation to employee inventors.[46] Since Germany attempted to harmonise legislation in its territory including Austria, 'it is fairly safe to assume that the provisions of the Austrian Patents Act ... had a marked influence on the development of German law' on this specific issue.[47] Subsequent to a series of ordinances issued by the wartime German government between 1942 and 1944 that provided for the payment of reasonable compensation to employee inventors, a basis for the calculation of its amount and the procedures both employers and employees must follow when employee inventions were made, the post-war Federal Republic of Germany passed the current Act on Employees' Inventions in 1957, which has adopted a system modelled after that implemented by the wartime ordinances.[48] The concept of 'company inventions' was finally repudiated in section 4 of the new Act, according to which inventions made by German employees are now categorised either as 'service inventions' (*Diensterfindungen*), namely 'those made during the term of employment which: (i) either resulted from the employee's tasks in the private enterprise ... , (ii) or are essentially based upon the experience or activities of the enterprise', or 'free inventions' (*freie Erfindungen*), namely those other than service inventions.[49]

The historical account of the German law above shows that German employees were not always recognised as the original owner of employee inventions before

---

[41] ibid 45 (citation omitted).

[42] ibid 44.

[43] ibid. See also text to ch 3, nn 218, 219.

[44] Patentgesetz vom 5 Mai 1936 (RGBl II S 117), s 36(1) (the current Patent Act, s 63(1)). See also text to ch 3, n 217.

[45] Brennan (n 15) 46 (citation omitted).

[46] Federal Law of 2 July 1925 on the Amendment and Supplement of the Provisions of the Patent Act (Patent Act Amendment 1925, Federal Law Gazette 219/1925), ss 5(a)–(o).

[47] Frederick Neumeyer, 'Employees' Rights in Their Inventions: A Comparison of National Laws' (1962) 44 *Journal of the Patent Office Society* 674, 679.

[48] ibid 698; Brennan (n 15) 47.

[49] Act on Employees' Inventions, s 4(1)–(3); Neumeyer (n 47) 699.

the Act on Employees' Inventions took effect in 1957; not only before 1936, when 'application principle' governed the German patent system, but also from that time on, when some courts still approved the concept of 'company inventions'. Germany repudiated the 'application principle' because of the concern that it would adversely affect the morale of employee inventors if their creative contribution to the inventions would go unnoticed. However, it is questionable whether German policy makers actually intended to secure for employee inventors the property rights in inventions they have made in order to maintain their morale. For example, on the assumption that 'inventions of workforce' would 'primarily serve armour' and boost national economy,[50] the 1942 ordinance adopted the principle that in return for reasonable compensation '[e]very member of a company [was] obliged to make available to the employer inventions he [had] made insofar as they [had] arisen from his work in the company'.[51] Today, according to the amendment to the Act on Employees' Inventions in 2009, an employer automatically acquires the ownership of a service invention even if the employer does not claim it with the lapse of four months after the receipt of the notification of the invention from its inventor.[52] This simplification of the Act has practically set forth the principle that employers exercise the property rights in employee inventions. Viewed in this light, the German legislature is unlikely to have intended that employee inventors should retain the ownership of service inventions as an essential prerequisite to building their morale.

On the basis of the 'inventor principle' the German legislature adopted 'monopoly theory' (*Monopoltheorie*) as the rationale for additional compensation to be received by employee inventors under the Act on Employees' Inventions.[53] It holds that an employee inventor should share in the monopoly profits attributable to a service invention claimed by his employer since he is not contractually obliged to let his employer acquire the monopoly power in the market.[54] It claims that employee inventors should receive additional compensation for the transfer of a service invention in the same way as those who have made a free invention are able to enter into an agreement to share in the benefits of the invention on equal terms with their employers in theory.[55] However, the Guidelines specifying the methods for the calculation of 'reasonable compensation' substantially deviate from the theory.[56] According to the licence analogy, which is the most commonly

---

[50] Verordnung über die Behandlung von Erfindungen von Gefolgschaftsmitgliedern vom 12 Juli 1942 (RGBl I S 466) [Ordinance on the Treatment of Inventions of Workers], preamble.

[51] Ordinance on the Treatment of Inventions of Workers, s 2.

[52] Act on Employees' Inventions, s 6(2).

[53] Brennan (n 15) 48.

[54] Helga Knauer, *Möglichkeiten und Nutzen einer Vereinheitlichung des Arbeitnehmererfinderrechts in der Europäischen Union und Schlussfolgerungen für die diesbezügliche deutsche Gesetzgebung* [Possibilities and Benefits of the Harmonisation of Employee Invention Law in the European Union and the Implications for the Related German Legislation] (München, Herbert Utz, 2007) 24.

[55] ibid 184.

[56] ibid.

used method for the calculation, when a service invention has contributed to 'high turnover', the applicable royalty rate is reduced on a sliding scale according to the turnover[57] on the assumption that 'efforts from the sphere of the employer (reputation of the company, advertisement, sales management, etc) are increasingly decisive for high turnovers'.[58] Besides, compensation due to the employee inventor is further reduced by 'share factor',[59] in which his contribution to the invention is discounted in view of various benefits and resources he has received from his employer in the process of making it[60] so that '[s]enior inventors in the research and development areas usually receive ... between 7% ... and 10%' of the applicable royalty rate.[61] This amount is far less than the monopoly profits that they could have gained if they had licensed the invention to a third party in theory.

By contrast, 'special benefit theory' (*Sonderleistungstheorie*) holds that employee inventors receive additional compensation because they have conferred a special benefit on their employers when they have made a patentable invention.[62] Whilst a patentable invention itself may be regarded as a special benefit to employers ('result-based special benefit theory'),[63] it may be argued instead that there is no special benefit that triggers the additional compensation to employee inventors unless they do more than contractually agreed work quantitatively or qualitatively ('activity-based special benefit theory').[64] Although the legislature 'consciously argued against' the 'special benefit theory',[65] it would appear that the theory can also account for the current Act on Employees' Inventions by virtue of the fact that the amount of 'reasonable compensation' depends, inter alia, on the value of the invention, that is to say on the portion attributable to the inventor's contribution.[66] It may be said that that amount is the worth of an employee inventor's performance which is regarded as a special benefit conferred on his employer.[67] However, according to the view that employers' special benefit should be recognised in terms of employees' activity rather than its result, it is reasonable to conclude that employers are not required to pay additional compensation to employees working in R&D departments because it is their contractual duty to

---

[57] Guidelines for the Remuneration of Employees' Inventions in Private Employment, nos 6, 11.

[58] Michael Trimborn, *Employees' Inventions in Germany: A Handbook for International Businesses* (Alphen aan den Rijn, Kluwer Law International, 2009) para 161.

[59] Guidelines for the Remuneration of Employees' Inventions in Private Employment, nos 30–33, 37, 39.

[60] Trimborn (n 58) para 175. Considered here 'are the facts that the object of the invention is set on the grounds of his employment, that he receives intellectual and material aid for the solution, and that he does not become active at his own economic risk but is economically and socially secured by continuous payments of salary'.

[61] ibid para 180.

[62] Knauer (n 54) 25.

[63] ibid.

[64] ibid 26.

[65] Trimborn (n 58) para 125.

[66] Act on Employees' Inventions, s 9(2); Knauer (n 54) 26.

[67] Knauer (n 54) 184.

solve a given technical problem and thus the resultant inventions are not 'special benefit' to their employers.[68]

In sum, despite the 'inventor principle', the German legislature is unlikely to intend that employee inventors should exercise the property rights in employee inventions. In addition, the actual calculation of compensation according to the Guidelines substantially deviates from the 'monopoly theory' adopted by the legislature. The rationale for compensation to employee inventors is highly debatable according to the '(activity-based) special benefit theory', which arguably has some validity. The 'inventor principle' has been virtually undermined under the current Act on Employees' Inventions, which shakes the assumption that the payment of compensation for employee inventions is required as a fixed principle in Germany.

II. Japan

A legal provision regarding the ownership of employee inventions in Japan first appeared in the Patent Act enacted in 1909 according to which the right to patent an invention made in the course of an employee's duties was vested in his employer in principle.[69] By contrast, according to the Patent Act enacted in 1921, that right originally accrued to the employee himself, whilst his employer was entitled to a non-exclusive licence on the patent obtained by him.[70] The 1921 Act adopted the 'inventor principle', which presumed that only a natural person capable of making an invention could apply for a patent, but allowed an employer to exploit the invention without paying compensation in view of the employer's contribution to the invention.[71] The Act also provided that an employee had the right to receive 'reasonable remuneration' where he transferred his right to obtain a patent or the obtained patent to his employer in accordance with a contract or workplace regulations.[72]

These basic rules remained almost intact in the Patent Act enacted in 1959,[73] and there were few, if any, disputes over the remuneration for employee inventions until around 2000.[74] However, the course of things changed when the

---

[68] ibid 26.

[69] Patent Act (Act No 23 of 1909), art 3(1).

[70] Patent Act (Act No 96 of 1921), art 14(2).

[71] Japan Patent Office, 'Shokumu hatsumei kitei no rekishi-teki hensen ni kakaru sankō shiryō' [The Background Information on the Historical Changes of the Provision for Employee Inventions] (30 April 2014) 3–4 (citations omitted), www.jpo.go.jp/shiryou/toushin/shingikai/pdf/newtokkyo_shiryou004/04.pdf.

[72] Patent Act (Act No 96 of 1921), art 14(3).

[73] Patent Act (Act No 121 of 1959, as amended up to Act No 36 of 2014), art 35(1)(3).

[74] Minoru Takeda, 'Shokumu hatsumei seido no arikata' [The State of the Employee Invention System] in Institute of Intellectual Property, *Kigyō-tō ni okeru tokkyo-hō dai 35-jō no seido un'yō ni kakaru kadai oyobi sono kaiketsu hōhō ni kansuru chōsa kenkyū hōkoku-sho: heisei 25-nendo tokkyo-chō sangyō zaisan-ken seido mondai chōsa kenkyū hōkoku-sho* [A Report of Investigation and Research

Supreme Court of Japan held in 2003 that an employer was obliged to meet the difference between 'reasonable remuneration' determined according to the Patent Act and the amount to be paid according to its workplace regulations which fell short of that standard specified in the Act (the *Olympus* case).[75] Furthermore, a Tokyo District Court decision in 2004 ordered a company to pay ¥20 billion (then over £10.3 million) to its ex-employee who had invented the blue Light-Emitting Diode during his tenure (the *Blue LED* case).[76] These decisions made Japanese policy-makers recognise the need to clarify how 'reasonable remuneration' would be determined. According to the Act as amended in 2004, the remuneration was determined according to the relevant terms in a contract, workplace regulations or other stipulation, as long as its payment would not be regarded as unreasonable in the light of the relevant circumstances such as how the negotiation between the parties took place, how those terms were disclosed and how the employee's opinions were heard.[77] Otherwise, the amount was to be fixed in consideration of such factors as the employer's benefits gained from the invention, share of the expenses, contribution to the invention and treatment of the inventor.[78] In short, the new provision approved the amount determined through appropriate procedures stipulated in contracts or workplace regulations in principle, and thus courts were expected to decide the amount for the parties concerned only when the procedures were unfair to employee inventors or when there were no established procedures whatsoever.[79]

Although few lawsuits had been filed over employee inventions under the Act as amended in 2004, the Patent System Subcommittee, an advisory body to the Minister of Economy, Trade and Industry of Japan, discussed further amendment to the Act in 2014 on the assumption that the Act still did not consider the reality of innovation taking place in companies.[80] The discussion focused on two main problems: (1) whether the right to patent employee inventions is initially vested in their employers; and (2) whether the law should oblige employers to offer financial incentives to employee inventors.

---

on the Problems of Implementing Article 35 of the Patent Act in Companies etc. and Their Solutions: Japan Patent Office Reports of Investigation and Research on the Issues concerning the Industrial Property Right System, the 2013 Fiscal Year] (February 2014) 437, www.jpo.go.jp/shiryou/toushin/kenkyukai/pdf/syokumu_hatsumei/honpen.pdf.

[75] Supreme Court, judgment on 22 April 2003, 57 *Minshū* 477.

[76] Tokyo District Court, judgment on 30 January 2004, 1852 *Hanrei jihō* 36.

[77] Patent Act (as amended up to Act No 79 of 2004), art 35(4).

[78] ibid art 35(5).

[79] A similar provision was enacted in the Republic of Korea in 2006 and was amended in 2013 to stipulate procedures an employer must follow: Invention Promotion Act (as amended up to Act No 11661 of 22 March 2013), art 15(2); Invention Promotion Act (as amended up to Act No 11960 of 30 July 2013), art 15(2)–(4)(6).

[80] Patent System Subcommittee, (Intellectual Property Committee of the Industrial Structure Council, hereinafter omitted), *Wagakuni no inobēshon sokushin oyobi kokusai-tekina seido chōwa no tame no chiteki zaisan seido no minaoshi ni mukete* [Recommendations for Reforming the Intellectual Property System to Facilitate Innovation in Japan and Achieve International Harmonisation] (January 2015) 2, www.jpo.go.jp/shiryou/toushin/toushintou/pdf/innovation_patent/houkokusho.pdf.

Delegates from the industrial circles claimed that the law should give employers the right to patent such inventions, not just the automatic right to a non-exclusive licence, on the premise that employers could make the most of the patents as business assets only if they could exploit or dispose of them on their own.[81] They pointed out that an employer might fail to secure the rights in an employee invention should the employee inventor sign them away to a third party,[82] and that in the case of joint research an employee inventor could not transfer his share in the patent to his employer if co-inventors from other companies or research institutions should not consent to it.[83] They argued that these problems would not arise if employee inventions should *ab initio* belong to employers. The delegates also expressed their concern that if 'reasonable remuneration' must be paid for the transfer of the inventions initially owned by employee inventors, employers could face an enormous and unforeseeable amount of compensation claim because the amount should in theory correspond to profits brought by these inventions.[84] Meanwhile, the delegates claimed that employers should not be compelled by law to offer financial incentives to named inventors, citing the need to reward not only individuals but project teams as a whole, sometimes with non-pecuniary benefits.[85] They pointed out that employers were often unable to reward employees who greatly boosted company profits, such as those working in the production and marketing departments, because employers must set aside funds for the mandatory compensation to named inventors.[86] They also argued that the priorities would be grossly wrong if companies facing bankruptcy would still be required to offer financial incentives to employee inventors.[87]

Arguing against changing the rule on the ownership of employee inventions in the Act, a committee member from the largest national trade union centre said that the ownership vested in employee inventors would serve as an incentive to invent.[88] A competent official in the Japan Patent Office pointed out that, apart from some large companies, the vast majority of small and medium businesses did not find it necessary to change the statutory rule.[89] The official also expressed his

[81] Japan Patent Office, *Minutes of the 3rd Meeting of the Patent System Subcommittee* (14 April 2014) 5 (comment by Tsuneaki Hagiwara), www.jpo.go.jp/shiryou/toushin/shingikai/pdf/tokkyo_seido_menu/newtokkyo_003.pdf.
[82] Patent System Subcommittee (n 80) 3.
[83] ibid.
[84] Japan Patent Office, *Minutes of the 3rd Meeting* (n 81) 6 (comment by Tsuneaki Hagiwara).
[85] ibid 10 (comment by Tsuneaki Hagiwara).
[86] ibid 9–10 (comment by Tsuneaki Hagiwara).
[87] Japan Patent Office, *Minutes of the 5th Meeting of the Patent System Subcommittee* (14 May 2014) 23 (comment by Yoichi Okumura), www.jpo.go.jp/shiryou/toushin/shingikai/pdf/tokkyo_seido_menu/newtokkyo_005.pdf.
[88] Japan Patent Office, *Minutes of the 3rd Meeting* (n 81) 33 (comment by Yumiko Doi); Japan Patent Office, *Minutes of the 6th Meeting of the Patent System Subcommittee* (29 May 2014) 20 (comment by Yumiko Doi), www.jpo.go.jp/shiryou/toushin/shingikai/pdf/tokkyo_seido_menu/newtokkyo_006.pdf.
[89] Japan Patent Office, *Minutes of the 7th Meeting of the Patent System Subcommittee* (18 June 2014) 6, 10, 11, 14 (comment by Masato Yamada), www.jpo.go.jp/shiryou/toushin/shingikai/pdf/tokkyo_seido_menu/newtokkyo_007.pdf.

concern that if the ownership should automatically shift to their employers as a fixed rule, it could trigger numerous compensation claims by employee inventors working for such businesses, most of which have not specified their policy about compensation for employee inventions in contracts or workplace regulations.[90] University researchers requested that even if employers should become the initial owner of employee inventions in principle, those made by academics should be treated differently because of the broad discretion they are given in carrying out their research.[91] They also pointed out that universities would not be able to bear high administration costs should they be required to manage all the inventions made by academics.[92] Regarding incentives for employee inventors, some committee members demanded that the amendment should not sacrifice the benefits of workers,[93] and that the amendment should not convey the impression that Japan would make light of employee inventors when many countries are trying to attract inventive talents from all over the world.[94] Finally, on the understanding that the Japanese Patent Act was intended to give both employers and employees incentives for encouraging innovation,[95] the committee members agreed that this issue should not be left to the complete discretion of employers.[96]

The Patent Act as amended in 2015 allows employers, including universities, to claim the initial ownership of employee inventions with a proviso that they offer some economic incentives to employee inventors where they obtain the rights in employee inventions. The essential feature of the new provision is twofold. First, the right to patent an invention made in the course of an employee's duties is vested in his employer the instant it has been made, on condition that it has been provided for beforehand in a contract, workplace regulations or other stipulation;[97] otherwise the initial ownership of the invention rests with the employee inventor as before the amendment to the Act. Second, an employee has the right to receive 'a reasonable amount of money or other economic benefits' if his employer obtains the rights in the invention whether before or after it has been made.[98] The new provision has replaced the former term 'reasonable remuneration' to

---

[90] Japan Patent Office, *Minutes of the 9th Meeting of the Patent System Subcommittee* (17 October 2014) 8-9 (comment by Takeshi Nakano), www.jpo.go.jp/shiryou/toushin/shingikai/pdf/tokkyo_seido_menu/newtokkyo_009.pdf; Japan Patent Office, *Minutes of the 10th Meeting of the Patent System Subcommittee* (19 November 2014) 32 (comment by Takeshi Nakano), www.jpo.go.jp/shiryou/toushin/shingikai/pdf/tokkyo_seido_menu/newtokkyo_010.pdf.

[91] Japan Patent Office, *Minutes of the 9th Meeting* (n 90) 10 (comment by Kaori Iida).

[92] ibid 14 (comment by Takehiko Kitamori).

[93] Japan Patent Office, *Minutes of the 7th Meeting* (n 89) 29 (comment by Yumiko Doi); 32 (comment by Kazumi Miyajima); 34 (comment by Yuichiro Mizumachi).

[94] Japan Patent Office, *Minutes of the 6th Meeting* (n 88) 25 (comment by Takehiko Kitamori); 30–32 (comment by Michio Tsuchida); 33 (comment by Kazumi Miyajima).

[95] Japan Patent Office, *Minutes of the 4th Meeting of the Patent System Subcommittee* (30 April 2014) 28 (comment by Tetsuya Obuchi, Chair), www.jpo.go.jp/shiryou/toushin/shingikai/pdf/tokkyo_seido_menu/newtokkyo_004.pdf.

[96] Patent System Subcommittee (n 80) 3.

[97] Patent Act (as amended up to Act No 55 of 2015), art 35(3).

[98] ibid, art 35(4).

make it clear that what employees receive is not the payment for the transfer of the rights in inventions but incentives for them whether money or other economic benefits.[99] The 'economic benefits' offered to employees shall be determined in basically the same way as the amount of 'reasonable remuneration' was determined under the Act as amended in 2004,[100] but 'for the purpose of encouraging the creation of inventions' the Minister of Economy, Trade and Industry shall issue Guidelines on what both parties are expected to consider in the negotiation to determine those economic benefits.[101] According to the Guidelines, 'other economic benefits' include the following: to afford an opportunity to study abroad at the employer's expense; to grant stock options; to give a promotion and an increase in salary; to give more paid holidays than the employee is entitled to; and to grant an exclusive or non-exclusive licence to use the patent on the employee invention.[102] However, something without economic value, such as a certificate of commendation, and what employers offer regardless of the creation of the invention, are not regarded as 'economic benefits' employers are required to offer under the amended Act.[103]

It is important to note that the amended Act has not totally replaced the 'inventor principle' adopted in Japan since 1921. Although the opinion offered by the Subcommittee reads as if employers would own employee inventions as a rule under the amended Act,[104] the Act still provides that employee inventions do not *ab initio* belong to employers unless 'reasonable ... economic benefits' offered to employee inventors are specified in contracts or workplace regulations in advance. The amendment has thus created quite a unique system, where employee inventions initially belong to employers in some cases, whilst employees in the other. This is likely to cause serious confusion in practice.[105] Under the amended Act those who are going to have an interest in employee inventions still need to check if there is a clause on their ownership in contracts between employers and employees or workplace regulations. It should also be added that the Subcommittee put aside the issue of the ownership of inventions made by university researchers. To introduce a uniform policy on the ownership of academic inventions Japanese policy-makers will need to further discuss the relevant issues mentioned earlier such as the influence of the ownership policy on innovation and the 'conflict of interest' likely to be caused if academics become the owners of such inventions.[106]

---

[99] Japan Patent Office, *Minutes of the 9th Meeting* (n 90) 43 (comment by Tetsuya Obuchi, Chair); Japan Patent Office, *Minutes of the 10th Meeting* (n 90) 19 (comment by Tetsuya Obuchi, Chair).
[100] Patent Act (as amended up to Act No 55 of 2015), art 35(5)(7). See also text to nn 77–79.
[101] Patent Act (as amended up to Act No 55 of 2015), art 35(6).
[102] Public Notice of the Ministry of Economy, Trade and Industry No 131 of 2016, para 3-1-3.
[103] ibid, para 3-1-1.
[104] Patent System Subcommittee (n 80) 4.
[105] Japan Patent Office, *Minutes of the 6th Meeting* (n 88) 27 (comment by Tsuneaki Hagiwara); Japan Patent Office, *Minutes of the 7th Meeting* (n 89) 21 (comment by Yasuhiro Suzuki).
[106] See ch 8, s III.

Nevertheless, the 'inventor principle' no longer justifies a huge amount of compensation for employee inventions even if they initially belong to employees under the amended Act. Since employee inventors receive 'economic benefits' not as the payment for the transfer of the inventions but as incentives for them, it is now clear that what employers have to offer to employee inventors does not need to be commensurate with the economic value of employee inventions, which can sometimes bring a huge commercial success to the employers. Under the amended Act, which has further developed the rule established in the 2004 amendment, employee inventors are expected to secure some sort of economic incentives acceptable to both parties according to the relevant provisions in contracts or workplace regulations rather than in a court battle.[107] Accordingly, Japanese courts are unlikely to order employers to pay an enormous amount of money to employee inventors under the amended Act as in the *Blue LED* case mentioned earlier.[108]

In the opinion of the chair of the Subcommittee, economic incentives worth up to about ¥100 million (around £0.65 million) may be given to an employee inventor when he has made an invention under the amended Act.[109] However, the Subcommittee did not discuss whether economic incentives offered to individual inventors would really boost their motivation and the creation of inventions. For example, a committee member pointed out that inventors' minds are usually so occupied with solving technical problems that they cannot think about monetary rewards while inventing,[110] a fact illustrative of Herzberg's theory on the motivation to work discussed earlier.[111] Another member indicated that most Japanese researchers find pleasure in working in teams because they have a strong sense of belonging,[112] suggesting the collectivistic nature of the Japanese society confirmed by the studies in social psychology such as Hofstede's.[113] However, the implications of these views were never discussed in the Subcommittee, let alone the effect of economic incentives on the creativity of employee inventors, which may be more important for the success in inventing than their morale.[114] Since the amended Act has made it clear that the 'economic benefits' offered to employee inventors are not the price for the ownership of employee inventions that may *ab initio* belong to them, the 'inventor principle' should no longer be a barrier to the abolition of the legal provision for inventor remuneration, which is unlikely to boost the creation of inventions.

---

[107] Japan Patent Office, *Minutes of the 9th Meeting* (n 90) 30–31, 33 (comment by Tetsuya Obuchi, Chair).

[108] See text to n 76.

[109] Tetsuya Obuchi, 'Shokumu hatsumei ni kansuru kikkin no kadai' [Pressing Issues concerning Employee Inventions] in Institute of Intellectual Property (n 74) 465.

[110] Japan Patent Office, *Minutes of the 4th Meeting* (n 95) 4 (comment by Hideki Takahashi).

[111] See ch 2, ss II and IV.

[112] Japan Patent Office, *Minutes of the 1st Meeting of the Patent System Subcommittee* (24 March 2014) 18-19 (comment by Yoichi Okumura), www.jpo.go.jp/shiryou/toushin/shingikai/pdf/tokkyo_seido_menu/newtokkyo_001.pdf.

[113] See ch 3, s III.A.

[114] See ch 4.

Nevertheless, the immediate abolition of the legal provision may adversely affect the morale of employee inventors in practice. Although I have argued that monetary rewards are unlikely to stimulate their motivation to invent, it is another question whether their morale will be undermined when the abolition of legal schemes to require employers to give inventor remuneration inevitably leads to the loss of their benefits. In Germany, for example, employee inventors may claim their vested interests in the additional compensation they have received on a regular basis under the Act on Employees' Inventions. In the PatVal-EU Survey (PatVal-I) mentioned earlier, on average German respondents had received from their employers compensation equivalent to 1.8 per cent of their annual gross income for a single invention, and 8.3 per cent for all the inventions they had made in their career.[115] One per cent of them had received inventor remuneration that amounted to more than their annual gross income throughout their career.[116] The abolition of the Act may take away the motivation of prolific German inventors because they can no longer expect to receive a fair amount of inventor remuneration, though it will not seriously damage the morale of most German inventors who have received only a nominal amount of inventor remuneration.

In Japan, the Subcommittee was cautious of the negative message the abolition of the legal provision for inventor remuneration could deliver to employee inventors and the general public.[117] Thus the amended provision should be recognised for the moment as an 'exit strategy' to minimise judicial involvement in remuneration for employee inventions without damaging the morale of employee inventors seriously. The new provision encourages the concerned parties to establish applicable rules for themselves, whilst showing the legislature's minimal commitment to guaranteeing employee inventors some economic incentives.

III. Summary of Part II

The ownership of employee inventions in various jurisdictions was discussed to examine whether employers are required to pay compensation for the transfer of the inventions that may initially belong to employee inventors in theory. As between employers and employees, employee inventions should belong to employers for the sake of innovation; otherwise it is likely to cause named inventors to pursue the holdup strategy contrary to the interests of their employers who invest funds in R&D and other employees who have also made a contribution to the invention. Despite the Patent and Copyright Clause in the US Constitution which vests the ownership of inventions in their inventors, US courts virtually accept for

---

[115] Dietmar Harhoff and Karin Hoisl, 'Institutionalized Incentives for Ingenuity – Patent Value and the German Employees' Inventions Act' (2007) 36 *Research Policy* 1143, 1153.
[116] ibid.
[117] See text to nn 93, 94.

the sake of innovation that employers own or exploit inventions made by employees without paying additional compensation. In other common law countries, employers naturally become the initial owner of employee inventions according to employment contracts.

However, inventions made by university researchers do not belong to universities on the ground of employment contracts because they do not generally owe a duty to invent. In terms of open science universities should be involved in patenting only on a limited basis to promote the commercial exploitation of inventions made incidentally in the course of academic research, though at present many university TTOs are not efficient enough to encourage technology transfer. Meanwhile, academics may pursue their personal interests at the sacrifice of research if they can retain the rights in the inventions. To eliminate such conflict of interest the ownership of academic inventions should be vested in universities by legislation or intellectual property policies at universities on condition that an academic grace period is introduced to protect their patentability and ensure academics their freedom to publish at the same time.

The ownership of employee inventions is vested in employee inventors according to the 'inventor principle' that is traditionally adopted in some civil law countries. However, the current legal schemes in Germany and Japan are virtually departing from that principle, which shakes the assumption that that principle demands the payment of compensation for the transfer of employee inventions in theory. In terms of encouraging innovation employee inventions should *ab initio* belong to employers in principle, so that they can acquire and exploit them without paying additional compensation to employee inventors in accordance with the fundamental principle in employment law that employers can naturally enjoy the fruits of labour expended by employees.

10

General Conclusion

In this final chapter I will give the main points of this book and explain their policy and theoretical implications.

I. Summary of the Argument

This book set out to test the assumption rarely questioned in existing legal literature that the laws on inventor remuneration currently implemented in many jurisdictions actually give employee inventors an incentive to invent, thereby boosting the creation of inventions. I examined the effect of financial incentives on the motivation, productivity and creativity of employee inventors, citing the results of the extensive empirical surveys on inventors' motivation and studies in social psychology and econometrics. In addition, I discussed the ownership of employee inventions to examine whether employers are still required to pay compensation for inventions acquired from their employees because their initial ownership may be vested in the employee inventors themselves in theory. Special consideration was given to inventions made by university researchers and the 'inventor principle' adopted in some civil law countries.

The key finding of this research is that inventor remuneration offered to employee inventors is unlikely to have a positive effect on their motivation, productivity and creativity. It will even hinder the creation of inventions because of its adverse effect on teamwork in inventing. In addition, it was concluded that the initial ownership of employee inventions should be vested in employers in principle in accordance with the fundamental principle in employment law that the fruits of the labour expended by employees naturally belong to their employers. Given that the 'inventor principle' has been undermined in Germany and Japan in the face of the need to encourage innovation by employers, it is doubtful that that principle still justifies the payment of additional compensation for employee inventions. Although inventions made by university researchers, who do not owe a duty to invent under their employment contracts, do not naturally belong to their employers, it is desirable to vest their ownership in universities to eliminate the academics' 'conflict of interest', introducing an academic grace period to reconcile their freedom to publish with the need to maintain the patentability of academic inventions.

It is important to remember that inventing is creative activity that essentially differs from routine work like assembling parts of a product. Even though financial incentives may improve the productivity of routine work in general, they do not boost the creation of inventions in the same way. Meanwhile, those who argue for the employee inventors' right to additional compensation may have in mind the image of independent 'hero-inventors' prevalent until the late nineteenth century who made great inventions on their own and often set up companies to popularise their inventions. However, today inventions are made through the teamwork of scientists and engineers from various backgrounds in organisations, whilst their employers are responsible for innovation, or the process of delivering the fruits of inventions to the society. Even if only a few employees are named as inventors, there are other employees who assist them in perfecting the invention or who contribute to innovation in the company such as workers in the production and marketing department. Given that employee inventions do not generate profits by themselves without the contribution of these employees, there is no cogent reason for allowing only the named inventors to share in the profits derived from exploiting the inventions. Meanwhile, it is reasonable for employers to take the profits because they bear all the financial risk involved in innovation.

Employee inventors may want to exploit the legal provision for inventor remuneration to press the management for better conditions, but it would run counter to the main purpose of the law to encourage the creation of inventions, which is utilitarian in nature. Although this book did not discuss collective agreements that are meant to improve the social status of employees as a whole,[1] it is doubtful that today employee inventors form a special category of workers who require significant protection in the society like part-time workers.

II. Policy Implications

It is recommended from what has been discussed in this book that compensation for employee inventions should not be made mandatory regardless of jurisdiction because it is unlikely to encourage the creation of inventions by employee inventors. It should be recalled that workplace creativity depends greatly on not only the creative talents and diversity of individual employees but also communication among colleagues and the vision and leadership of supervisors and top management as indicated by the aforementioned recent research in social psychology.[2] Since employers can exert a direct influence on these determinants of workplace creativity, the practical way to encourage the creation of inventions is to let them devise strategies for innovation on their own. Rather, it is anachronistic to enforce

[1] Yet I referred to the recent collective agreement concluded in Sweden: see ch 1, n 22; ch 9, n 20.
[2] See ch 4, Figs 18, 19 and accompanying text.

them to offer monetary rewards to employee inventors by legislation across the board because inventors' pecuniary motives may have little to do with the success in inventing in fact. A recent research in social psychology suggests that workers' 'prosocial motivation', or 'the desire to expend effort based on a concern for helping or contributing to other people',[3] is likely to increase the positive effect of intrinsic motivation on creativity, thereby encouraging them to produce novel and useful ideas.[4]

In Europe, divergent laws on compensation for employee inventions among the EU Member States have been a barrier to strengthening the European single market. This issue should resolve itself for the most part if all the Member States abolish legal provisions for inventor remuneration, though there will remain the need to harmonise rules on incidental inventions. The abolition will eliminate the adverse effect of monetary rewards on teamwork in inventing and workplace creativity, so that it will eventually help to encourage the creation of inventions in each country. In Germany, however, abolishing the Act on Employees' Inventions is likely to adversely affect the morale of employee inventors who have received inventor remuneration on a regular basis under the Act. To reduce the negative impact on the inventors' morale the German legislature may need to introduce a transitional measure similar to the rule adopted in the 2015 amendment to the Japanese patent law, according to which employee inventors still secure some 'economic benefits' that are not limited to monetary rewards.

In its report published in 1970, the aforementioned Banks Committee in the UK already called attention to the problem of secrecy among employee inventors caused by the offer of inventor remuneration.[5] Although the Committee opposed the introduction of the inventor remuneration scheme, citing the lack of evidence that such a scheme had been effective in other countries, notably Germany,[6] the Patents Act 1977 contains a provision that allows courts to award compensation to an employee inventor where 'the invention ... is of outstanding benefit to the employer'[7] as a result of a compromise between the industry and workers when a Labour government was in power.[8] Since this requirement for awarding inventor remuneration is essentially irrelevant to the issue of incentives for employee inventors, the legislature should immediately repeal this poorly-drafted provision,

---

[3] Adam M Grant and James W Berry, 'The Necessity of Others Is the Mother of Invention: Intrinsic and Prosocial Motivations, Perspective Taking, and Creativity' (2011) 54 *Academy of Management Journal* 73, 77 (citation omitted).

[4] ibid 81–82 Table 2, 83 Fig 2.

[5] *The British Patent System: Report of the Committee to Examine the Patent System and Patent Law* (Banks Report, Cmnd 4407, 1970) para 461.

[6] ibid para 465.

[7] Patents Act 1977, s 40(1).

[8] Jeremy Phillips and Michael J Hoolahan, *Employees' Inventions in the United Kingdom: Law and Practice* (Oxford, ESC, 1982) 49–50; William R Cornish, 'Rights in Employees' Inventions – The United Kingdom Position' (1990) 21 *International Review of Industrial Property and Copyright Law* 298, 301.

which causes confusion over the meaning of the vague term 'outstanding benefit' as was disputed in a recent case.[9]

Since 2014 the Russian government has implemented an ordinance that requires employers to pay a certain amount of inventor remuneration to employees where employee inventions are created and they are used, licensed and/or assigned by employers unless the parties agree otherwise.[10] In 2015 a Chinese government agency published the latest draft regulations on service inventions which proposed to significantly increase the minimum amount of compensation which all entities, whether state-owned enterprises or not, must pay to those who have made inventions in the course of duties assigned to them unless the parties agree otherwise.[11] However, these schemes are unlikely to be effective in encouraging the creation of inventions. If the legislature in these countries should make the payment of inventor remuneration mandatory regardless of whether there is an agreement on the matter between the parties, the countries may face the difficulty in attracting investment from foreign companies which fear that they might need to set aside substantial funds for inventor remuneration.

III. Theoretical Implications

When it is said that the patent system provides 'inventors' with an 'incentive to invent',[12] the conventional assumption has been that 'inventors' here means natural persons who have creative skills to make inventions. However, given that most inventions are made in organisations today, it should be clearly recognised that

---

[9] Whilst it appears that in theory an invention is less likely to bring 'outstanding benefit' to a big company which ordinarily posts large profits, the court in *Shanks* held that the hearing officer in the case had dismissed the inventor's claim for inventor compensation after properly considering various factors, including 'the size and nature of the employer's undertaking', in accordance with s 40(1) of the Patents Act 1977, not on the grounds that the employer was 'too big to pay' inventor compensation: *Shanks v Unilever Plc (No 2)* [2017] EWCA Civ 2, [2017] RPC 15 [64]. The case was distinguished from the *Kelly and Chiu* case, where it was held that the patent in question had been 'of outstanding benefit' to the employer because without it the company would have faced a crisis: *Kelly and Chiu v GE Healthcare Ltd* [2009] EWHC 181 (Pat), [2009] RPC 12 [148]–[150].

[10] Civil Code, art 1370(4); Order of the Government of the Russian Federation of 4 June 2014 No 512.

[11] Patent Law, art 16; Implementing Regulations of the Patent Law of the People's Republic of China, arts 77, 78; Regulations on Service Inventions (Draft for Review, published by the State Council Legislative Affairs Office on 2 April 2015), arts 20, 21. Whilst the regulations on service inventions have not been enacted so far, Art 45 of the Law on Promoting the Transformation of Scientific and Technological Achievements (as amended in 2015) sets the minimum amount of compensation entities must pay to 'personnel who have made important contributions to the completion and transformation of scientific and technological achievements', which presumably include inventions and other technical intellectual property such as software, in the absence of an agreement between the parties.

[12] The argument that the patent system encourages inventors to disclose their inventions to the society has been criticised on several grounds: Fritz Machlup and Edith Penrose, 'The Patent Controversy in the Nineteenth Century' (1950) 10 *The Journal of Economic History* 1, 25–28. This book did not discuss this 'incentive to disclose' theory.

the main purpose of the patent law is now to provide employers with an 'incentive to innovate', which subsumes an 'incentive to invent'. Apart from the lead-time or first-mover advantage,[13] patents enable companies to recoup the investment in R&D by preventing competitors from exploiting the patented technology for 20 years. Although employers do not invent on their own, thanks to the 'incentive to innovate' guaranteed by the patent system they can put their human, material and capital resources into inventive activities so that inventions are created by their employees.

Meanwhile, this book has shown that the patent system does not need to give incentives to employee inventors since the vast majority of them are naturally motivated to make inventions by their intellectual craving to solve technical problems. Although they will not be able to concentrate on inventing if they are not paid a minimal level of salary, this is a matter which should be addressed by employment law. If the legislature still adopts a policy to reward employee inventors for their efforts, this would be only justified by the 'reward theory' of the patent system, which attracts little support,[14] because it is unlikely that such rewards encourage the creation of inventions and thus serve as 'incentive to invent'.

[13] See text to ch 5, n 8.
[14] See text to ch 1, n 27.

BIBLIOGRAPHY

Books

—— *Pooling of Patents: Appendix to Hearings before the House Committee on Patents on H.R. 4523, Part I, 74th Congress* (Washington DC, United States Government Printing Office, 1935)

3M, *A Century of Innovation: The 3M Story* (Saint Paul, 3M Company, 2002)

Alger PL, *The Human Side of Engineering: Tales of General Electric Engineering over 80 Years* (Schenectady, Mohawk Development Service, 1972)

Amabile TM, *Creativity in Context* (Boulder, Westview Press, 1996)

Bader MA, *Intellectual Property Management in R&D Collaborations: The Case of the Service Industry Sector* (Heidelberg, Physica, 2006)

Berenstein A, Mahon P and Dunand JP, *Labour Law in Switzerland* (Alphen aan den Rijn, Kluwer Law International, 2011)

Bush V, Science, *The Endless Frontier: Report to the President on a Program for Postwar Scientific Research* (Washington DC, United States Government Printing Office, 1945)

Clark R, Smyth S and Hall N, *Intellectual Property Law in Ireland*, 3rd edn (Haywards Heath, Bloomsbury Professional, 2010)

Collins JC and Porras JI, *Built to Last: Successful Habits of Visionary Companies*, 3rd edn (London, Random House Business, 2000)

Cornish W, Llewelyn D and Aplin T, *Intellectual Property: Patents, Copyright, Trade Marks and Allied Rights*, 8th edn (London, Sweet & Maxwell, 2013)

Craft EB, *Bell Educational Conference, 1925* (New York, Bell System, 1925)

Csikszentmihalyi M, *Creativity: Flow and the Psychology of Discovery and Invention* (New York, Harper Perennial, 1997)

Dancey CP and Reidy J, *Statistics without Maths for Psychology*, 5th edn (Harlow, Pearson Education, 2011)

Deci EL and Ryan RM, *Intrinsic Motivation and Self-Determination in Human Behavior* (New York, Plenum Press, 1985)

Folk GE, *Patents and Industrial Progress: A Summary Analysis and Evaluation of the Record of Patents of the Temporary National Economic Committee* (New York, Harper & Brothers, 1942)

Hamilton A, Madison J and Jay J, *The Federalist Papers* (originally published 1788, New York, Cosimo Classics, 2006)

Hayes N and Stratton P, *A Student's Dictionary of Psychology*, 4th edn (London, Arnold, 2003)

Heine HG and Rebitzki H, *Die Vergütung für Erfindungen von Arbeitnehmern im privaten Dienst* [The Remuneration for Inventions of Employees in Private Employment] (Weinheim, Chemie, 1960)

Herzberg F, *Work and the Nature of Man* (originally published 1968, London, Staples Press, 1972)

—— Mausner B and Snyderman BB, *The Motivation to Work*, 2nd edn (New York, John Wiley & Sons, 1967)

Hillman RA, *Principles of Contract Law* (Saint Paul, West, 2004)

Hofstede G, *Culture's Consequences: Comparing Values, Behaviors, Institutions, and Organizations across Nations*, 2nd edn (originally published 1980, Thousand Oaks, SAGE, 2001)

Kelley HH, Holmes JG, Kerr NL, Reis HT, Rusbult CE and Van Lange PAM, *An Atlas of Interpersonal Situations* (Cambridge, Cambridge University Press, 2003)

Knauer H, *Möglichkeiten und Nutzen einer Vereinheitlichung des Arbeitnehmererfinderrechts in der Europäischen Union und Schlussfolgerungen für die diesbezügliche deutsche Gesetzgebung* [Possibilities and Benefits of the Harmonisation of Employee Invention Law in the European Union and the Implications for the Related German Legislation] (München, Herbert Utz, 2007)

Lam J, *Enterprise Risk Management: From Incentives to Controls* (Hoboken, John Wiley & Sons, 2003)

Leptien C, *Anreizsysteme in Forschung und Entwicklung: unter besonderer Berücksichtigung des Arbeitnehmererfindergesetzes* [Incentive Systems in Research and Development: With Special Reference to the Employee Invention Law] (Wiesbaden, Deutscher Universitätsverlag, 1996)

Marden OS, *How They Succeeded: Life Stories of Successful Men Told by Themselves* (Boston, Lothrop, 1901)

McLaurin WR, *Invention and Innovation in the Radio Industry* (New York, Macmillan, 1949)

McSherry C, *Who Owns Academic Work? Battling for Control of Intellectual Property* (Cambridge, Massachusetts, Harvard University Press, 2001)

Merges RP, *Justifying Intellectual Property* (Cambridge, Massachusetts, Harvard University Press, 2011)

Merton RK, *The Sociology of Science: Theoretical and Empirical Investigations* (Chicago, The University of Chicago Press, 1973)

Monotti A and Ricketson S, *Universities and Intellectual Property: Ownership and Exploitation* (Oxford, Oxford University Press, 2003)

Noble DF, *America by Design: Science, Technology, and the Rise of Corporate Capitalism* (Oxford, Oxford University Press, 1979)

OECD, *Turning Science into Business: Patenting and Licensing at Public Research Organisations* (Paris, OECD, 2003)

—— *Frascati Manual 2015: Guidelines for Collecting and Reporting Data on Research and Experimental Development* (Paris, OECD, 2015)

—— *OECD Science, Technology and Industry Scoreboard 2017: The Digital Transformation* (Paris, OECD, 2017)

Ouchi WG, *Theory Z: How American Business Can Meet the Japanese Challenge* (Reading, Massachusetts, Addison-Wesley, 1981)

Phillips J and Hoolahan MJ, *Employees' Inventions in the United Kingdom: Law and Practice* (Oxford, ESC, 1982)

Pink DH, *Drive: The Surprising Truth about What Motivates Us*, pbk edn (Edinburgh, Canongate, 2011)

Reischauer EO and Jansen MB, *The Japanese Today: Change and Continuity* (Cambridge, Massachusetts, Harvard University Press, 1977)

Schumpeter JA, *Capitalism, Socialism and Democracy*, new edn (originally published 1943, London, Routledge, 1994)

Scotchmer S, *Innovation and Incentives* (Cambridge, Massachusetts, The MIT Press, 2004)

Steiner ID, *Group Process and Productivity* (New York, Academic Press, 1972)

Stern B, *Inventors at Work: The Minds and Motivation behind Modern Inventions* (Berkeley, Apress, 2012)

Taylor FW, *The Principles of Scientific Management* (New York, Harper & Brothers, 1911)

Triandis HC, *Individualism and Collectivism* (Boulder, Westview Press, 1995)

Trimborn M, *Employees' Inventions in Germany: A Handbook for International Businesses* (Alphen aan den Rijn, Kluwer Law International, 2009)

Vroom VH, *Work and Motivation* (originally published 1964, Malabar, Robert E Krieger, 1984)

Contributions to Edited Books

Alencar EMLS, 'Creativity in Organizations: Facilitators and Inhibitors' in Mumford MD (ed), *Handbook of Organizational Creativity* (Amsterdam, Academic Press, 2011) 87–111

Arrow KJ, 'Economic Welfare and the Allocation of Resources for Invention' in National Bureau of Economic Research, *The Rate and Direction of Inventive Activity: Economic and Social Factors* (Princeton, Princeton University Press, 1962) 609–26

Deci EL, 'Motivation Research in Industrial/Organizational Psychology' in Vroom VH and Deci EL (eds), *Management and Motivation: Selected Readings*, 2nd edn (Harmondsworth, Penguin, 1992) 167–78

DeMatteo JS, Eby LT and Sundstrom E, 'Team-Based Rewards: Current Empirical Evidence and Directions for Future Research' in Staw BM and Cummings LL (eds), *Research in Organizational Behavior*, vol 20 (Greenwich, Connecticut, JAI Press, 1998) 141–83

Feather NT, 'Values and Cultures' in Lonner WJ and Malpass RS (eds), *Psychology and Culture* (Boston, Allyn & Bacon, 1994) 183–89

Flynn FJ and Chatman JA, 'Strong Cultures and Innovation: Oxymoron or Opportunity?' in Cooper CL, Cartwright S and Earley PC (eds), *The International Handbook of Organizational Culture and Climate* (Chichester, John Wiley & Sons, 2001) 263–87

Gelfand MJ, Bhawuk DPS, Nishii LH and Bechtold DJ, 'Individualism and Collectivism' in House RJ, Hanges PJ, Javidan M, Dorfman PW and Gupta V (eds), *Culture, Leadership, and Organizations: The GLOBE Study of 62 Societies* (Thousand Oaks, SAGE, 2004) 437–512

George JM, 'Creativity in Organizations' in Walsh JP and Brief AP (eds), *The Academy of Management Annals*, vol 1 (Abingdon, Routledge, 2007) 439–77

Gupta V and Hanges PJ, 'Regional and Climate Clustering of Societal Cultures' in House RJ, Hanges PJ, Javidan M, Dorfman PW and Gupta V (eds), *Culture, Leadership, and Organizations: The GLOBE Study of 62 Societies* (Thousand Oaks, SAGE, 2004) 178–218

House RJ, 'Illustrative Examples of GLOBE Findings' in House RJ, Hanges PJ, Javidan M, Dorfman PW and Gupta V (eds), *Culture, Leadership, and Organizations: The GLOBE Study of 62 Societies* (Thousand Oaks, SAGE, 2004) 3–8

Janssens MC, 'Belgium' in Kono T (ed), *Intellectual Property and Private International Law: Comparative Perspectives* (Oxford, Hart, 2012) 347–423

—— 'EU Perspectives on Employees' Inventions' in Pittard M, Monotti AL and Duns J (eds), *Business Innovation and the Law: Perspectives from Intellectual Property, Labour, Competition and Corporate Law* (Cheltenham, Edward Elgar, 2013) 111–30

Lincoln A, 'Second Lecture on Discoveries and Inventions' in Basler RP (ed), *The Collected Works of Abraham Lincoln*, vol 3 (New Brunswick, Rutgers University Press, 1953) 356–63

Nelsen L, 'Technology Transfer in US Universities and Research Institutions' in Breznitz SM and Etzkowitz H (eds), *University Technology Transfer: The Globalization of Academic Innovation* (Abingdon, Routledge, 2016) 451–59

Oldham GR and Baer M, 'Creativity and the Work Context' in Mumford MD (ed), *Handbook of Organizational Creativity* (Amsterdam, Academic Press, 2011) 387–420

Paulus PB, Dzindolet M and Kohn NW, 'Collaborative Creativity – Group Creativity and Team Innovation' in Mumford MD (ed), *Handbook of Organizational Creativity* (Amsterdam, Academic Press, 2011) 327–57

Richards G, 'Bayh-Dole-Thatcher' in Richards G (ed), *University Intellectual Property: A Source of Finance and Impact* (Petersfield, Harriman House, 2012) 17–21

Zhou J and Shalley CE, 'Expanding the Scope and Impact of Organizational Creativity Research' in Zhou J and Shalley CE (eds), *Handbook of Organizational Creativity* (New York, Lawrence Erlbaum Associates, 2008) 347–68

Encyclopaedias

Black's Law Dictionary, 9th edn (Saint Paul, West, 2009)

Chisum on Patents, vol 8 (New York, LexisNexis Matthew Bender, 2012)

Journal Articles

Adams JS, 'Toward an Understanding of Inequity' (1963) 67 *Journal of Abnormal and Social Psychology* 422

Amabile TM, 'How to Kill Creativity' (1998) 76(5) *Harvard Business Review* 77

Baer M, Oldham GR and Cummings A, 'Rewarding Creativity: When Does It Really Matter?' (2003) 14 *The Leadership Quarterly* 569

Bakacsi G, Sándor T, András K and Viktor I, 'Eastern European Cluster: Tradition and Transition' (2002) 37 *Journal of World Business* 69

Baldini N, Fini R, Grimaldi R and Sobrero M, 'Organisational Change and the Institutionalisation of University Patenting Activity in Italy' (2014) 52 *Minerva* 27

Barnes CM, Hollenbeck JR, Jundt DK, Derue DS and Harmon SJ, 'Mixing Individual Incentives and Group Incentives: Best of Both or Social Dilemma?' (2011) 37 *Journal of Management* 1611

Bassett-Jones N and Lloyd GC, 'Does Herzberg's Motivation Theory Have Staying Power?' (2005) 24 *Journal of Management Development* 929

Bechtoldt MN, Choi HS and Nijstad BA, 'Individualism in Mind, Mates by Heart: Individualistic Self-Construal and Collective Value Orientation as Predictors of Group Creativity' (2012) 48 *Journal of Experimental Social Psychology* 838

Belenzon S and Schankerman M, 'University Knowledge Transfer: Private Ownership, Incentives, and Local Development Objectives' (2009) 52 *The Journal of Law and Economics* 111

Bénabou R and Tirole J, 'Intrinsic and Extrinsic Motivation' (2003) 70 *The Review of Economic Studies* 489

Bond MH, Leung K and Wan KC, 'How Does Cultural Collectivism Operate? The Impact of Task and Maintenance Contributions on Reward Distribution' (1982) 13 *Journal of Cross-Cultural Psychology* 186

Brand A, 'Knowledge Management and Innovation at 3M' (1998) 2(1) *Journal of Knowledge Management* 17

Brayfield AH and Crockett WH, 'Employee Attitudes and Employee Performance' (1955) 52 *Psychological Bulletin* 396

Brennan JW, 'The Developing Law of German Employee Inventions' (1962) 6 *The Patent, Trademark and Copyright Journal of Research and Education* 41

Brockhoff K, 'Ist die kollektive Regelung einer Vergütung von Arbeitnehmererfindungen wirksam und nötig?' [Is the Collective Regulation of Remuneration for Employees' Inventions Effective and Necessary?] (1997) 67 *Zeitschrift für Betriebswirtschaft (ZfB)* 677

Burhop C and Lübbers T, 'Incentives and Innovation? R&D Management in Germany's Chemical and Electrical Engineering Industries around 1900' (2010) 47 *Explorations in Economic History* 100

Byron K and Khazanchi S, 'Rewards and Creative Performance: A Meta-Analytic Test of Theoretically Derived Hypotheses' (2012) 138 *Psychological Bulletin* 809

Caldwell P, 'Employment Agreements for the Inventing Worker: A Proposal for Reforming Trailer Clause Enforceability Guidelines' (2006) 13 *Journal of Intellectual Property Law* 279

Chen CC, Meindl JR and Hunt RG, 'Testing the Effects of Vertical and Horizontal Collectivism: A Study of Reward Allocation Preferences in China' (1997) 28 *Journal of Cross-Cultural Psychology* 44

Cherensky S, 'A Penny for Their Thoughts: Employee-Inventors, Preinvention Assignment Agreements, Property, and Personhood' (1993) 81 *California Law Review* 595

Cohen-Charash Y and Spector PE, 'The Role of Justice in Organizations: A Meta-Analysis' (2001) 86 *Organizational Behavior and Human Decision Processes* 278

Colquitt JA, Conlon DE, Wesson MJ, Porter COLH and Ng KY, 'Justice at the Millennium: A Meta-Analytic Review of 25 Years of Organizational Justice Research' (2001) 86 *Journal of Applied Psychology* 425

Colquitt JA, Rodell JB, Zapata CP, Wesson MJ, Scott BA, Long DM and Conlon DE, 'Justice at the Millennium, a Decade Later: A Meta-Analytic Test of Social Exchange and Affect-Based Perspectives' (2013) 98 *Journal of Applied Psychology* 199

Conceição P, Hamill D and Pinheiro P, 'Innovative Science and Technology Commercialization Strategies at 3M: A Case Study' (2002) 19 *Journal of Engineering and Technology Management* 25

Conti A and Gaule P, 'Is the US Outperforming Europe in University Technology Licensing? A New Perspective on the European Paradox' (2011) 40 *Research Policy* 123

Cornish WR, 'Rights in Employees' Inventions – The United Kingdom Position' (1990) 21 *International Review of Industrial Property and Copyright Law* 298

Crespi G, D'Este P, Fontana R and Geuna A, 'The Impact of Academic Patenting on University Research and its Transfer' (2011) 40 *Research Policy* 55

Cross SE and Madson L, 'Models of the Self: Self-Construals and Gender' (1997) 122 *Psychological Bulletin* 5

Damsgaard EF and Thursby MC, 'University Entrepreneurship and Professor Privilege' (2013) 22 *Industrial and Corporate Change* 183

Dasgupta P and David PA, 'Toward a New Economics of Science' (1994) 23 *Research Policy* 487

Daun Å, 'Individualism and Collectivity among Swedes' (1991) 56 *Ethnos* 165

David PA, 'Understanding the Emergence of "Open Science" Institutions: Functionalist Economics in Historical Context' (2004) 13 *Industrial and Corporate Change* 571

Deci EL, 'Effects of Externally Mediated Rewards on Intrinsic Motivation' (1971) 18 *Journal of Personality and Social Psychology* 105

—— 'Intrinsic Motivation, Extrinsic Reinforcement, and Inequity' (1972) 22 *Journal of Personality and Social Psychology* 113

—— 'The Effects of Contingent and Noncontingent Rewards and Controls on Intrinsic Motivation' (1972) 8 *Organizational Behavior and Human Performance* 217

—— Koestner R and Ryan RM, 'A Meta-Analytic Review of Experiments Examining the Effects of Extrinsic Rewards on Intrinsic Motivation' (1999) 125 *Psychological Bulletin* 627

Deutsch M, 'Equity, Equality, and Need: What Determines Which Value Will Be Used as the Basis of Distributive Justice' (1975) 31(3) *Journal of Social Issues* 137

Dratler J Jr, 'Incentive for People: The Forgotten Purpose of the Patent System' (1979) 16 *Harvard Journal on Legislation* 129

Dunnette MD, Campbell JP and Hakel MD, 'Factors Contributing to Job Satisfaction and Job Dissatisfaction in Six Occupational Groups' (1967) 2 *Organizational Behavior and Human Performance* 143

Earley PC, 'Social Loafing and Collectivism: A Comparison of the United States and the People's Republic of China' (1989) 34 *Administrative Science Quarterly* 565

—— 'East Meets West Meets Mideast: Further Explorations of Collectivistic and Individualistic Work Groups' (1993) 36 *Academy of Management Journal* 319

Eisenberg RS, 'Public Research and Private Development: Patents and Technology Transfer in Government-Sponsored Research' (1996) 82 *Virginia Law Review* 1663

Eisenberger R, 'Learned Industriousness' (1992) 99 *Psychological Review* 248

—— and Armeli S, 'Can Salient Reward Increase Creative Performance Without Reducing Intrinsic Creative Interest?' (1997) 72 *Journal of Personality and Social Psychology* 652

—— Armeli S and Pretz J, 'Can the Promise of Reward Increase Creativity?' (1998) 74 *Journal of Personality and Social Psychology* 704

—— and Aselage J, 'Incremental Effects of Reward on Experienced Performance Pressure: Positive Outcomes for Intrinsic Interest and Creativity' (2009) 30 *Journal of Organizational Behavior* 95

—— Haskins F and Gambleton P, 'Promised Reward and Creativity: Effects of Prior Experience' (1999) 35 *Journal of Experimental Social Psychology* 308

—— Pierce WD and Cameron J, 'Effects of Reward on Intrinsic Motivation – Negative, Neutral, and Positive: Comment on Deci, Koestner, and Ryan (1999)' (1999) 125 *Psychological Bulletin* 677

—— and Rhoades L, 'Incremental Effects of Reward on Creativity' (2001) 81 *Journal of Personality and Social Psychology* 728

—— Rhoades L and Cameron J, 'Does Pay for Performance Increase or Decrease Perceived Self-Determination and Intrinsic Motivation?' (1999) 77 *Journal of Personality and Social Psychology* 1026

—— and Selbst M, 'Does Reward Increase or Decrease Creativity?' (1994) 66 *Journal of Personality and Social Psychology* 1116

—— and Shanock L, 'Rewards, Intrinsic Motivation, and Creativity: A Case Study of Conceptual and Methodological Isolation' (2003) 15 *Creativity Research Journal* 121

Erez M, 'Interpersonal Communication Systems in Organizations, and Their Relationships to Cultural Values, Productivity and Innovation: The Case of Japanese Corporations' (1992) 41 *Applied Psychology* 43

Ernst H, Leptien C and Vitt J, 'Inventors Are Not Alike: The Distribution of Patenting Output among Industrial R&D Personnel' (2000) 47 *IEEE Transactions on Engineering Management* 184

Ewen RB, Smith PC, Hulin CL and Locke EA, 'An Empirical Test of the Herzberg Two-Factor Theory' (1966) 50 *Journal of Applied Psychology* 544

Fabrizio KR and Di Minin A, 'Commercializing the Laboratory: Faculty Patenting and the Open Science Environment' (2008) 37 *Research Policy* 914

Fang M and Gerhart B, 'Does Pay for Performance Diminish Intrinsic Interest?' (2012) 23 *International Journal of Human Resource Management* 1176

Fasse WF, 'The Muddy Metaphysics of Joint Inventorship: Cleaning Up after the 1984 Amendments to 35 U.S.C. § 116' (1992) 5(2) *Harvard Journal of Law and Technology* 153

Fellmeth AX, 'Conception and Misconception in Joint Inventorship' (2012) 2 *New York University Journal of Intellectual Property and Entertainment Law* 73

Fischer R and Smith PB, 'Reward Allocation and Culture: A Meta-Analysis' (2003) 34 *Journal of Cross-Cultural Psychology* 251

Fischer R, Smith PB, Richey BE, Ferreira MC, Assmar EML, Maes J and Stumpf S, 'How Do Organizations Allocate Rewards? The Predictive Validity of National Values, Economic and Organizational Factors Across Six Nations' (2007) 38 *Journal of Cross-Cultural Psychology* 3

Fish FP, 'The Patent System in its Relation to Industrial Development' (1909) 28 *Transactions of the American Institute of Electrical Engineers* 315

Fisk CL, 'Removing the 'Fuel of Interest' from the 'Fire of Genius': Law and the Employee-Inventor, 1830–1930' (1998) 65 *The University of Chicago Law Review* 1127

Franzoni C and Scellato G, 'The Grace Period in International Patent Law and its Effect on the Timing of Disclosure' (2010) 39 *Research Policy* 200

Frey BS and Jegen R, 'Motivation Crowding Theory' (2001) 15 *Journal of Economic Surveys* 589

Garbers Y and Konradt U, 'The Effect of Financial Incentives on Performance: A Quantitative Review of Individual and Team-Based Financial Incentives' (2014) 87 *Journal of Occupational and Organizational Psychology* 102

Garud R, Gehman J and Kumaraswamy A, 'Complexity Arrangements for Sustained Innovation: Lessons from 3M Corporation' (2011) 32 *Organization Studies* 737

Gerhart B and Fang M, 'Pay for (Individual) Performance: Issues, Claims, Evidence and the Role of Sorting Effects' (2014) 24 *Human Resource Management Review* 41

Geuna A and Nesta LJJ, 'University Patenting and its Effects on Academic Research: The Emerging European Evidence' (2006) 35 *Research Policy* 790

Geuna A and Rossi F, 'Changes to University IPR Regulations in Europe and the Impact on Academic Patenting' (2011) 40 *Research Policy* 1068

Giummo J, 'German Employee Inventors' Compensation Records: A Window into the Returns to Patented Inventions' (2010) 39 *Research Policy* 969

Giuri P, Mariani M, Brusoni S, Crespi G, Francoz D, Gambardella A, Garcia-Fontes W, Geuna A, Gonzales R, Harhoff D, Hoisl K, Le Bas C, Luzzi A, Magazzini L, Nesta L, Nomaler Ö, Palomeras N, Patel P, Romanelli M and Verspagen B, 'Inventors and Invention Processes in Europe: Results from the PatVal-EU Survey' (2007) 36 *Research Policy* 1107

Glucksberg S, 'The Influence of Strength of Drive on Functional Fixedness and Perceptual Recognition' (1962) 63 *Journal of Experimental Psychology* 36

Goncalo JA and Duguid MM, 'Follow the Crowd in a New Direction: When Conformity Pressure Facilitates Group Creativity (and When It Does Not)' (2012) 118 *Organizational Behavior and Human Decision Processes* 14

Goncalo JA and Kim SH, 'Distributive Justice Beliefs and Group Idea Generation: Does a Belief in Equity Facilitate Productivity?' (2010) 46 *Journal of Experimental Social Psychology* 836

Goncalo JA and Staw BM, 'Individualism-Collectivism and Group Creativity' (2006) 100 *Organizational Behavior and Human Decision Processes* 96

Graham SJH, Merges RP, Samuelson P, and Sichelman T, 'High Technology Entrepreneurs and the Patent System: Results of the 2008 Berkeley Patent Survey' (2009) 24 *Berkeley Technology Law Journal* 1255

Grant AM and Berry JW, 'The Necessity of Others Is the Mother of Invention: Intrinsic and Prosocial Motivations, Perspective Taking, and Creativity' (2011) 54 *Academy of Management Journal* 73

Hackman JR and Oldham GR, 'Motivation through the Design of Work: Test of a Theory' (1976) 16 *Organizational Behavior and Human Performance* 250

Harhoff D and Hoisl K, 'Institutionalized Incentives for Ingenuity – Patent Value and the German Employees' Inventions Act' (2007) 36 *Research Policy* 1143

Hershovitz MB, 'Unhitching the Trailer Clause: The Rights of Inventive Employees and Their Employers' (1995) 3 *Journal of Intellectual Property Law* 187

Hettinger EC, 'Justifying Intellectual Property' (1989) 18 *Philosophy & Public Affairs* 31

Hoffman JR and Rogelberg SG, 'A Guide to Team Incentive Systems' (1998) 4 *Team Performance Management* 22

Honeywell-Johnson JA and Dickinson AM, 'Small Group Incentives: A Review of the Literature' (1999) 19 *Journal of Organizational Behavior Management* 89

Honig-Haftel S and Martin LR, 'The Effectiveness of Reward Systems on Innovative Output: An Empirical Analysis' (1993) 5 *Small Business Economics* 261

Hoppe HC and Ozdenoren E, 'Intermediation in Innovation' (2005) 23 *International Journal of Industrial Organization* 483

House RJ and Wigdor LA, 'Herzberg's Dual-Factor Theory of Job Satisfaction and Motivation: A Review of the Evidence and a Criticism' (1967) 20 *Personnel Psychology* 369

Hovell WP, 'Patent Ownership: An Employer's Right to His Employee's Invention' (1983) 58 *Notre Dame Law Review* 863

Hughes JP, Rees S, Kalindjian SB and Philpott KL, 'Principles of Early Drug Discovery' (2011) 162 *British Journal of Pharmacology* 1239

Hui CH, Triandis HC and Yee C, 'Cultural Differences in Reward Allocation: Is Collectivism the Explanation?' (1991) 30 *British Journal of Social Psychology* 145

Hülsheger UR, Anderson N and Salgado JF, 'Team-Level Predictors of Innovation at Work: A Comprehensive Meta-Analysis Spanning Three Decades of Research' (2009) 94 *Journal of Applied Psychology* 1128

Hunter ST, Bedell KE and Mumford MD, 'Climate for Creativity: A Quantitative Review' (2007) 19 *Creativity Research Journal* 69

Irons ES and Sears MH, 'The Constitutional Standard of Invention-The Touchstone for Patent Reform' [1973] *Utah Law Review* 653

Javidan M and Dastmalchian A, 'Culture and Leadership in Iran: The Land of Individual Achievers, Strong Family Ties, and Powerful Elite' (2003) 17(4) *The Academy of Management Executive* 127

Jensen R and Thursby M, 'Proofs and Prototypes for Sale: The Licensing of University Inventions' (2001) 91 *American Economic Review* 240

Jesuino JC, 'Latin Europe Cluster: From South to North' (2002) 37 *Journal of World Business* 81

Kamprath RA, 'Patent Reversion: An Employee-Inventor's Second Bite at the Apple' (2012) 11 *Chicago Kent Journal of Intellectual Property* 186

Kaplow L, 'The Patent-Antitrust Intersection: A Reappraisal' (1984) 97 *Harvard Law Review* 1815

Karau SJ and Williams KD, 'Social Loafing: A Meta-Analytic Review and Theoretical Integration' (1993) 65 *Journal of Personality and Social Psychology* 681

Kenney M and Patton D, 'Reconsidering the Bayh-Dole Act and the Current University Invention Ownership Model' (2009) 38 *Research Policy* 1407

Kesten R, 'Innovationen durch eigene Mitarbeiter: Betriebswirtschaftliche Aspekte zur monetären Beurteilung von Diensterfindungen nach dem Gesetz über Arbeitnehmererfindungen' [Innovations by Individual Employees: Economic Aspects of Monetary Evaluation of Employee Inventions under the Law on Employee Inventions] (1996) 66 *Zeitschrift für Betriebswirtschaft* (*ZfB*) 651

Kim YK, Ryu TK and Jung CS, 'Employees' Invention Compensation Plan as a Determinant of Patent Quality and Quantity: Findings of Inventor Survey in Korea' (2011) 6(1) *The Journal of Intellectual Property* 133

Kirstein R and Will B, 'Efficient Compensation for Employees' Inventions' (2006) 21 *European Journal of Law and Economics* 129

Lach S and Schankerman M, 'Incentives and Invention in Universities' (2008) 39 *The RAND Journal of Economics* 403

LaFrance M, 'Nevada's Employee Inventions Statute: Novel, Nonobvious, and Patently Wrong' (2002) 3 *Nevada Law Journal* 88

Lazear EP, 'Performance Pay and Productivity' (2000) 90 *American Economic Review* 1346

Leavy B, 'A Leader's Guide to Creating an Innovation Culture' (2005) 33(4) *Strategy & Leadership* 38

Leptien C, 'Incentives for Employed Inventors: An Empirical Analysis with Special Emphasis on the German Law for Employee's Inventions' (1995) 25 *R&D Management* 213

Lerner J and Wulf J, 'Innovation and Incentives: Evidence from Corporate R&D' (2007) 89 *The Review of Economics and Statistics* 634

Leung K and Bond MH, 'The Impact of Cultural Collectivism on Reward Allocation' (1984) 47 *Journal of Personality and Social Psychology* 793

Leung K and Iwawaki S, 'Cultural Collectivism and Distributive Behavior' (1988) 19 *Journal of Cross-Cultural Psychology* 35

Liden RC, Wayne SJ, Jaworski RA and Bennett N, 'Social Loafing: A Field Investigation' (2004) 30 *Journal of Management* 285

Lissoni F, Pezzoni M, Potì B and Romagnosi S, 'University Autonomy, the Professor Privilege and Academic Patenting: Italy, 1996-2007' (2013) 20 *Industry and Innovation* 399

Lotka AJ, 'The Frequency Distribution of Scientific Productivity' (1926) 16 *Journal of the Washington Academy of Sciences* 317

Lowe S, 'Culture and Network Institutions in Hong Kong: A Hierarchy of Perspectives. A Response to Wilkinson: 'Culture, Institutions and Business in East Asia'' (1998) 19 *Organization Studies* 321

Machlup F and Penrose E, 'The Patent Controversy in the Nineteenth Century' (1950) 10 *The Journal of Economic History* 1

Mandel GN, 'To Promote the Creative Process: Intellectual Property Law and the Psychology of Creativity' (2011) 86 *Notre Dame Law Review* 1999

Manly DG, 'Inventors, Innovators, Compensation and the Law' (1978) 21(2) *Research Management* 29

Mannix EA, Neale MA and Northcraft GB, 'Equity, Equality, or Need? The Effects of Organizational Culture on the Allocation of Benefits and Burdens' (1995) 63 *Organizational Behavior and Human Decision Processes* 276

Mariani M and Romanelli M, '"Stacking" and "Picking" Inventions: The Patenting Behavior of European Inventors' (2007) 36 *Research Policy* 1128

Matal J, 'A Guide to the Legislative History of the America Invents Act: Part I of II' (2012) 21 *Federal Circuit Bar Journal* 435

Merges RP, 'The Law and Economics of Employee Inventions' (1999) 13 *Harvard Journal of Law and Technology* 1

Miller BC and Gerard D, 'Family Influence on the Development of Creativity in Children: An Integrative Review' (1979) 28 *The Family Coordinator* 295

Mislow CM, 'Necessity May Be the Mother of Invention, but Who Gets Custody?: The Ownership of Intellectual Property Created by an Employed Inventor' (1985) 1 *Santa Clara Computer & High-technology Law Journal* 59

Mitchell TR and Silver WS, 'Individual and Group Goals When Workers Are Independent: Effects on Task Strategies and Performance' (1990) 75 *Journal of Applied Psychology* 185

Morris CR Jr, 'Patent Rights in an Employee's Invention: the American Shop Right Rule and the English View' (1960) 39 *Texas Law Review* 41

Mowery DC, Nelson RR, Sampat BN and Ziedonis AA, 'The Growth of Patenting and Licensing by U.S. Universities: An Assessment of the Effects of the Bayh-Dole Act of 1980' (2001) 30 *Research Policy* 99

Mowery DC and Sampat BN, 'University Patents and Patent Policy Debates in the USA, 1925-1980' (2001) 10 *Industrial and Corporate Change* 781

Mühlemeyer P, 'R&D – Personnel Management by Incentive Management: Results of an Empirical Survey in Research & Development' (1992) 21(4) *Personnel Review* 27

Myers MS, 'Who Are Your Motivated Workers?' (1964) 42(1) *Harvard Business Review* 73

Narin F and Breitzman A, 'Inventive Productivity' (1995) 24 *Research Policy* 507

Nelson MR and Shavitt S, 'Horizontal and Vertical Individualism and Achievement Values: A Multimethod Examination of Denmark and the United States' (2002) 33 *Journal of Cross-Cultural Psychology* 439

Nelson RR, 'The Simple Economics of Basic Scientific Research' (1959) 67 *Journal of Political Economy* 297

Neumeyer F, 'Employees' Rights in Their Inventions: A Comparison of National Laws' (1962) 44 *Journal of the Patent Office Society* 674

Nicholson GC, 'Keeping Innovation Alive' (1998) 41(3) *Research-Technology Management* 34

Onishi K, 'The Effects of Compensation Plans for Employee Inventions on R&D Productivity: New Evidence from Japanese Panel Data' (2013) 42 *Research Policy* 367

Oyserman D, Coon HM and Kemmelmeier M, 'Rethinking Individualism and Collectivism: Evaluation of Theoretical Assumptions and Meta-Analyses' (2002) 128 *Psychological Bulletin* 3

Parker HD, 'Reform for Rights of Employed Inventors' (1984) 57 *Southern California Law Review* 603

Pila J, '"Sewing the Fly Buttons on the Statute": Employee Inventions and the Employment Context' (2012) 32 *Oxford Journal of Legal Studies* 265

Polanyi M, 'Patent Reform' (1944) 11 *The Review of Economic Studies* 61

Rahmatian A, 'Make the Butterflies Fly in Formation? Management of Copyright Created by Academics in UK Universities' (2014) 34 *Legal Studies* 709

Ramsey G, 'The Historical Background of Patents' (1936) 18 *Journal of the Patent Office Society* 6

Rhoten D and Powell WW, 'The Frontiers of Intellectual Property: Expanded Protection versus New Models of Open Science' (2007) 3 *Annual Review of Law and Social Science* 345

Rich GS, 'The Relation between Patent Practices and the Anti-Monopoly Laws' (1942) 24 *Journal of the Patent Office Society* 159

Rivard PM, 'Protection of Business Investments in Human Capital: Shop Right and Related Doctrines' (1997) 79 *Journal of the Patent and Trademark Office Society* 753

Roberts EB, 'What We've Learned: Managing Invention and Innovation' (1988) 31(1) *Research-Technology Management* 11

Román FJ, 'An Analysis of Changes to a Team-Based Incentive Plan and its Effect on Productivity, Product Quality, and Absenteeism' (2009) 34 *Accounting, Organizations and Society* 589

Rosenberg N and Nelson RR, 'American Universities and Technical Advance in Industry' (1994) 23 *Research Policy* 323

Rossman J, 'The Motives of Inventors' (1931) 45 *The Quarterly Journal of Economics* 522

—— 'Rewards and Incentives to Employee-Inventors' (1963) 7 *The Patent, Trademark and Copyright Journal of Research and Education* 431

Rynes SL, Gerhart B and Minette KA, 'The Importance of Pay in Employee Motivation: Discrepancies between What People Say and What They Do' (2004) 43 *Human Resource Management* 381

Salancik GR and Pfeffer J, 'An Examination of Need-Satisfaction Models of Job Attitudes' (1977) 22 *Administrative Science Quarterly* 427

Sandrock SP, 'The Evolution and Modern Application of the Shop Right Rule' (1983) 38 *The Business Lawyer* 953

Sauermann H and Cohen WM, 'What Makes Them Tick? Employee Motives and Firm Innovation' (2010) 56 *Management Science* 2134

Savitsky TR, 'Compensation for Employee Inventions' (1991) 73 *Journal of the Patent and Trademark Office Society* 645

Schettino F, Sterlacchini A and Venturini F, 'Inventive Productivity and Patent Quality: Evidence from Italian Inventors' (2013) 35 *Journal of Policy Modeling* 1043

Sears MH, 'The Corporate Patent: Reform or Retrogression' (1979) 61 *Journal of the Patent Office Society* 380

Shalley CE, Zhou J and Oldham GR, 'The Effects of Personal and Contextual Characteristics on Creativity: Where Should We Go from Here?' (2004) 30 *Journal of Management* 933

Shane SA, 'Why Do Some Societies Invent More Than Others?' (1992) 7 *Journal of Business Venturing* 29

Shaw JD, Duffy MK and Stark EM, 'Interdependence and Preference for Group Work: Main and Congruence Effects on the Satisfaction and Performance of Group Members' (2000) 26 *Journal of Management* 259

Shaw JD, Gupta N and Delery JE, 'Pay Dispersion and Workforce Performance: Moderating Effects of Incentives and Interdependence' (2002) 23 *Strategic Management Journal* 491

Shipley DD and Kiely JA, 'Industrial Salesforce Motivation and Herzberg's Dual Factor Theory: A UK Perspective' (1986) 6(1) *The Journal of Personal Selling & Sales Management* 9

Simmons AL, 'The Influence of Openness to Experience and Organizational Justice on Creativity' (2011) 23 *Creativity Research Journal* 9

Stallberg CG, 'The Legal Status of Academic Employees' Inventions in Britain and Germany and its Consequences for R&D Agreements' (2007) *Intellectual Property Quarterly* 489

Stark EM, Shaw JD and Duffy MK, 'Preference for Group Work, Winning Orientation, and Social Loafing Behavior in Groups' (2007) 32 *Group & Organization Management* 699

Staudt E, Bock J, Mühlemeyer P and Kriegesmann B, 'Anreizsysteme als Instrument des betrieblichen Innovationsmanagements – Ergebnisse einer empirischen Untersuchung im F+E-Bereich' [Incentive Systems as an Instrument of Corporate Innovation Management – Results of an Empirical Study in the R&D Sector] (1990) 60 *Zeitschrift für Betriebswirtschaft (ZfB)* 1183

Staudt E, Bock J, Mühlemeyer P and Kriegesmann B, 'Der Arbeitnehmererfinder im betrieblichen Innovationsprozeß – Ergebnisse einer empirischen Untersuchung' [The Employee Invention in Corporate Innovation Process – Results of an Empirical Study] (1992) 44 *Schmalenbachs Zeitschrift für betriebswirtschaftliche Forschung (zfbf)* 111

Summers CW, 'Employment at Will in the United States: The Divine Right of Employers' (2000) 3 *University of Pennsylvania Journal of Labor and Employment Law* 65

Swan KR, 'Patent Rights in an Employee's Invention' (1959) 75 *The Law Quarterly Review* 77

Tabarrok A, 'Patent Theory versus Patent Law' (2002) 1(1) *Contributions to Economic Analysis & Policy* 1

Takano Y and Osaka E, 'An Unsupported Common View: Comparing Japan and the U.S. on Individualism/Collectivism' (1999) 2 *Asian Journal of Social Psychology* 311

Taras V, Kirkman BL and Steel P, 'Examining the Impact of *Culture's Consequences*: A Three-Decade, Multilevel, Meta-Analytic Review of Hofstede's Cultural Value Dimensions' (2010) 95 *Journal of Applied Psychology* 405

Taylor FW, 'A Piece-Rate System' (1896) 1 *Economic Studies* 89

Toubia O, 'Idea Generation, Creativity, and Incentives' (2006) 25 *Marketing Science* 411

Triandis HC, 'Collectivism and Individualism as Cultural Syndromes' (1993) 27 *Cross-Cultural Research* 155

Ubell FD, 'Assignor Estoppel: A Wrong Turn from *Lear*' (1989) 71 *Journal of the Patent and Trademark Office Society* 26

Valentin F and Jensen RL, 'Effects on Academia-Industry Collaboration of Extending University Property Rights' (2007) 32 *The Journal of Technology Transfer* 251

van Caenegem W, 'VUT v Wilson, UWA v Gray and University Intellectual Property Policies' (2010) 21 *Australian Intellectual Property Journal* 148

Voronov M and Singer JA, 'The Myth of Individualism-Collectivism: A Critical Review' (2002) 142 *The Journal of Social Psychology* 461

Wageman R, 'Interdependence and Group Effectiveness' (1995) 40 *Administrative Science Quarterly* 145

—— and Baker G, 'Incentives and Cooperation: The Joint Effects of Task and Reward Interdependence on Group Performance' (1997) 18 *Journal of Organizational Behavior* 139

Wagner DG, 'Gender Differences in Reward Preference: A Status-Based Account' (1995) 26 *Small Group Research* 353

Wagner JA III, 'Studies of Individualism-Collectivism: Effects on Cooperation in Groups' (1995) 38 *The Academy of Management Journal* 152

Walterscheid EC, 'To Promote the Progress of Science and Useful Arts: The Anatomy of a Congressional Power' (2003) 43 *IDEA: The Journal of Law and Technology* 1

Wernimont PF, 'Intrinsic and Extrinsic Factors in Job Satisfaction' (1966) 50 *Journal of Applied Psychology* 41

Witte RC and Guttag EW, 'Employee Inventions' (1989) 71 *Journal of the Patent and Trademark Office Society* 467

Wolk S, 'Remuneration of Employee Inventors – Is There a Common European Ground? A Comparison of National Laws on Compensation of Inventors in Germany, France, Spain, Sweden and the United Kingdom' (2011) 42 *International Review of Intellectual Property and Competition Law* 272

Wrzesniewski A, Schwartz B, Cong X, Kane M, Omar A and Kolditz T, 'Multiple Types of Motives Don't Multiply the Motivation of West Point Cadets' (2014) 111 *Proceedings of the National Academy of Sciences of the United States of America* 10990

Zenger TR and Lazzarini SG, 'Compensating for Innovation: Do Small Firms Offer High-powered Incentives That Lure Talent and Motivate Effort?' (2004) 25 *Managerial and Decision Economics* 329

Working Papers

Bowles S and Reyes SP, 'Economic Incentives and Social Preferences: A Preference-Based Lucas Critique of Public Policy' (2009) *CESifo Working Paper Series No 2734*

Cohen WM, Nelson RR and Walsh JP, 'Protecting Their Intellectual Assets: Appropriability Conditions and Why U.S. Manufacturing Firms Patent (or Not)' (2000) *NBER Working Paper 7552*

Czarnitzki D, Hussinger K and Leten B, 'The Market Value of Blocking Patent Citations' (2011) *ZEW Discussion Paper No 11-021*

Nagaoka S, Tsukada N, Onishi K and Nishimura Y, 'Innovation Process in Japan in the Early 2000s as Seen from Inventors: Agenda for Strengthening Innovative Capability' (in Japanese) (2012) *RIETI Discussion Paper Series 12-J-033*

Nagaoka S and Walsh J, 'The R&D Process in the US and Japan: Major Findings from the RIETI-Georgia Tech Inventor Survey' (2009) *RIETI Discussion Paper Series 09-E-010*

Onishi K and Owan H, 'Incentive Pay or Windfalls: Remuneration for Employee Inventions in Japan' (2010) *RIETI Discussion Paper Series 10-E-049*

Owan H and Nagaoka S, 'Intrinsic and Extrinsic Motivations of Inventors' (2011) *RIETI Discussion Paper Series 11-E-022*

Walsh JP and Nagaoka S, 'Who Invents?: Evidence from the Japan-U.S. Inventor Survey' (2009) *RIETI Discussion Paper Series 09-E-034*

Official Documents

—— *The British Patent System: Report of the Committee to Examine the Patent System and Patent Law* (Banks Report, Cmnd 4407, 1970)

—— *Lambert Review of Business-University Collaboration: Final Report* (HM Treasury 2003)

Board of Trade, *Patent Law Reform* (White Paper, Cmnd 6000, 1975)

—— *Patents and Designs Acts: Final Report of the Departmental Committee* (Swan Report, Cmd 7206, 1947)

Commission, 'Promoting Innovation through Patents: Green Paper on the Community Patent and the Patent System in Europe' COM (97) 314 final

—— 'Promoting Innovation through Patents: The Follow-Up to the Green Paper on the Community Patent and the Patent System in Europe' COM (1999) 42 final

Japan Patent Office, *Minutes of the 1st Meeting of the Patent System Subcommittee* (24 March 2014)

—— *Minutes of the 3rd Meeting of the Patent System Subcommittee* (14 April 2014)

—— *Minutes of the 4th Meeting of the Patent System Subcommittee* (30 April 2014)

—— *Minutes of the 5th Meeting of the Patent System Subcommittee* (14 May 2014)

—— *Minutes of the 6th Meeting of the Patent System Subcommittee* (29 May 2014)

—— *Minutes of the 7th Meeting of the Patent System Subcommittee* (18 June 2014)

—— *Minutes of the 9th Meeting of the Patent System Subcommittee* (17 October 2014)

—— *Minutes of the 10th Meeting of the Patent System Subcommittee* (19 November 2014)

National Science Board, *Science and Engineering Indicators 2018* (National Science Foundation 2018)

Patent System Subcommittee, Intellectual Property Committee of the Industrial Structure Council, *Wagakuni no inobēshon sokushin oyobi kokusai-tekina seido chōwa no tame no chiteki zaisan seido no minaoshi ni mukete* [Recommendations for Reforming the Intellectual Property System to Facilitate Innovation in Japan and Achieve International Harmonisation] (January 2015)

WIPO, *Patent Cooperation Treaty Yearly Review 2017: The International Patent System* (WIPO 2017)

Reports and Conference Papers

—— 'The 2007 Georgia Tech Inventor Survey Questionnaire'

Bouvet T, 'Employee-Inventor Rights in France' (Loyola Law School IP Special Focus Conference, Los Angeles, September 2006)

Bruun N, Heikkinen P, Karttunen J, Kivi-Koskinen T, Martikainen S, Rapinoja B, Salomaa P, Tommila M and Weckman A, 'Finland Group Report Q 183: Employers' Rights to Intellectual Property' (39th World Intellectual Property Congress, AIPPI, Geneva, June 2004)

Committee on Engineers and Scientists for Federal Government Programs, 'Summary Report of Survey of Attitudes of Scientists and Engineers in Government and Industry' (Washington DC, United States Government Printing Office, 1957)

CMS Patents Team, 'Employee Inventor Rewards Survey' (CMS 2014)

InnoS&T, 'Final Report of PatVal-EU II Survey: Methods and Results' (2010)

—— 'Final Report of PatVal-US/JP II: Survey Methods and Results US and JP' (2011)

—— 'Final Report of the Inventor Survey in Europe, the US and Japan' (2012)

Intellectual Property Owners Association, 'Employee Inventor Compensation Practices Survey: Report of the IPO Asian Practice Committee' (2004)

Japan Patent Office, 'Shokumu hatsumei kitei no rekishi-teki hensen ni kakaru sankō shiryō' [The Background Information on the Historical Changes of the Provision for Employee Inventions] (30 April 2014)

Laney OE, 'Intellectual Property and the Employee Engineer' (IEEE-USA Professional Guideline Series, The Institute of Electrical and Electronics Engineers 2001)

Montobbio F, 'Intellectual Property Rights and Knowledge Transfer from Public Research to Industry in the US and Europe: Which Lessons for Innovation Systems in Developing Countries?' in WIPO, *The Economics of Intellectual Property: Suggestions for Further Research in Developing Countries and Countries with Economies in Transition* (2009)

Obuchi T, 'Shokumu hatsumei ni kansuru kikkin no kadai' [Pressing Issues concerning Employee Inventions] in Institute of Intellectual Property, *Kigyō-tō ni okeru tokkyo-hō dai 35-jō no seido un'yō ni kakaru kadai oyobi sono kaiketsu hōhō ni kansuru chōsa kenkyū hōkoku-sho: heisei 25-nendo tokkyo-chō sangyō zaisan-ken seido mondai chōsa kenkyū hōkoku-sho* [A Report of Investigation and Research on the Problems of Implementing Article 35 of the Patent Act in Companies etc. and Their Solutions: Japan Patent Office Reports of Investigation and Research on the Issues concerning the Industrial Property Right System, the 2013 Fiscal Year] (February 2014)

PatVal-EU, 'The Value of European Patents: Evidence from a Survey of European Inventors (Final Report of the PatVal EU Project)' (2005)

Takeda M, 'Shokumu hatsumei seido no arikata' [The State of the Employee Invention System] in Institute of Intellectual Property, *Kigyō-tō ni okeru tokkyo-hō dai 35-jō no seido un'yō ni kakaru kadai oyobi sono kaiketsu hōhō ni kansuru chōsa kenkyū hōkoku-sho: heisei 25-nendo tokkyo-chō sangyō zaisan-ken seido mondai chōsa kenkyū hōkoku-sho* [A Report of Investigation and Research on the Problems of Implementing Article 35 of the Patent Act in Companies etc. and Their Solutions: Japan Patent Office Reports of Investigation and Research on the Issues concerning the Industrial Property Right System, the 2013 Fiscal Year] (February 2014)

The University of Manchester Institute for Science, Ethics and Innovation, 'Who Owns Science? The Manchester Manifesto' (2009)

Vroom VH, 'Some Observations Regarding Herzberg's Two-Factor Theory' (American Psychological Association Convention, New York, September 1966)

Zimmer FJ and Sethmann S, 'What Makes a Co-Worker a Co-Inventor?' (Grünecker 2005)

Websites and Social Media

3M, '3M Business Groups'
—— '3M Performance'
CORDIS, 'InnoS&T'
—— 'PATVAL-EU'
Gammelby PF, 'Aarhus University and Industry Open Patent-Free Playground' (24 July 2017)
TED, 'The Puzzle of Motivation | Dan Pink' (*YouTube*, 25 August 2009)
USPTO Patent Technology Monitoring Team, 'U.S. Colleges and Universities – Utility Patent Grants 1969–2012: Ownership Category Breakout'

INDEX

CPSIA information can be obtained
at www.ICGtesting.com
Printed in the USA
LVHW021955170321
681769LV00004B/143